Place name discoveries

on Upper Deeside and the far Highlands

Best Wishes Ian Murray

Adam Watson

Adam Watson and Ian Murray

Publication of this book was aided by the generous sponsorship of Bert McIntosh of Crathes, Banchory and of McIntosh Plant Hire (Aberdeen) Ltd, Birchmoss, Echt, Westhill, Aberdeenshire AB32 6XL, www.mphltd.co.uk

Published by Paragon Publishing, 4 North Street, Rothersthorpe, Northants, NN7 3JB, UK

First published 2015
© Adam Watson* and Ian Murray^ 2015

*Clachnaben, Crathes, Banchory, Aberdeenshire AB31 5JE, Scotland, UK, adamwatson@uwclub.net
^Altnacraig, Braemar Road, Ballater, Aberdeenshire AB35 5RQ, Scotland, UK, ianlochnagar1@btinternet.com

ISBN 978-1-78222-328-3

Book design, layout and production management by Into Print
www.intoprint.net +44 (0) 1604 832149

Printed and bound in UK, USA and Australia by Lightning Source

Contents

Foreword

The first three words in the title of this book are Place name discoveries. To us, that implies not just the facts in each discovery, but the excitement of hearing and recording how each name is said in the native indigenous tongue, and also the delight in meeting local folk who appreciated what we were doing.

Now that we are near publication of our book, it is a fitting time to look back on how it has come about. We are interested in place names as part of our great affection for Upper Deeside and the Cairngorms. Many names go back hundreds of years, in Gaelic, Scots or English. Some are at grave risk of disappearing.

One of us (AW), raised on lowland Deveronside, first became interested in place names during 1939, when he read Seton Gordon's *Cairngorm Hills of Scotland* (1925). Gordon's experience of the names went back almost to 1900, and from 1944 onwards he told AW many names. AW also heard names back to 1941 from folk on Spey and Dee. However, it was only in 1973 that he and John Duff decided to collate a score of unpublished Deeside names that they had heard. To check whether there might be one or two more, they interviewed deerstalker Colin McIntosh at Braemar. Colin told them far more unpublished names than their 20, and said he had more for a second visit. This was the tip of an iceberg, leading 11 years later to *The place names of Upper Deeside* with Elizabeth Allan (1984). It included nearly 7000 names, after interviews with 260 residents.

IM had a different background, raised at Ballater in Upper Deeside from 1970, so he heard names from residents during ordinary conversation. Around 1988 he decided to interview people who had lived in remoter parts of Upper Deeside, about folklore and history. This led to his first book *In the shadow of Lochnagar* (1992). Some of those he visited were the same as AW had interviewed years earlier.

Before finishing that book, he contacted AW with queries on names, and then asked AW to write the Foreword. Initially, place names had been a side interest to IM, and he knew that many names that he heard matched those already published in the 1984 book. However, he then began to notice several names not recorded there. Sometimes this referred to a single stone or feature, known now to only one remaining person. Because a few new names had been uncovered, he contacted AW again. We decided to go to the hill together to check the new names. After a trip we retired to IM's house. Over tea and cake, we discussed what we had seen. Our excitement rose because there was now a small but growing list of unpublished and nearly extinct old names. We felt a sense of responsibility to preserve them.

This book is the result. It has been decades in the making, mainly because we both kept discovering new names and did not want to publish before we had caught most of them. As well as Upper Deeside, we visited Strathdon and Speyside. Independently we went to the hills hundreds of times for different reasons, but place-name collection always added an additional interest. Though the human population is fairly stable on Upper Deeside these days, down the centuries people have moved from remote glens into villages and towns. In some glens the entire population left many decades ago, and so numerous names have been lost or were about to disappear. This provided urgency to our work. Because place names are often good descriptions of the landscape or feature, there is added interest in visiting the place to see whether the name fits the location. In addition, this helped us try as accurately as we could to translate Gaelic or Scots names into English. Each author knew that the other would be pleased by discovery of a new name. This propelled us to work on with enthusiasm.

As we near completion of this book, still we find the odd name to insert just in time. It is a good feeling to look back on the folk whom we have met whilst compiling this work. Many of them, as well as many places, appear in the colour photographs that illustrate the book.

Languages, dialects and customs have been changing for a long time and continue to alter. Place names therefore are like invisible bench marks on hill or glen, preserving in some cases intricate detail and transcending the generations, each one a brief reminder of folk, language or culture, often long departed. We hope that this book, a culmination of two lifetimes of study of the place names of Upper Deeside, will preserve some of that detail for generations to come.

Preface

Structure of the book

We regard this book as a natural sequel to *The place names of Upper Deeside* by AW & Elizabeth Allan (1984). That book presented nearly 7000 names, thousands of which were unpublished.

Later, AW and IM came across 235 names not in the 1984 book, plus 24 from Glen Tanar of mid Deeside and Glen Carvie of Don, just outside the area of Upper Deeside. We collated these in an article in the *Cairngorm Club Journal* (October 2011). The club membership is small. To make the article available to more readers, we republish it here as Chapter 1. The Introduction and Methods of the two republished articles in Chapters 1 and 6 involve some repetition with the account in this Preface. That is especially so for the sections on 'Our methods of collection' and 'Our methods for presenting the names'. Readers should regard this Preface and the two sections mentioned as our definitive statement.

Chapter 2 shows extra information that we have learned since, about some names in the 1984 book and in the article.

Since 2011 we have discovered 56 more unpublished names in Upper Deeside, and have seen some more in old documents. These are in Chapter 3. We have excluded the many names of plantations and other woods. These names are used by staff on estates and land owned by the Forestry Commission, as well as by loggers, and are recorded in managers' files and maps.

Author AW and John Robertson with his Labrador at the Sgairneach Well, named after An Sgairneach (the heap of stones), a bouldery slope above this well in Glen Girnock, 15 May 1983 (Adam Christopher Watson)

The river of unpublished names in the 1984 book dwindled to a large burn in the 2011 article, and now in 2014 a small burn. There will be other unpublished names to find. Those who read this book may be encouraged to look further.

Chapter 4 lists errors in names on modern Ordnance Survey maps of Upper Deeside. The OS did a great work in the mid 1800s by collecting place names, and this has proved invaluable now that the local dialect of Gaelic has died out in Upper Deeside. However, it has long been known that the OS collectors made many errors in different parts of the Highlands (e.g. Watson 1904, MacBain 1922). To its credit, the OS has since printed correct versions on later maps, for instance, correcting many errors shown by the above two authors. In the last few years there has been a renewal of interest in Gaelic place names across Scotland, and the OS is cooperating with staff of Comunn na Gaidhlig and students of place names in considering more corrections. This is commendable.

In Chapter 5 we re-publish a review paper on 'A study of the place-names of Upper Deeside' (*Nomina* 8). This was delivered at the 16th Annual Conference of the Council for Name Studies in Britain and Ireland, held at University of Aberdeen in 1983. The organisers made the Deeside study a centrepiece of the Conference, calling it the 'Deeside Project', and the field trip by bus took the participants to Upper Deeside, where they met several of the main informants. Again, the readership was small, so we now make the review available more widely.

In Chapter 6 is re-published an article on 'Some place names from areas near Upper Deeside' (*Deeside Field*, 1988). The Deeside Field Club had very few members, so again we use this book to make the content open to a wider readership. The article gives many names not in Upper Deeside, but it originated from the study for the 1984 book, because Watson and Allan searched for new names on the boundary of Upper Deeside, and heard a few that they had not heard from Deeside folk.

Now we turn to names outside Upper Deeside, a smaller but important part of our book. In Chapter 7 we present a selective list of 'Some incorrect Gaelic names on OS maps outside Upper Deeside'.

Chapter 8 is a collation of information outside Upper Deeside, on a highly selective list of many place names, heard from residents (mostly indigenous) back to 1941 in the counties of Sutherland, Ross, Inverness, Argyll, Perth, Moray, and Banff. Nearly all are of Gaelic origin and some of lowland Scots or English, but the list includes a few Pictish names, and a fair number of names of Norse or part Norse origin in the west Highlands and especially Sutherland. Most are published, but many not, and local pronunciations should be of interest. Nearly all were heard by AW, who visited these locations. However, Davie Duncan contributed in 2013 and 2014 some unpublished Badenoch and Perthshire names that he heard from residents, including a few Badenoch names at locations not visited by AW since then. Also he uncovered many Badenoch names that he did not hear from residents but found in old estate papers. In addition, IM heard two unpublished names of bays near Arisaig in 2013 from residents Audrey Macdonald, and Ewen Nicholson of Grimsay.

In Chapter 9, a selective list shows misleading Anglicised spellings of names on OS maps of north-east Scotland. This includes names of villages and inhabited houses, such as Aboyne and Hopeman, where the official pronunciations follow the OS spelling and not the local version. The latter would fit Anglicised spellings Abyne and Howdman. These incorrect names will probably remain, because they are on road signs, postal addresses and other official designations. Indigenous local residents know that they are incorrect and use the authentic local versions when speaking Scots. However, the chapter should be of interest to incomers, and to indigenous folk as a reminder.

Historical background on methods for collecting names

For all of this book, our philosophical rationale and methods have followed those of excellent early accounts (Joyce 1869, Watson 1904, 1904–05, 1926, posthumously 2002, MacBain 1922, Nicolaisen 1979, see final Bibliography). These authors described and recommended the only methods that can produce reliable accurate results, particularly to hear and record pronunciations by local residents, search for earlier written spellings, and make field visits to check whether each name fitted its location. The books and papers by these four authors set a standard for sound reliable methods in recording information on the place names of a county or region, a standard as important today as a century ago. Watson (1904–05) commented on the lack of a satisfactory account of Scottish place names, 'Nothing on the subject so far approaches, for example, the work of Dr Joyce on the names of Ireland, or of Canon Isaac Taylor on English Village Names. This may be ascribed partly to the great difficulty of the subject, aggravated as it is by the comparative scantiness of ancient and reliable written forms of names, partly to the fewness of investigators possessing the necessary qualifications of scholarship and opportunity. It must be admitted, however, that much of the work actually attempted is sadly lacking in trustworthiness from no other reason but defective method.'

Likewise, MacBain criticised three earlier authors of books, two on counties and one on Scotland, calling them as from the 'old school of etymologists', and in one case referring to books such as this as being 'worthless'. These three authors had not asked local residents for pronunciations, the key method for accurate reliable study, and had paid scant or no attention to the other methods recommended as necessary by W. J. Watson and MacBain, especially the searching of old records with early spellings, and the importance of visiting each place to check whether possible interpretations of the name fit the location. We hold firmly to the recommendations of these early pioneers. For instance, in a review criticising a book on Scottish hill names by Drummond (1991) where the author had not personally studied local pronunciations, one of us (AW) wrote, 'Reliable publications in this field must involve careful study of local pronunciations, old written sources and ground inspection, and the many publications that ignore these basic rules are worthless' (Watson 1992). AW used the term 'worthless' here, in relation to MacBain's principles. The MacBain criticism would also apply to John Murray (2014), a recent all-Scotland book that ignores local pronunciations. We hasten to add that neither Drummond nor Murray set out to further place-name research with their books, which instead were written for much more general purposes that are to be commended.

Poll na Buitsich, pool of the witch, in birchwood W of the foot of Gairn, April 2012 (IM)

In the last few decades there have been some fine studies based on sound methods. Also, since 1995 there has been a Scottish Place-name Society, issuing its seasonal newsletter *Scottish Place-name News* and its own journal, the *Journal of Scottish Name Studies*. Nicolaisen (1979) wrote that the days of the method of map and dictionary leading straight to publication were over, i.e. ignoring the early essential steps of recording local pronunciations, old written sources, and visits to inspect the locations. However, in Chapter 8 we note a few names in recent books where authors omitted that first essential step. Mentioning this we believe is necessary because the books cited are widely used by hill-walkers and other tourists.

Our methods of collection

Watson & Allan (1984), under their sub-heading on *Methods of collection* (p. xiv), wrote 'The widely-accepted early methods of Joyce (1869) and Watson (1926) were used, along with the standard modern methods reviewed by Nicolaisen (1979). We concentrated throughout the study on visiting people who had lived locally all their lives. The total number of residents seen was 260. Some lived in surrounding areas such as Speyside, and gave a few boundary names not heard from Deeside folk. A collection of the place names of an area can never be complete. More informants provide more names, and informants seen repeatedly may give further names on return visits. We halted the collection when we had asked for the names of every field, ruin, hill, corrie, stream, and wood, and when over half the new informants were producing no further names for our list. By then we had searched all graveyards in Upper Deeside, all maps and papers pertaining to the study area in Register House and other archive collections at estate offices and charter rooms, the central and university libraries at Aberdeen, the National Library of Scotland, and other sources given below in the References section.

During each interview we asked whether informants knew names and locations shown on maps and other documents. If they did not, we offered only the first letter or syllable as a prompt. Only after this did we show them the OS (Ordnance Survey) map to get precise locations. Next we asked them for names of other obvious features such as small hillocks and river pools which were not on maps. Few of them were accustomed to reading maps, so if they pointed to a location on the map we checked with further questions, asked for places to be shown from window or garden, and took many people out to field and hill. We recorded pronunciations and key parts of interviews with tape-recorders, and made notes.

Informants who had forgotten some names often recalled them on later visits On return visits we mentioned names since heard from others, to check whether the current informant knew them. This indicated relatively how widely known the names were. Where only one person or family had given a name, or an informant was uncertain about a name or location, we always checked particularly carefully with other people.

All parts of the area were visited to see whether our derivations of the name fitted the appearance of the places. Every place in the list whose approximate or precise location is known was visited by Adam Watson and many by Elizabeth Allan also.

To conclude, a large difference from the early accounts was that Watson & Allan named informants and their locations in terms of the area for which each informant gave names. This was usually near where each informant lived, but sometimes also other areas where they had worked as deerstalkers or gamekeepers. Another important difference was that they used the International Phonetic Alphabet to note pronunciations and tape-recorded most of these.

In the current book we have followed the above detailed *Methods of collection* in Watson & Allan 1984). We continued the naming of informants in our article in the *Cairngorm Club Journal* (Watson & Murray 2011) and in the rest of this book, as did Watson (2013) in his recent book on place names.

There are two exceptions where we did not follow the above rule of recording pronunciations as a second step as well as hearing them first. One was in AW's experience back to 1941, where many of the names in Chapter 8 were heard and often checked against what he heard from other residents, but where he did not write down the names or use a tape-recorder with residents. He did, however, visit all the places named in the lists. Only in the last few years did he look for early spellings, check against the reliable works of excellent past

Gaelic place-name scholars such as Watson (1904, 1926, 2002) and MacBain (1922), and finally collate the evidence for Chapter 8.

In the Badenoch part of the Inverness-shire section, which forms the main part of Chapter 8, as well as for many in north-west Perthshire, AW checked names and pronunciations in 2013 with Davie Duncan of Kingussie, and Seumas Grannd of Inverdruie also helped with valuable comments. For Sutherland he checked pronunciations and English meanings with Bobby Macleod, who gave many more names for the book by AW (Watson 2013) than are in the current book. For west Sutherland he checked some pronunciations with Davie Duncan, and for Ross with Calum Anton, Dick Balharry, Alex Murray, John Pottie and Mark Stewart. For north Inverness-shire he checked with Alex Murray and John Pottie, for Strathspey in Inverness-shire with Davie Duncan, Seumas Grannd, and Donnie Smith, and for north-west Perthshire with Davie Duncan, Alex Murray and John Robertson.

The other exception where the second step of recording did not immediately follow the first step of hearing the name, involved Elizabeth Allan for the 1984 book and IM after 1990. As IM well expressed in the Foreword, he grew up at Ballater in Upper Deeside, as did Elizabeth Allan earlier, and so like AW in the Highlands before 1973 they heard many names from local residents in ordinary conversations. Only years afterwards did EA and later still IM become interested in place names. After 1973, when AW began a detailed study in Upper Deeside, EA told AW several names not previously heard by him, but in common use by local Ballater residents in and near the village. The second step of recording and checking with others and visiting the places immediately followed.

Sandy Walker, John Robertson, Rodney Heslop at the Tillage, Glen Girnock (Gleann Goirneig or glen of little crier referring to Girnock Burn), beside stones cleared from an area used for cultivating barley centuries ago, 2 November 2007 (AW)

After 1990, IM noticed an occasional name that was not in the book *The place names of Upper Deeside* by Watson & Allan (1984). This led to his deciding to contact AW, and thence sprang a further fruitful cooperation. Again there was an immediate move to the second step of recording and checking with others and visits to the places. There followed many visits by IM and AW to residents, with notebook and tape-recorder, and often field trips with informants, yielding new names not previously published or heard by us.

With every name that is not in the book by Watson & Allan (1984), we followed the same methods as in that book, to the letter. There is no final end to it, for our best informant is still telling us what we call 'new' names, just in the course of ordinary conversations, so his stock seems limitless! At least we will have recorded the bulk of the remaining unpublished names for posterity in this book.

Our methods for presenting the names

Here we follow the main principles stated by Watson & Allan in their section *Brief guide to use of main list.* If a name is on current Ordnance Survey maps we give the OS spelling even where we judge it incorrect. For correct spelling of Gaelic names, we use Dwelly's dictionary except for changes in a list of Gaelic spellings in Ordnance Survey (1973), following advice by Dr W.F.H Nicolaisen of the School of Scottish Studies. In a few cases we refer to the website of Ainmean-Aite na h-Alba (Place names of Scotland). We spell Lowland Scots as in the *Scottish National Dictionary* by Grant & Murison. For names of Norse origin, we followed the brief list by Nicolaisen in OS (1973) and earlier accounts by MacBain and Watson (1926, 2002), but all

John Robertson, Rodney Heslop and Sandy Walker investigate soils at the Birk Bush (Scots birch copse) above Loch Muick, the Stulan Falls (Steallan a little cataract) beyond, July 2002 (AW)

this was checked and supplemented by reference to dictionaries by Cleasby & Vigfusson (1874, republished 2011 by compiler Agnarsson, and by Zoega 2013). Our listed pronunciations use the phonetic symbols of the International Phonetic Association (See Chapter 1, Table 1).Whether a name was known to 1-3 of the informants interviewed, or 4–6, or more than 7, we allocate symbols U, F and C. We ignore the definite article when allocating a name's alphabetical position in a list.

Bob Scott hangs up fox tails on an old pine outside Luibeg Cottage, footbridge over Luibeg Burn (from Laoigh Beag or little calf-one) later swept away by flood, and cottage now uninhabited most of the year, beyond lies Derry (from Doire a copse) pinewood, leading to Meall an Lundain, locally Meall Lundain (rounded hill at marshy ground or at green place), April 1952 (Tom Weir)

Bob Scott with his pony Punchie about to sledge five miles from Luibeg to the village of Inverey (Inbhir Eidh or mouth of Ey) for provisions when snow blocked the road, ancient pines towards the Lairig Ghru (from Lairig Dhru, pass of the stream Allt Dhru on the Spey side of the pass, which becomes the River Druie) beyond and the rocks of Coire na Poite (corrie of the pot) on Carn a' Mhaim (hill of the pass) under heavy snow on a morning of hard frost, February 1954 (AW)

Chapter 1. Unpublished place names from Upper Deeside
(from *Cairngorm Club Journal* 2011)

Introduction

Below we list and discuss names that we have found since the publication of a book *The Place Names of Upper Deeside* by Watson & Allan (1984), for the sake of brevity called Wa below. One of us (IM) came across a few while interviewing local residents for his own book on local history and folklore (1992) and he told AW. It excited us to find a few 'new names', and we thought that a brief note about them would be worth publishing. To make sure, however, we decided to do more interviews and more searching of old papers and maps. This was the tip of a wee iceberg, revealing scores of new names. Below we give the results of our two decades of intermittent effort, involving many visits to places as well as numerous interviews and searches of old sources. Our collection is unusual in containing much history in addition to place names, for instance connections between some names and Queen Victoria at Balmoral, such as the Eagle Hoose, the Elephant's Graveyard, and the Irons.

If readers know or come across any name in upper Deeside that appears to be absent from the lists in Watson & Allan (1984, 1988) and the present account, we would be pleased to be informed. Place names are an important part of local identity, but many are disappearing with the passing of older generations. It is good that the names of places in this fine part of Scotland be recorded, now and in future.

In 1984, one of us (AW) was first author of *The Place Names of Upper Deeside*, published by Aberdeen University Press. The study rested on interviews with 260 local residents, supplemented by maps and other historical sources. That book documented nearly 7000 place names, a high proportion of them previously unpublished. It might have been thought that afterwards there would be no other place names to be found in Upper Deeside. However, one can never be certain that one has heard all of even a single informant's place names, let alone those of all others interviewed and the far bigger numbers not interviewed.

One of the most outstanding informants for the 1984 book was retired farmer Willie Downie of the Lebhall farm at Micras east of Crathie. During work for the 1984 book, AW interviewed him on many days, including two day-long trips in the field. At the end of the last day, he announced with a smile, "Adam, I have no more names to give you. You have milked me dry!"

Years later, however, Ian Murray of Ballater was recording information about local folklore from old folk, including Willie Downie, and heard him in the course of conversation mention a few place names that seemed new to Ian and that he could not recall seeing in AW's 1984 book. IM then phoned AW and came to see him around 1990, and we realised that Willie had not been milked dry after all! This led to the two of us interviewing him again and to other interviews with informants visited by AW in the 1970s and 1980s. We also interviewed new informants discovered by IM and found names in historical sources unavailable to AW earlier.

We present 235 place names from Upper Deeside that did not appear in the 1984 book and 24 from lower Glen Tanar and Glen Carvie outside Upper Deeside. Also we make corrections to some names in the 1984 book and add extra information on names listed there.

The 235 new names are an interesting set, some Gaelic, some Scots, some English, reflecting Upper Deeside's rich variety of language and tradition. Mrs Jean Bain, the last fluent native speaker of the Aberdeenshire dialect of Gaelic, died at Crathie as recently as 1984.

However, Gaelic is in decline, and so is Scots, as incomers with neither language form a rapidly increasing proportion of the local population. Meanwhile, several of our best informants such as Willie Downie, Charlie Wright and Rob Bain have died. It is timely to publish this article so that their place names are not forgotten.

Stags tamed by Bob Scott with potato peelings stand beside free-range poultry outside Luibeg Cottage, stags have shed grey winter coats for resplendent red summer coats and have large new antlers, beyond, the old pines of Glen Derry stand below Beinn Bhreac (speckled hill) on left, June 1952 (AW)

Methods

Most names in the first list below are to our knowledge unpublished. IM noted a few in his three books on folklore in Upper Deeside, but not the full data on pronunciations, meanings and other aspects as we do here.

Upper Deeside, the study area for the 1984 book and the present book, covers the two parishes of Crathie & Braemar and Glenmuick, Tullich & Glengairn. We include a few names from just outside these parishes, in lower Glen Tanar and Glen Carvie of Strathdon. These were not in the paper by Watson & Allan (1988) on place names around the boundaries of the study area for their 1984 book.

Since 1984 the Duff archive has become available (University of Aberdeen, Special Collections MS 3175), including many old papers from Mar Lodge and other land up from Braemar. The archive has been searched (Dixon & Green 1995, Ewen 1996, 2001, S. Mitchell letter to A. Watson, Jamieson 1998). In the archive we inspected one plan and one paper (note that two maps re-drawn by Ewen contain errors that were not in the originals). In addition, Roy's maps (1747–55) are now available online in high quality, and inspection of these revealed a few names that Watson & Allan had not seen earlier.

We spell Scots as in Grant & Murison and give pronunciations that follow the standard phonetics of the International Phonetic Association (Table 1). Table 2 explains the abbreviations that we use in the lists. The Gaelic term Ruighe has different meanings that are hard to separate (Fraser 1995), so for convenience we translate all cases of it as cattle-run. For locations we give grid references, but omit them in a few cases involving minerals, where this might lead to ground disturbance by digging.

Upper Deeside names not in Watson & Allan 1984

Alltdoire Park (Jm), the Alltdourie Park (U), field at Alltdourie by Invercauld House

The Arns (U ðɪˈarnz), Scots alders, 298955, trees by Dee at Micras

The Auinward Foord (Im3), Avinard Foord (Tw), Athan Bhard, little ford of fields, Scots Fuird a ford, 094896, on Dee at Inverey

The Auld Regions (U ðɪˈalˈridʒənz), Scots old, 283965, long-disused former cultivated fields on Geallaig Hill above Wester Micras

Aultannich (Im5), after the nearby burn Allt an t-Sionnaich (OS), 012878, former farm township by Geldie-Dee confluence

Back Island (Fi), SE of 085894, former island at Inverey, not an island now

The Back Park (AS), 344979, a field at Culsh by Gairn

The Back Road (JR), 243947, high road to Invergelder from Balmoral

Baddachubber (Im3), Bad a' Chabair, clump of the pole, 096804, copse near Mar Lodge

The Bad Fiantaige Burn (F ðɪˌbadˈfjantəkˈbʌrn), part of the Coulachan Burn at Bad Fiantaige

The Bad Fiantaige Brig (F brɪg), Scots bridge, at above burn

The Badgers' Hillock (F ˈbadʒērzˈhëlək), 337901, below Linn of Muick

Balineonan (A), Baile an Eoinean, stead of the little bird, same as Dail a' Chata up Clunie

Ballniloan (Im5), Baile nan Lon, stead of the wet meadows, W of Wester Tullochcoy

The Balmoral Bonnet (F ðɪˌbəlˈmorəlˈbonët), 232898, a pine with foliage shaped like a Balmoral bonnet, tree now toppled by wind but still alive, NW of Lochnagar

Balnialt (Roy), Baile an Uillt, stead of the burn, shown as a farm on E side of Muick SE of Toldhu, on N side of a burn near its entry to Muick

The Banks of Inverey (J), 'a place with pine', probably E of Muir Cottage

The Barns o Beinn Mheadhoin (F ˈbarnzaˌbenˈmen), tors

The Bear's Fit, (JR ðɪˈberzˈfët), SW of 227832, a rock outcrop with indentation like the imprint of a bear's foot, W of Dubh Loch

Binlea (in 1602 Rms), 'the Blakhillok callit Garchory or Binlea, i.e. the top at 358017, noted as Tom Dubh Garbh-choire by Wa, Binlea suggests Beinn Liath or grey hill

Bob Scott, retired after leaving Luibeg, stands on his former Derry beat as mist rolls up Coire an Dubh-lochain (corrie of the black lochan) on Beinn a' Bhuird, 19 October 1975 (AW)

The Black-strip Burn (Im3), Scots Stripe a small burn, 094899, at Mar Lodge

The Blue Stane (EG ðɪˈbluˈstin), Scots stone, NE of 221937 beside former Aberarder school, schoolchildren slid down the boulder's E face (published M)

The Blue Stane (WD as above), 344965, Polhollick ferryman Benton refused to put his boat out if the river Dee ran above this boulder

The Boars' Holes (WD ðɪˈborzˈholz) at two places mentioned collectively. IM transcribed it as The Boar's Holes (M1, p. 92) but it seems likely that there was more than one boar. The sites were traps for killing wild boars that had been driven uphill. WD said the family Morgan who formerly farmed Rinabaich used both holes as hides for hunting wild boar from the bogs below, and in the late 1800s they were used again as hides to shoot deer. Both were well-built with stones, The one at 291962 had its uppermost wall set into a vertical bank, lower side-walls, and a floor level with the ground on either side, situated at the top of a long curved hollow where animals could have been driven from below. The hole at 309973 had a wall of the same height all the way round in a circle, with a floor well below ground-level and the top of the wall at ground level on flat ground on a hill-spur, among naturally regenerated Scots pines. There were no trees at either site in the late 1800s or even in the 1940s at the second site.

Bog Farral (WD bogˈfarəl), 269015, a bog, and the nearby former Gairnside farm of Bog Farral (Wa) was named after it

Bogrossalich (Ma, RB bogˈrɔsləx), Bog Rosailich, bog of reddish place, 320020 up Fenzie

The Bomb Hole (C ðɪˈbɔmˈhol), 278024, hole from a bomb dropped on Gairnside by a German plane in early 40s (photo M1)

The Boolin Green (Do, F ðɪˈbulənˌgrin), Scots bowling, summit green on Lair of Aldararie, where men from different glens formerly bowled with a round stone

The Bouchts (U ðɪˈbʌxts), Scots pens, NW of 300966, stone pens at Micras

Brae Riggs (Fi), 091896, farmland at a bank near Inverey

Brechohill (Roy), Breacach, speckled place, with Hill, shown as the long shank E of Allt an Uisge in Glen Muick

The Bridge Pool (U), same as the Gairnshiel Puil of Wa

The Brig o Dams Wuid (PG ˈbrɪgəˈdamzˈwɪd), wood on both sides of road at bridge by Gairnshiel kirk, the Brig o the Dam was in Wa as the name of the bridge, and PG gave it as the Brig o Dams

Bull's Nose (Gregory), to judge from its position in a list, was half way between Sean Spittal Bridge and the top of the Cairnwell road

The Burn o Coire Slugain (U ðɪˈbʌrnəˌkorˈslugən), 208807, in Callater

The Burn of the Dail Ceorc (Jm, U ðɪˈbʌrnəðɪˌdalˈhork), 172917, at Dail a' Choirce opposite Invercauld House

The Butchers' Walk (JR ðɪˈbutʃˈɛrzˈwak, M1), 287939 to 302920, path used in late 1800s by butchers from Khantore to Bovaglie and back for sheep to feed Balmoral household

Cairn Craganaglown (Im3), Carn Creagan nan Gleann, cairn of Creagan of the glens, 112904, where a former track reached a gap in a stone dyke above the former farm of Creagan at Mar Lodge, cairn and some of the dyke later removed for road-metal

The Canadian Bank (C), was on S side of railway shortly E of Ballater Station, used for loading timber cut by Canadians near Ballater during the Second World War (PD)

The Carding Mill (Jm), the Lint Mill later became a carding mill, at Milltoun of Invercauld

Castle Park (Im4a), 157925, field by Braemar Castle

The Chapel in the Valley (JR), humorous nickname (because the wooden hut was so small) for Victor's Hut in Ballochbuie, named after Victor McIntosh from Braemar

Charlie Clais Bhacaidh's Stane (WD ˈtʃarleˌklaʃˈvaxezˈstin), boulder SE of 297968, favoured by one who lived at nearby house Clais Bhacaidh at Micras, was nicknamed after his house-name and buried beside the boulder, which has since split, and vegetation now covers his house 40 m NW.

The Circle (WD), NW of 294966, small boulders in a circle on heather E of Crathie

Willie Downie tells AW about place names, Ballater, 1996 [IM]

Clais a' Mhadaidh (F klaʃ'vate), hollow of the dog, 988932 on burn's W side c100 m up from ford, Clashmattie (Roy), Clashmaddy (A), shiels S of a hollow of the same name, same as Gordon's (1925) 'ruined bothy'

The Cnoc Chalmac Parks (F), three fields in Glen Gairn

Cnoc Phlocaich or Phlocaid, (WD 'flokəx or 'flokətʃ), hill of the lad, WD in his 90s said a keeper had told him this name a long time ago, but he was now uncertain of the location; his place names were predominantly between Bridge of Gairn and Crathie on the N side, and up Glen Gairn

The Cobbler's Walk (U 'koblɛrz'wak), also The Souter's Road (U ðɪ'sutɛrz'rod), Scots Souter a cobbler, 266944, track from Crathie to Dee suspension bridge, used by a former cobbler walking to his shop at Easter Balmoral

Coire Slugain (U kor'slugən), corrie of gullet, 209807, Callater corrie with narrow funnel

The College (WD ðɪ'kolədʒ), Watson & Clement (1983) quoted WD, and M1 (p. 81) gives some detail, former Micras school on site of Hazel Cottage garden

The Communal Well (WD ðɪˌkom'junəl'wel), former public well at Queen's Road in Ballater

Corn na ?hullor or ?lullow (Fife 1798), handwriting uncertain, to judge from Earl's description of a hunt, by elimination was at 977932 on Beinn Bhrotain, Coire na h-Iolaire, corrie of the eagle

The Cornamuich Road (J), 'hill pathway' for Inverey folk going to Braemar by Coire nam Muc before present public road was made

The Cots (U ðɪ'kots), 298968 and E of burn, stone-cots largely overgrown, near Micras

Country Road (Im5), 114901, former track from Inverey to Braemar on Dee's N side

The Crafties (F 'kraftez), Scots little crofts, anglicised name for Bad Fiantaige by Coulachan Burn

The Craig (U kreg), also The Little Craig, rocky hill W of Bridge of Gairn

Craig Maud (Roy), Creag Madaidh, rocky hill of fox, shown at site of Craig of Tulloch OS, and note Fox Cairn OS nearby to the N, which raises the possibility that the local story of Fox Cairn being named after a man of that name may be a case of popular etymology, and the possibility that Fox Cairn was an anglicised form of Craig Maud

Craig of Alchulie (Mc), from the description, Alchulie was Allt Cholzie, and the Craig a hill between Craig Hillock and Auchnacraig Hill, maybe the rocky slope at 350885

The Craig of Arderg (Im3), 125807, crag W of Braemar

The Croft (U ðɪ'kroft), former house near Aucholzie, at a field called the Croft (I, Wa)

Croft Glass (D, 1682), Crote Glass (Im3), Croit Ghlas, green croft, N of 110901, former croft near Mar Lodge, stones later removed

Croislish (D, 1763), Croit Lise, croft of garden, a former Lui farm-township, thought by elimination (D) to be S of 055925, if so, was near Bad an t-Suidhe

Crom Lands or the Forked rigs (Fi), Crom crooked, Lands maybe from Lann, enclosure or land, but note Na Crom-raon at Braemar now pronounced Cromlins (Wa), 091897, former farmland at Inverey

Cross Lands (Fi), 086894, farmland at Inverey

The Crystal Diggers' Path (U), was near Shelter Stone Crag

The Cuarsag of Ben Avon (Jm, said to mean curve), A' Chuarsgag, the curve, location not known, maybe a whirlpool at Clach Bhan. Seamus Grannd thought it a common name for a whirlpool, and IM has seen one in a hollow at this place

Cutaway Cottage (OS, C), a house W of Cambus o' May Hotel, with a corner cut off to make room for the railway, see The Docket Hoose

The Dark Walk (Jm), was SE of a water course taken from Allt Dourie, an area below the stables and N of Invercauld House, still dark because of thick coniferous trees

The Deer Park (Jm), former field for keeping deer near Invercauld House, probably to NW

The Deil's Darnin Needle, see Farquharson's Needle

Delbreack (Im4a), Dail Bhreac, speckled haugh, 174919, former Invercauld field

Derleks Well (R), at Dail Choirce, later called Derleks (Wa) at Aberarder

The Docket Hoose (F 'dokət), Scots Docket is clipped or cut, the house later called Cutaway Cottage

The Doupin Stane (F ðɪ'dʌupənˌstin), Scots where novices visiting marches or property for the first time were initiated by a ceremony in which 'doup-free' members dumped novices down smartly on their buttocks against a march stone (Gm). This is a boulder that was taken from Aberarder to Tamidhus of Crathie

Duncan's Hoose (JR 'dʌnkənzˌhus), 267810, ruined divot-shelter named after a Moulzie stalker of the late 1800s

The Eagle Hoose (F ðɪ'igəlˌhus), SE of 244938, wooden hut with wire-netting, attached to an outdoor cage, carries a plaque informing that eagles were from a nest in 1885, and eagles kept till c1950, building still there but cage removed, near Balmoral

The Eagle Rock (U ðɪ'igəl'rok), 913842, eagle perch on Carn an Fhidhleir

The Eagle Stanes (F ðɪ'igəlˌstinz), 223028 and 231035, two rocks on Brown Cow Hill, each with a metal ring bolted into the rock to hold a trap formerly set to catch eagles

East Bridge (A), 147865, house SW of the Clunie bridge now called Fraser's Brig (Wa), stones removed later, maybe for road-metal

The East Muir (F mir), E part of Muir of Dinnet towards Dinnet House

David Patterson junior of Glenshee Ski Centre, who was raised there and now lives there, happy on his home hills at Meall Odhar (dun hill), Carn Aosda to left and the Cairngorms beyond, 31 July 2012 (AW)

Eelen gues (Im3), Eilean Giubhas, island with fir, N of 088897, by Dee N of Inverey

The Elephant's Graveyard (U, ðɪˈeləfənts ˈgrevˌjard), where an elephant was buried in Victoria's time at Balmoral

Ellen Begg (Im3, Tw), Eilean Beag, little island, 104896, at riverside by Victoria Bridge

The Eileruig Wood (Jm, U ˈelrəkˈwɪd), plantation S of Little Elrick at Invercauld

Ernie's Moss (F ˈɛrnezˈmos), Scots peat-bog, SW of 205995 on track's E side, where Balnault farmer Ernie Fraser dug his peat

The Eskie Pond (F ðɪˈeskeˈpond), Scots Esk a newt, Eskie diminutive, 270952, a mire with newts

The Fairy Hillock (U), same as Tom an t-Sidhein near Daldownie

The Falls o Allt Fileachaidh (F ðɪˈfalzəˌaltˈfiləxi), anglicisation of Linn of Allt Fileachaidh

The False Corrie (U ðɪˈfɔlsˈkore), anglicisation by some members of Braemar Mountain Rescue Team for Coire na Saobhaidhe on Lochnagar, named because if they were walking on a rescue mission to the Corrie of Lochnagar from Glen Gelder and were not sufficiently careful they could easily go to this corrie, the next one to the W

Farquharson's Needle (C), also The Deil's Darnin Needle (F ˈdilzˈdarnënˌnidəl), same as Monaltrie Monument

Faunoran (OS 1:10 000, C fənˈuərən), Feith an Fhuarain, bog-stream of the well, 269948, house at Crathie with a good well beside it

The Flats o the Black Burn (U), plateau on upper part of Black Burn above Loch Muick

The Forkins (U ðɪˈforkənz), Scots Forkings a fork, W of 248008 where two Gairnside roads join

The Gairden Brae (U), 357936, a hill on a track past former walled garden of old Glenmuick House

The Gauger's Lookoot (PG ˈgedʒərz ˈlukut), Scots gauger an exciseman, 273045, a stone shelter, name was well known to Willie Gordon of Sleach and PG's father, overlooks an old track from Gairn to Corgarff

The General Smuts, see Gladstone's Heid

George Mackay's Roadie (RB ˈdʒordʒməˈkaezˈrodi), Scots Roadie a path, N of 296009, after a Gairnshiel man

Glac Begg (Im3), Glac Bheag, little hollow, 106897, near Mar Lodge

Glacnabea (Im3), Glac na Beithe, hollow of the birch, S of 113902, a rock there has a centuries-old birch still growing, its roots in cracks in the rock, near Mar Lodge

The Glack o Tomnavey (Ma), Scots Glack a hollow between two hills, in Glen Gairn

Gladstone's Heid (JR hid), Scots head, refers to Prime Minister Gladstone, a boulder with a face carved by a former Rinasluick man (photo M), SW of Rinasluick, WG gave it as General Smuts, after South African leader Jan Smuts who visited the area (U)

The Glas-choille Moss (U ðɪˈglasxəlˈmos), 304042, peat-bog with cart-track still visible, same as Bruach Dhubh (OS)

The goat cott stance (Im3, shown on map as a dark blob, so was probably a rock, name printed in lower case), E of 110905, a prominent rock in this location overlooks a rough slope formerly enclosed on its E and W sides by a stone dyke, and abutting on its N side against steep screes, near Mar Lodge, so presumably someone stood there, watching over goats

Greynose (J), a place with pinewood on Mar Lodge estate, probably translation of Sron Liath, grey hill-nose

The Gully (F), defile of a burn behind cafe at Glenshee Ski Centre

The Haugh of Dellmore (J), Scots Haugh a streamside meadow, at Mar Lodge

The Haugh o' Delnabo (Ma), on Gairn

The High Road (U), from Blairglass to Daldownie on Gairn, above the Low Road

The Hill Park (AS), N of 345975, a field at Culsh in Glen Gairn

Hillie's Brae, (C ˈhëlezˈbre), Scots Brae here a hill on a road, after a Hill family who had a shop there (nicknamed Hillie), 369959, road from station square at Ballater up to the bridge over former railway

The Howe (AS), 334984, Scots Howe a hollow, here a moorland basin in Glen Gairn

The Howe Burn (WD), the low part of Torgalter Burn

The Howe o Megen (U ðɪˈhʌuəˈmegən), 325895, flat area E of Craig Megen

The Howe o the Gweemlin (R), at Ach nan Cuithe Iomlan in Glen Feardar

John Anderson, farmer of Loinmore, on the Lang Hillock, Glen Carvie, with the gap of Slacks of Glencarvie on skyline, leading to Morven Lodge and Glen Gairn, 2005 (we omitted to include The Lang Hillock in the 2011 publication; its grid reference is 346074) (IM)

Rob Bain with Selina Scott during TV filming on the Strone (An t-Sron or the hill-nose) south-west of Gairnshiel, July 1985 (AW)

The Hut (Ian Mitchell), 418981, ruin of former small drystane house above fields at Cambus o' May

The Indian Graveyard (JR ðɪˈɪndjənˈɡrevˌjard), NW of 250943, where one or more Indian servants of Queen Victoria were buried beside a small pool with a ditch running to it, now overgrown by rhododendron, SW of Balmoral Castle

Invercauld Forest (C), Wa gave The Forest of Invercauld (I) but omitted to state that Invercauld Forest is a common name for the deer-forest on Invercauld Estate (in Scots a forest was an area for hunting, not necessarily wooded and often treeless, the modern usage for a wood being an anglicisation, and other terms formerly widely used in Deeside were forester for a deerstalker, forestry for the process of hunting, afforested for an area being turned into a hunting area by introducing and protecting deer, and free forester for a local deer-hunter who did not work for a landowner and poached for a living)

The Irons (Whitehead 1960, JR ðɪˈɛirənz), SE of 210911, where Prince Albert shot a big stag in 1858 at the site of a derelict sawmill where big pieces of iron lay on the ground (JR). A nearby burn had been dammed to power the mill, and the dam remains are still visible (now altered to form a trout pond), while the track to the mill is also visible. Although published, the name is worth including here for its historical interest.

Janet's Hoosie (AnnS), same as The Muir at Gairnshiel, Janet Anderson a former inhabitant

John Ewen's Sawmill (Jm), was near Milltoun of Invercauld

The Kame o Morven (U kem), Scots Kame a terraced hillock, on Morven's S side

Kichaderg (Im3, J), Caochan Dearg, red burn, 109903, runs on and among reddish rocks, most of water now diverted to Cragan house

The King's Briggie (WD ˈbrɪɡi), Scots little bridge, W of 298968, turf-covered so that King George's horse was unaware of it when he rode to nearby butts

The King's Road, (C), private road up Muick's W side when kings reigned in the 1900s

Kinnavey (A), Cinn Bheith, end of birches, differs from Ceann an t-Sean-bhaile (shown by A as Kenheneval), 231936, former house near Inver

Lady Sinclair's School (Jm), was at Milltoun of Invercauld in late 1700s

The Laird o Glen Muick (JR), SE of 295826, a rock on Creag Bhiorach like a man's head when viewed from the side, later fell in a landslide, now on Balmoral but was on Glen Muick estate till late 1940s

The Larches (U), 268002, larch wood W of Gairnshiel

The Lecht (U lext), An Leachd, the declivity, 260007, slope near Cnoc Chalmac

The Lecht Roadie (U ˈlextˈrodi), 261006, path on above slope

The Lime Quarry (JR ˈkware), 248946, former quarry SW of Balmoral Castle

The Lint Mill (Jm), established at Milltoun of Invercauld, W of Alltdourie Cottage, in late 1700s

The Little Hillie (U), a double diminutive, 255002, W of Gairnshiel

The Loch Braes (F ˈloxˈbrez), steep slopes on Loch Muick's E side

The Loch Braes (F, as above), steep slopes on Loch Builg's W side

Long-field (Fi), 087892, at Inverey

The Long Water Track (Jm), water course cut from Glas Allt Beag to near Alltdourie, to supply a former pond where many trout were kept in hollow NW of Alltdourie

The Loupin-on Stane (McConnochie 1891, JR ˌlʌupənˈonˈstin), a stone that was at the back of the house at Spittal of Glenmuick, where the last landlady of the former pub in a building on the other side of the road from the house mounted her horse, locally was usually The Mountin Stane (JR ˈmʌuntənˌstin), no longer there, JR can remember the building that formerly held the pub, and said that most of the stones and slates were used for renovating the house at the Spittal in 1928

The Lowps (JR lʌups), Scots fish-jumps, turbulent part of Muick below the Linn

The Low Road (U), from Daldownie down Gairn to Braenaloin

Lundie's Corner (U ˈlʌndiz), NW of 318883, in road up W side of Glen Muick, after a Birkhall keeper of that name

Lundie's Cottage (U), former house opposite the bothy at Corndavon Lodge, was for decades the home of a

Rob Bain holds kittens at his Ardoch farmhouse (from Ardach or high place), 1999 (IM)

keeper named Lundie who was keeper there for 50 years

Mackintosh's Hut (U), same as Victor's Hut in Ballochbuie (Victor Mackintosh)

mac na Bracha, son of the malt, or whisky (Jm) in a list of hills, corries and burns on Invercauld Forest, Mac na Bracha, son of the malt

The Mairch Dyke (RB ˈmertʃ), Scots march, 258011, stone-wall at Wester Sleach

The Mairch Road (CW ˈmertʃ), 181900, path at Balmoral march near Invercauld Bridge

The Mairch Stanes (F ˈmertʃˈstinz), marker stones on Abergeldie-Balmoral march

The Mam (Gordon 1941), Gaelic Mam a pass, here the pass S of Carn a' Mhaim, traversed by Lairig Ghru path

The Maple-leaf Wuid (C wɪd), Scots wood, 096904, uncut by Canadians in the 1940s because the plantation trees were too young, to the fanciful the Canadians left a wood uncut in the shape of a maple leaf as a mark of their presence, the shape resembles vaguely a maple-leaf, still obvious from Inverey, and the metal strainer posts around the former plantation are still there

Meall Eal Buidhe (Jm), hill of the herb, called St. John's Wort is how Jm described it in a list of hills, corries and burns in Invercauld Forest. Meall Eala-bhuidhe, hill of St John's wort, this plant favours rich soils over base-rich bedrock

The Middle Valley (C), name used by Glenshee ski staff for valley W of Meall Odhar

Mill Croft (Fi), 087887, an arable field with buildings nearby, at Inverey

The Monega Brig (C monˈegə), recent new footbridge across the Cairnwell Burn near the foot of the Monega track to Glen Isla

AW senior left, Charlie Wright centre and Ray Parr beside Alt-na-giubhsaich (Allt na Giubhsaich or burn of the pinewood) at the start of a trip with pointing dogs to find ptarmigan nests on Lochnagar, deer skins drying on the fence, June 1963 (AW)

Morgans' Burn (WD 'mɔrgənzs'bʌrn), named after a Rinabaich family, same as Easter Micras Burn (OS)

The Moss Road (U ðɪ'mɔs'rod), 262002, track to a Gairnside peat-bog

The Mountin Stane, see The Loupin-on Stane

The Muckle Stane Hotel (U ðɪ'mʌkəl'stin,hə'tel), Scots big stone, hotel is humour for a shooters' lunch-spot at the Muckle Stane or Clach Mhor Bad a' Chabair up Girnock

The Muckle Stane o the Mairch (WD mertʃ), 300969, boulder on Rinabaich-Lebhall march

The Muir (U ðɪ'mir), Scots moor, same place as the Black Muir, W of Gairnshiel

The Mullach Fuird (C ðɪ'ımʌləx'fjurd), Scots Fuird a ford, 198022, on road W of Corndavon

The Mustard Stane (RB stin), a boulder with a hollow on top for grinding mustard seed, stood in front of Torran house on Gairn, now overgrown or removed

The Mutton Larder (JR, M1), building formerly used for storing mutton for Balmoral

Newton Cottage (OS, C), N of 396980, above Newton of Tullich or Drylea

The Newton Face (F), 335975, hill-face N of Newton of Gairn

The New Walk (JR ðɪ'nju'wak), 270815, path built c1910 for Edward VII by Loch Muick, later also the Diagonal Path (Wa), and to some walkers the Streak o Lichtnin (a name used by other walkers for the zigzag path and later vehicle track at 286820 that stalkers call the Snob Road), to JR the Streak o Lichtnin is at the loch end and the same as the New Walk

Norman's Tree (F 'normənz,tri), 086938, an old pine of spiral growth in Glen Quoich

The Nose o the Capel (U ðɪ'nozɪðɪ'kepəl), An t-Sron (OS), meaning the nose, on N side of Capel Road

The Old Schoolhouse Pool (U), in Gairn at the Auld Schoolhouse of Wa

The Old Man 'as the Garbh Choire Mor is locally known' (Hudson 1976), but Wa, Wa88 and we found no indigenous folk who knew it, so this error probably originated in Firsoff's (1946, p. 231) reference to perennial snow there as the 'Old Snow', but Firsoff often over-used quotation marks, such as 'pockets' and 'froth', and, following Hudson's paper on snow, Spink (1980) in a paper on snow reported that he saw 'the Old Man (Garbh Choire)' and Gilbert (1984) took this further by stating that snow in 'Choire Garbh' (sic) is 'known locally as The Old Man', and Gilbert & Fox (1985) by writing of 'the permanent snowfield, known locally as The Old Snowman', but these are not authentic names

The Packman's Grave (JL who lived nearby at Braenaloin), said to be a man called Macfarlane, same spot as the Tinker's Grave

The Peat-stack Hut (F), W of 315871, former shed up Muick, used for storing cut peats

The Peat Foord (Im3), Scots Fuird a ford, 118900, near Mar Lodge

The Planks (U), S of 268017, where W. Gordon of Sleach used planks to cross Gairn (M)

The Poacher's Corrie (F), recent anglicised name for Coire an Lochain Uaine of Derry, where William Smith of Abernethy stayed while poaching deer

The Pointoul Foord (Im3, J), Pointoul Foord (Tw), Poll an t-Sabhail, pool of the barn, Scots Fuird a ford, 093897, on Dee near Inverey

The Priest's Stane (U stin), anglicisation of Clach an t-Sagairt at Loch Callater

The Prince's Stane (JR stin), 324838 near Allt Fileachaidh, same Prince of Wales as in the Prince's Stone on Lochnagar

The Private Side (F), upper Glen Muick's W side with its private road

The Pulpit Stane (RB stin), 299013, a pulpit-like boulder near Gairnshiel

The Queen's Road (McConnochie 1897), road by Loch Muick to Glas-allt-shiel, referred to Queen Victoria

The Queen's Seat (JR), 285820 on track's S side, three boulders form a natural seat at Loch Muick

The Rams' Park (AS), 345977, field in front of Culsh house in Glen Gairn

The Raon Gate (WD 'ren), gateway in a stone-dyke at top of the Raon Parks

The Raon Parks (WD), a collective for more than the one field An Raon at Micras

The Red Bank (U), a pool in Gairn about 225018, near Corndavon Lodge

The Red Lands (Fi) noted as 'poor Soil', 090896, at Inverey

Elizabeth Allan, Sandy Esson, Rob Bain at the bus excursion for the 16th Annual Conference of the Council for Name Studies in Great Britain and Ireland, beside the farm at the Bush near Crathie, 1 April 1984 (AW)

The Reid Wall (U ðɪˈridˈwal), Scots red well, 298968, iron-ore well near Crathie

Rettie's Corrie (U ˈretez), after a former Gairnside man, same as Coire an t-Slugain

The Riverside Walk (JR wak), path for Queen Victoria beside Dee at Balmoral Castle

The Roadmen's Hut (JL), 271991, stone foundation above the road's N side, was a hut where they kept their tools before the days of tarred roads

Robertson's Park (U), 205935, field named after a Ballachlaggan man

The Rocks of Creagcluaine (Jm), the Rocks of Creag Clunie (U), cliffs above main road

Fly fisherman Dr Christopher Bateman casts a rod at Broch Roy pool on Dee east of Crathie (Anglicised from A' Bhruach Ruadh or the red bank), which is the steep gravelly bank to the left, wooded hill on right is Creag nam Ban (rocky hill of the women), the one beyond Creag Ghiubhais, September 2012 (IM)

The Ruch Corner (U ˈrox), Scots rough, same as Loinn Aitinn at Blairglass, a rocky field

Ruigh Fionnladh (Jm, who wrote that it means Fionnladh Sheiling), Ruighe Fionnlaigh, Finlay's shiel, Fionnladh Mor, by tradition the first Farquharson of Invercauld, was said to have been born at this house on a knoll close to the path up Gleann an t-Slugain, on W side of Glas Allt Beag

The Sanctuary (U), the private salmon water at Invercauld House

Sand Rigs (Fi), 093897, sandy former farmland by Dee at Inverey

Sandy Spout (McCoss 1921), same as the Red Spout on Lochnagar

The Sappers' Bothy (C, Watson 1975), SE of 990989, ruin of hut used for OS survey, also The Sappers' Hut (Alexander 1928) and The Sappers' Kitchen (U) on Ben Macdui

The Scob (JR skob), Scots Scob is a rod, and in place-names a point projecting from a hill, 276916, ridge between Creag nan Gall and Tom Bad a' Mhonaidh

The Sentry Box (F), 380906, stone-shelter on Cairn Leuchan near Ballater

Shannoch (A), Seanach, old place, house E of burn at Balnault, now three houses

Sheanusk (D 1700s), Sean-uisge, old water, 113901, old course of Dee near Mar Lodge after river changed course (E)

Sherlaid (Roy), Sear-leathad or east slope, the slope of Carn a' Mhaim on E side of Lairig Ghru, Wa misread this as Sherluich and thought it might be for Sgeir Fliuch, but Roy showed it clearly further N on Carn a' Mhaim above the E side of Lairig Ghru

Sherref Yard (Fi), Scots Sherref a sheriff, or personal name, 088895

The Shenwell Park (J), Sean-bhaile, old stead, Scots Park a field, 096896 by Mar Lodge

The Shouder o Inchnabobart (U ˈʃudër), Scots shoulder, 309868, a low hill-ridge in Glen Muick

The Shoppie Road (RB ˈʃope), 323016, track past former little shop up Fenzie

Skinner's Moss (U), Skinner personal name, Scots Moss a peat-bog, same as Moine Taibhseach on Glas Choille

The Smugglers Garret (Jm), was a long upstairs room, the only pub in Braemar, replaced by Fife Arms Hotel

Charlie Wright, stalker at the nearby house of Garbh Allt Shiel (Garbh-allt is rough burn), pours food pellets out of a bag for stags at the former farm of Ach a' Ghiuthais (field of the pine), a farm enclosed by a stone dyke visible in the photo, March 1971 (AW)

The Slate Quarry (Jm)

The Snob Road (F snob), track from Black Burn up to the Snob at Loch Muick

The Snow Corrie (F), a stalkers' name for Coire an t-Sneachda of Beinn Bhrotain

The Sodger's Cairn (F ðɪ'sodʒɛrz'kern), Scots soldier, resembles a soldier when viewed from above, W of 373904 in Glen Muick

The Souter's Road, see Cobbler's Walk

Sput Clach (McCoss), Sput-chlach, stone-spout, same as climbers' later name Chokestone Gully in An Garbh Choire

The Spying Cairn (JR ðɪ'spaeən'kern), 303819, a built cairn at a good spot to spy for deer by the Capel Road

The Staghorn Wreath (U riθ), snow in Lochnagar corrie in spring is like a stag's head, with snow in Douglas-Gibson Gully as one antler and in Raeburn's Gully the other

The Target Stane (WD stin), boulder at E side of burn beside and N of the Lebhall

The Three Graves (RR), SW of 344907, marks in the ground from graves at Aucholzie

The Tinks' Place (AS), SE of 343983, where tinkers stayed at the roadside in Glen Gairn

Tom na Moine (U ˌtamnə'moin), hillock of the peat-bog, 356928, ruin in Glen Muick

Tomantian (Im3), Tom an t-Sidhein, hillock of the fairy knoll, NW of 109903 by Mar Lodge

The Torgalter Brig (F), carries main road below Torgalter

Tornaleat (D late 1700s), Torr na Leathaid, hillock of the slope, a Mar tack

The Tulloch Corrie (Ma, U), near Tullochmacarrick, same as Coire na Cloiche

The Wall-ee (PG ðɪ'wal'i), Scots well-eye or spring, same as the Buailteach Wall

The Wallie o the Crofts (JR 'wale), Scots small well, same as the Crofts Wall but less anglicised, in Glen Muick

The Water Course (Jm), dug from Allt Dourie burn by a lime kiln towards the Keiloch and passing through the Deer Park so that the deer could have water to drink, at Invercauld

The Waulkmiln of Dellmore (J), near Mar Lodge

The Wee Craig (U), Scots small, same as Creag na h-Eaglaise E of Crathie

IM's son Ruaraidh on the Muckle Stane o the Mairch above Micras east of Crathie, 2004 (IM)

IM at the Eagle Stane on Brown Cow Hill, 1999 (Paddy Duncan)

The West Muir (F mir), west part of Muir of Dinnet towards Cambus

The White Wuidie (F ˈwɪdi), Scots small wood, at Craigendarroch Walk in Ballater

The Wolf Cairn (JR ðɪˈwulfˈkern), SE of 327887, said to be where the last wolf in Glen Muick was killed, was at road's E side at Wolf Corner, later demolished for road widening

The Wolf Pit (WG ðɪˈwulfˈpët), c325044, hollow for wolf-trapping, with stones set into the ground near grouse-butts, but not found by us

The Wolf Pit (as above), not seen by WG but the late Willie Ross told him it was a hollow S of the E-W track on Morven at very approximately 354026

A place-name rhyme from Cromar runs *Fae Faandhu ti Tamgleddie, Fae Paddockpuil ti Allalagie, There nivver dwelt an honest body*, ˈfeˌfanˈduˌtɪˌtamˈgledi, ˈfeˈpadəkˈpilˌtɪˌalaˈlagi, ðërˈnɪvərˈwɪzˌənˈonəstˈbʌdi. Tam Gleddie is in Wa under Tom Gleadaidh and Allalogie OS in Watson & Allan (1988). We have no information on locations of the other names, but obviously they are in Cromar near the two places that are still well known. Faandhu is likely to be Gaelic Fan Dubh or dark plain.

Changes to names in Watson & Allan 1984

Ach a' Mhadaidh, delete Easter and Wester Ach a' Mhaigh, same as Easter & Wester Auchavrie, Easter 052925, Wester 051926 (D), Auchavairy (D late 1700s), Achavenie (E, but note that handwritten *n* and *r* are often hard to distinguish with certainty), Achavadie (Roy), Achavairie (Im5)

Ach nan Saighdear, pronunciation favours the singular Ach an t-Saighdeir, field of the soldier (Thomson)

Bad a' Mheig Wood, Im3 shows it at 109906 as Pat Vaich, so should be Bad Bhathaich, clump of the sheltered place, a pine copse near Mar Lodge

The Cave is N of 087871, first rocky pool on Ey Burn N of Colonel's Bed

Coire Bhronn and Allt Bhronn with the same derivation Bhronn, meaning of bulges

Creag Curraigh, delete, it is The Craig Quarry, a quarry W of Bridge of Gairn

Creag na Saobhaidhe, detailed inspection of Roy's maps shows it to be the 702 m top at 011860 S of White Bridge, not near Linn of Dee as stated in Wa

Derleks, should read 'see Dail Choirce', not 'see Dail a' Choirce'

The Horseshoe of the Lair is not OS, 314785 and also for 250 m W along the contour

The Little Craig, the entry Creag Curraigh should have been Creag Corraidh but both are wrong (see Creag Curraigh above), rocky hill W of Bridge of Gairn

Long Hill, shown by Roy as Cairn of Claise, not Glas Maol

The Lunndaidh Moss, maybe Lundie's Moss, given the name Lundie's Corner in the list above, map reference slightly wrong, should be at 318883 on W side of Muick

Meall is usually a masculine noun, so it would be classic Gaelic form that accompanying adjectives would not be aspirated, e.g. should be Gorm, not Ghorm

The Miners' Hut, map reference dubious, as IM found a stone foundation at a different spot nearby

Poacher's Cave, was above Miners' Hut, could shelter six men (McConnochie), IM now finds no cave but it may have vanished by boulder movement

Poll Tearlaich, pronunciation favours Poll Searlus, pool of Charles (Thomson)

Roinn a' Bhathaich, Roy gave Runavoch, not Runavach

The Sleach on Gairn, Insleugh in Campbell (1750), so An Sliabhach

Sron an Daimh, the spur is at 003999 SW of Loch Etchachan

Information to add to entries of names in Watson & Allan 1984

Abergeldie, Abergaldie (He)

The Admiral Tree, sometimes The Admiral's Tree, a Scots pine with a double trunk and spreading form, favoured by an Admiral who liked to stand under it beside a short path of sand from the nearby road up Glen Tanar (JO)

Allt a' Mhadaidh-allaidh, Alltvatigally (E), Altavatagally (D 1763), Aldvattigally in Roy, not Altvattigally

Allt Chernie, given as Aldchurn (Roy)

Allt Domhain, also Altmarlich (Archer) from Allt Mearlaich, burn of thief

Allt nam Meirleach, given as Altmarlich (Archer)

Baile an Eilein, Ballnilan (Roy), Im 3 shows Ballneilan E of 103901, N of burn where it turned S, but burn's course since straightened, former farm at Mar Lodge, stones later removed

Baile nan Taobhanach, Ballnantuanoch (Im3) shown as NW of 100900 on burn's S side, Ballintuanach (E), former farm at Mar Lodge

Beinn a' Bhuird, Ben y bourd (Pe)

Beinn Mheadhoin, Ben-Main (Mc), Ben Main (V)

Beinn nan Ciochan, Bennyhigh or Benchichin Mountains (He)

Charlie Clais Bhacaidh's Stane above Micras, hammer for scale, 15 January 1995 (IM)

The Beitheachan Burn, the Beachan Burn (Mc)

Ben Avon, Ben Awin (He)

Ben Macdui, hill of sons of Duff (Watson 1926) from Beinn Mac Duibh, fits pronunciation and old written forms better than Macduff's hill which would be Beinn Mhic Duibh

Braemar Castle, given as Castle Marr (Avery)

Braigh Mharr, shown Brea Marr along Morrone slopes W to Corriemulzie (Avery)

Bynack Burn, given as Water Alturan (Avery), which suggests perhaps Allt Dhobhrain or burn of the water or the otter

Cairn Geldie, given as Carnjoldy or the Devil's Carn (Avery)

Cairn of Claise, Carn of Glascha (Do, 1403), Cairn Glaishie (V)

Cairn of Gowal to local folk the Cairn o the Gowal (JR) is the 983-m top, not 991-m one to N or 927-m one to S as incorrectly shown on some past OS maps (Stewart 1998). Munro's Tables (Scottish

IM and AW on the Blue Stane at the former Aberarder (Obair Ardair or mouth of high water) kirk and later school, building was derelict when photo taken, now converted to modern dwelling, schoolchildren slid down the Stane and parents complained of ripped breeks (Scots trousers), 5 February 1995 (IM)

Mountaineering Trust 1997) incorrectly put Cairn of Gowal at the 991-m top, which is far from The Gowal that gives The Cairn of the Gowal its name.

The Cairnwell, given as Kern Vaalg (Archer)

Caochan nan Spold, given as Clachnaspaild (Roy)

Carn Aosda, maybe Carn Naois, Naois' hill (Diack 2006), which would fit with nearby names of Fingalian legend such as Carn an Tuirc, Ben Gulabin and Tom Diarmaid, but perhaps also Carn an Fhuathais, hill of the spectre, though Diack's note 'old age' and the name Moses' Cairn may suggest Carn an Aoise, hill of the age

Carn Bhac, given as Carnvaich (Roy)

Carn Leac Dubh, Caurnleachkadow (Im5)

Carn Meadhonach (U karn'menax)

Castle William, also Castle Willie (WD)

Castleton, Castalltoun of braymarr (Pont) and Casteletown of Brae Mar (Fi) indicate Gaelic Caisteal

Ceann Dalach, Im3 shows Cantalloch at 107901 on burn's S side, so it means end of haugh, not head of haugh as in Wa, former farm near Mar Lodge, stones later removed

Charter's Chest, the Charter House; hiding place of the rocks of Creagcluaine (Jm)

Clais Balgaire (WD), also Clais Bhalgair (RB 'valagër and WD in 1996)

Clais Bhalgair, (F often 'valagër to Balmoral stalkers), a hollow in Ballochbuie

Clunie Park, the Cluaine Park (Jm)

Cnoc na Teididh, Knockintid (E), Knocknatet, Knocknatete (D 1763)

Coireach Bhuth, given as Qurrevous (Archer)

Coire an Dubh-loch, the Corry of the Duloch (Mc)

Coire Mor (OS), Coire mhor na Lairige (Gordon 1921), Coire Mor na Lairige, big corrie of the pass, on Ben Macdui above Lairig Ghru

Coire na Poite, Muick one published; as Taylor (1981) gave Corrie na Poitch

The Coths, Coathes (Mc)

Craig Doin, Craig-an-dain (Mc)

Creag an Dail Mhor, Great or Mickle Craigandal, Larger Craigandal (Mc)

The Croft, W of Balmoral, often the Crofts locally (F)

Dail a' Choirce, Delfork (P, suggested as a Mar farm by Di), but no good evidence of its being on Mar, maybe was one of the Invercauld farms with this name or elsewhere in the Lordship of Mar which included land outside that which later became Forest of Mar, thought to be Dalvorar (Di) but seems unlikely

Dail Gainimh, Dalgenie (E), Dallgainy (D 1750)

Dail Rosaigh, Delnrosick (D 1739) suggests Dail an Rosaich, haugh of the rose bush

Derry Cairngorm, Cairngorm of Derrie, or the lesser Cairngorm (Anonymous 1847)

The Derry Dam Fuird, the Ford of the Derry (V)

The Devil's Point, given as Baden Divul (Roy)

Druim a' Chreagain former farm, Wa location wrong, Im 3 shows Drumachragin E of 111902 and NE of present Cragan, stones later removed

An Duibh-leathad, 'the heid of the Divilet' in 1602 (Rms)

Eilean Giubhas, Ellengues (Im3), 118903 was at riverside, now an island by Mar Lodge

Na Feadan, W of Feadan Odhar or Muckle Feadan on Conachcraig are three small gullies joined at the foot, their green vegetation contrasting with dark heather around. In 2002, JR pointed out to AW their resemblance to bagpipes. The gullies are green with blaeberry and mat-grass, associated with snow-lie and groundwater springs. Feadan is a bagpipe chanter, whistle, or gully where wind whistles.

The Fog House, Balmoral one, the Moss House (V)

Geldie, Guillie (D 1763)

The Ghillies' Hall at Allt-na-giubhsaich, also The Ghillie Hall (U)

Glas allt Beag, written as the glaisallt burn (Jm), at Invercauld

(The) Haugh, former farm W of Dinnet, given as The Haw (Roy), probably following the common pronunciation among older Scots of Haa for Haugh

The Horseshoe o the Lair, horseshoe-shaped hollow often holding snow till early summer, horseshoe in Scots lucky position with the ends up, and a pale horseshoe of mat grass is conspicuous after snow has gone (JR)

Inbhir Geallaidh, Invergeldie (D 1739)

Invercauld, Invercald (He), Inver Call (Avery)

Inverey, shown as Inneree (Avery)

Keiloch, written as Ceileach (Jm)

Lairig Mhor, the collective name The Lairig (C) is still well known to Invercauld gamekeepers as a peaty tract E of Tom Breac, S of Corndavon Lodge

Lochan Uaine (Cairn Toul), Loch na Youn or the Blue Lake (Anonymous 1847)

Lochnagar, the hill called Lochnagar (He), the mountain Laghin y gair (Pe)

Loch nan Stuirteag, given as Loch Na Stiurtag (Roy)

Milltoun of Auchendryne, Miltown of Achidrine (Im3) shown E of Mill of Coull

Monadh Ruadh, The Mona-rua, Monadh-ruadh (Mc, 'extending from the western base of Ben Vrotan to the eastern base of Ben-Aun')

Moor of the Inver, noted as the Muir of Inver by McConnochie 1895

The Park of Inis Lagaigh, Lagaigh at hollow-place, not at hollow, a birchwood with pasture, not an arable field

Pass of Ballater, Pass of Bollitir (Pe)

The Pass o Little Craig, usually The Pass o the Little Craig (F)

The Balmoral Bonnet, a windswept outpost above Ballochbuie pinewood, named from its shape and Royalty used to picnic there, 2001 (IM)

The Boar Hoose is demolished at Claybokie, Mar Lodge, 1970s (Robbie Mitchell)

The Play Cock (I, drawn as a small 'Green'), site of a blackcock lek or display-ground at least back into late 1880s and this is the meaning (JR), Scots Playcock a pastime or game

Poll na Buitsich, N of 338967 (JR), a pool with no inlet or outlet, W of Bridge of Gairn

Ricardo's Brig in Glen Ey, no local story heard on the name's origin, so Wa thought it might be Gaelic. This is not so. John Duff in December 2010 found that Ricardo was J. L Ricardo, MP, son in law of General The Hon. Sir Alexander Duff (Aberdeen Journal Notes and Queries 2011) 4, 288 and 318. Joe Dorward then saw in Wikipedia he was John Lewis Ricardo, an MP who died in 1862. Also McConnochie (1923) wrote 'Alltanodhar was for some years occupied by the Hon George Skene Duff', presumably a relative who tenanted the Glen Ey deer-beat of Mar. The OS 6-inch map of 1866 shows a footbridge at the site of Ricardo's Brig. Wa gave Drochaid an Leim a slightly different grid reference, but they were at the same place, where the river runs at a tiny gorge.

Richarkarie, given as Richurchy (Roy)

Sleac Ghorm (OS), three instances of this name, from An Sleaghach Gorm on Balmoral, An Sleaghach Gorm in Callater and An Sliabhach Gorm on Carn a' Mhaim may all be An t-Sleac Ghorm, meaning the blue slab at Balmoral and Callater where it is a slabby cliff, and the blue hill-face at Carn a' Mhaim where it is a steep slope of dark boulders. Badenoch folk used Sleac instead of Leac, and other Leac names in Wa suggest that Leac and Sleac may be alternatives.

Snout na Loinne (F)

Strath Dee (Avery) shown as main valley W of Braemar past Mar Lodge

The Timber Foord (Im3), Scots Fuird a ford, 140915 on Dee W of Braemar

Tobar Chuirn or Red Well of the Cairnwell, stated (Wa) to be under the top car-park at the Cairnwell but water seeps out on the E side. The water is still red from iron compounds, staining the gravel of the car-park immediately E of the road, 200 m N of the pass summit.

Tolmount, Watson (1926) suggested Tul meaning brow

Tom nan Sealgair, Tomnashallager (E), Thomshalager (D 1770)

Tullich, Tulloch (Pe)

Uisge Bhruidh, Vhrich-vhruich (Anonymous 1847), given as Water of Brouen (Archer), which suggests a form like Brown in Bridge of Brown near Grantown

Names in lower Glen Tanar and Glen Carvie

The Howe o Monawee (F ðɪˈhʌuəˌmonəˈwi), 505935, Wa88 suggested Moine a' Bhith, but Moine Bhuidhe or yellow peat-bog maybe more likely

Jock Milne's Stane (F stin), N of 484915, named after a former gamekeeper, beside Jock Milne's Well (Wa88) on E side of Water of Allachy

The Peat Stable (F pit), for horses pulling peat-carts on a track at Moss of Monawee

The Three-mile Tree (U ðɪˈθriˌmɛilˈtri), a big pine at third milestone from Glentanar House

Auld Francie's Stane or Francie Riach's Stane or the Francie Riach Stane (U aldˈfransizˈstin, ˌfransiˈriəxsˈstin), 346070

Breacon Hillocks (OS), The Breacon Knowes (ˈbrakənˈknʌuz), from Breacan or speckling, Scots Knowe a knoll or hillock

Cairnagour Hill (OS, ˌkjarnaˈgʌuən, other Strathdon informants F told AW ˌkjarnaˈgʌuər), which suggests Carn nan Gabhair, hill of the goats, JA's pronunciation suggests nan Gobhann of the smiths, or nan Gamhann of the stirks

Castle o Ha (ˈkasələˈha), i.e. Castle of Haugh, and in 2010 he said the Haa Castle (ˈhaˈkasəl), remnant of the dry-stone foundation still evident on haugh between Craigneach and Lochans at about 352087

The Cateran Howe ('ketərən'hʌu), Scots thief hollow, 349063, just E of main route from Morven Lodge to lower Carvie

The Crooked Rig ('krukət'rɪg), 350086, field S of Birkford

The Greens (grinz), centre of them is at 343067, grassy stretches on the hill

The Laird's Park (lerdz), 344076, large area enclosed by a stone dyke, said to be reserved for the laird to use in a crisis

The Lang Greens, Scots Lang is long and the Greens are the middle part of the Lang Greens

The Lead Mine ('ledmɛin), in upper glen, no mine there today but some signs of stone having been taken from there

Morven's Roadie ('morvənz'rodi), Scots Roadie a track or path, 347064, path towards Morven, following approximately the line of a burn

Pattie's Knowe ('patez'knʌu), Scots Knowe a knoll, Pattie personal nickname, 349089, hillock SW of Birkford

The Peat Hillock (pit'hëlək, but JA's uncle Frank Anderson called it pet'hëlək), a flat-topped hillock formerly used for drying peats dug from a moss on the hill behind

Rahosh, (rə'hoʃ), Ruighe Chois, cattle-run of the hollow, 345082, a well SW of Lynemore

The Ringin Stane ('rɪŋənstin), 348082, a stone about three feet across, rings when you roll a pebble along it or throw a pebble at it, S of Craigneach

The Rhubarb Yard ('rubarbjerd), 350084, at an old house S of Craigneach

The Sooth-rinnin Wallie ('suθrënən'wale), Scots south-running small well, 348084, SW of Craigneach

The Waster Hoose ('wastërhus), 344084, a ruin SW of Lynemore

Willie's Hoose ('wëlezhus), 344074, ruin of small square building built into a stone dyke, not remembered who Willie was

The Sappers' Bothy near the top of Ben Macdui, 9 July 2013 (Derek Pyper)

Acknowledgements

It is a pleasure to acknowledge information and hospitality from John Anderson, Bill Bain, Rob Bain, Paul Becky, Walter Coutts, Stewart Cumming, Willie Downie, Basil Dunlop, Isabel Duncan, Paddy Duncan, Willie Findlay, Alan Gibb, Margaret Gibb, Peter Gillan, Willie Gillanders, Ann Gordon, D. Grant, Elizabeth Grant, Ann Greig, Jean Leslie, Donnie Littlejohn, Colin McIntosh, Ian Mitchell, John M. Murray, N. Nicol, Jimmy Oswald, Peter Holden, Ernie Rattray, John Robertson, J. Scott, Alan Smith, Ann Swan and Charlie Wright. Alwyne Farquharson showed AW old plans and Charles McHardy and George McIntosh an old list (Gregory below), while Stuart Mitchell, John Duff and Joe Dorward sent notes from papers.

Bibliography

Alexander, H.A. (1928). The Cairngorms. Scottish Mountaineering Club, Edinburgh.

Anonymous (1847). Ben Nevis and Ben Muich Dhui. Blackwood's Magazine, August, 149-165, was written by J.H. Burton, as is obvious when one compares it with Burton (1864). The Cairngorm mountains. Blackwood's, Edinburgh.

Archer, J. (1749). A survey of the road made by the detachment of General Guise's Regiment in Brae Marr, beginning where General Blakeney's left off: continued to the Spittle of Glen Shee. Original is at the National Library of Scotland.

Arrowsmith, A. (1807). Map of Scotland. London.

Avery, J. (1735). A plan of the country where the new intended road is to be made from the Barrack at Ruthven in Badenoth to Inver Call. Original is at National Library of Scotland.

Lochan Feith nan Sgor (lochan of bog-stream of the peaks), with Carn Fiaclach Beag (little toothed hill) beyond Glen Dee and the west tops of Beinn a' Ghlo in far distance, 24 June 2013 (Derek Pyper)

Brown, G. (1807–09). Plans of the estate of Invercauld in Aberdeen-shire. Original at Invercauld House, copy RHP 3897 at Register House, Edinburgh.

Brown, G. (1808). Plans of the estate of Invercauld in Perthshire. Original at Invercauld House, copy RHP 3896 as above.

Campbell, G. (1750). Survey from the Water Aveun to Brae-marr Castle measuring 27 miles. British Library Maps, London.

Diack, A.M.G. with Grant, J.H. (2006). Place-names of the Cairngorms National Park. Leaflet, Cairngorms National Park Authority, Grantown on Spey.

Dixon, P.J. & Green, S.T. (1995). Mar Lodge Estate Grampian. An archaeological survey. Royal Commission on the Ancient and Historical Monuments of Scotland, Edinburgh.

Dorward, D. (2001). The glens of Angus. Names, places, people. Pinkfoot Press, Forfar.

Ewen, G. (1996). Dalmore. Cairngorm Club Journal 20, 190–194.

Ewen, G. (2001). Old maps of the Cairngorms. Cairngorm Club Journal 21, 32–39.

Farquharson, J. (1703). Plan of the Forest of Mar. National Library of Scotland, Edinburgh.

Fife, Earl of (1783–92). Journal of the weather at Marr Lodge, during shooting season 1783-. Also 1798 (MS 3175/1410/1), Special Collections, University of Aberdeen.

Fife, Earl of (1787). Plan of the lands of Inverey, drawn for the Earl. Special Collections, University of Aberdeen.

Firsoff, V.A. (1946). The Cairngorms on foot and ski. Robert Hale, London.

Fraser, I. (1995). The agricultural element in Gaelic place-names. Transactions of the Gaelic Society of Inverness 58, 223–246.

Gilbert, O. (1984). The lichens of Choire Garbh. New Scientist, 23 February, 2 pp.

Gilbert, O.L. & Fox, B.W. (1985). Lichens of high ground in the Cairngorm mountains, Scotland. Lichenologist 17, 53–66.

Gordon, R. (1636-52). MS maps, National Library of Scotland, Edinburgh.

Gordon, S. (1921). Wanderings of a naturalist. Cassell, London.

Gordon, S. (1925). The Cairngorm hills of Scotland. Cassell, London.

Gordon, S. (1941). In search of northern birds. Eyre & Spottiswoode, London.

Grant, W. & Murison, D.D. (1929–76). The Scottish National Dictionary. SND Association, Edinburgh.

Gregory, J. (late 1800s–early 1900s). Invercauld Arms Hotel, Braemar, list of charges for hiring. Showed places, distance, time and price for using a Landau Victoria or Waggonette drawn by two horses, or a Victoria Dogcart drawn by one.

Henderson, D.M. & Dickson, J.H. (Eds) (1999). A naturalist in the Highlands: James Robertson, his life and travels in Scotland 1767–1771. Scottish Academic Press, Edinburgh.

Hudson, I.C. (1976). Cairngorm snow-field report 1975. Journal of Meteorology 1, 284–286.

International Phonetic Association (1963). The principles of the International Phonetic Association. University College, London.

Invercauld map 3 (1743). River Dee from the boat of Braemar up to the foord called Dee Ford, by Thomas Winter, for Lord Braco.

Invercauld map 4a (c1750, similar to Im 4 of Watson & Allan 1984). Plan of the house, garden and policys at Invercauld in the county of Aberdeen one of the seats of James Farquharson Esquire.

Invercauld map 5 (1775). An eye sketch of Brae Marr to Strath Dee anno 1775.

Jamieson, F.M. (1998). Mar Lodge Estate documentary research. Vol. 1. Report to National Trust for Scotland.

McConnochie, A.I. (1891). Lochnagar. Wyllie, Aberdeen.

McConnochie, A.I. (1895). Deeside. Lewis Smith, Aberdeen.

McConnochie, A.I. (1896). The Cairngorm mountains. I. The eastern Cairngorms. Cairngorm Club Journal 1, 236–258.

McConnochie, A.I. (1897). Queen Victorias's Highland home and vicinity. Morgan, Aberdeen.

McConnochie, A.I. (1923). The deer and deer forests of Scotland. Witherby, London.

Slaughter Brae is the steep grassy slope at centre, to the left of the slabby rocks and to the right of a deep shadow, a 1920s avalanche killed a large number of red deer, sweeping many bodies into Loch Muick, 9 March 2012 (AW)

McCoss, J. (1921). Climbing notes. Cairngorm Club Journal 10, 119–127.

MacGillivray, W. (1855). The natural history of Dee side and Braemar. Ed. E. Lankester. Printed for private circulation for Queen Victoria, London.

McHardy. J. (1853–1900). Hand-written diary, unpublished. John McHardy was head deerstalker on Invercauld. Now published in Murray (2010)

Murray, I. (1992). In the shadow of Lochnagar. I. Murray, Alt na Craig, Ballater.

Murray, I. (1999). The Dee from the far Cairngorms. Lochnagar Publications, Alt na Craig, Ballater.

Murray, I. (2010). The Cairngorms and their folk. Lochnagar Publications, Alt na Craig, Ballater.

Pennant, T. (1771). A tour in Scotland, 1769. Monk, Chester, reprint (2000), Birlinn, Edinburgh.

Pont, T. (1583–1652). Descriptive notes to accompany maps, at National Library of Scotland, Edinburgh.

Roy, W. (1747–55). The military survey of Scotland. National Library of Scotland, Edinburgh.

Scottish Mountaineering Trust (1997). Munro's Tables. SMT, Glasgow.

Stewart, K. (1998). Tricky tops: obscurities in Munro's Tables. The Angry Corrie 40, 14.

Stuart, J. (Ed) (1844). List of pollable persons within the shire of Aberdeen. Spalding Club, Aberdeen.

Taylor, R. (1981). George Washington Wilson. Aberdeen University Press, Aberdeen.

Thomson, J.M. (Ed) (1984). The Register of the Great Seal of Scotland (Registrum Magni Sigilli Regum Scotorum). Scotland's National Archives. Reprinted and presented by Scottish Record Society.

Thomson, R.L. (1965). Review of Adam Watson & Elizabeth Allan, The Place Names of Upper Deeside. Nomina 9, 119–120.

Watson, A. (1975). The Cairngorms. Scottish Mountaineering Club, Edinburgh.

Watson, A. & Allan, E. (1984). The place names of upper Deeside. Aberdeen University Press, Aberdeen.

Watson, A. & Allan, E. (1988). Place names near upper Deeside. Deeside Field, 85–96.

Watson, A. & Clement, R.D. (1983). Aberdeenshire Gaelic. Transactions of the Gaelic Society of Inverness 52, 373-404.

The Broon Coo's White Calf is the middle and deepest snow wreath on Brown Cow Hill, with the green fields of Blairglass centre, and nearer on left the ruined farm and fields of Ruighe Chreichidh or shiel of Crathie beside scattered birches, eastern part of Ben Avon distant far left, Brown Cow Hill an OS Anglicisation, for the local name is the Broon Coo, a translation of the original Gaelic A' Bho Dhonn (the brown cow), May 1984 (AW)

Alan Dennis tries to lift Clach Thogalach (stone of the lifting) as Derek Pyper watches, Glen Luibeg, 1 May 2012 (AW)

Derek Pyper at Jimmy's Hoosie, a lookout for a former watcher paid by the Duke of Fife to prevent tourists in early 1900s from walking up the track, Glen Quoich, 23 September 2011 (AW)

Watson, A. & Murray, I. (1999). Letter in The Angry Corrie 41, 17.
Watson, W.J. (1911). Topographical varia. IV. Celtic Review 7, 68–81.
Watson, W. J. (1926). The history of the Celtic place-names of Scotland. Blackwood, Edinburgh.
Whitehead, G.K. (1960). The deerstalking grounds of Great Britain and Ireland. Hollis & Carter, London.

Table 1. Phonetic scheme, underlined letters in English words as pronounced by Scots indigenous to the area. For brevity in the lists we often omit phonetics of common English words such as 'the'.

Although not in Table 1, the IPA symbol ø is used in Chapter 8, a frequent sound in Gaelic, a common letter in modern Norwegian and Danish, and sounding like oeu in French.

a f<u>a</u>t	ɔ p<u>o</u>t	ð <u>the</u>	' main stress on following syllable
e d<u>ay</u>	u t<u>oo</u>	θ <u>th</u>in	, subsidiary stress on following syllable
ɛ g<u>e</u>t	ʌ s<u>u</u>n	ʃ <u>sh</u>e	· half-long vowel
ë h<u>er</u>	ae h<u>igh</u>	x lo<u>ch</u>	: long vowel
ə tak<u>e</u>n	ɛi h<u>eigh</u>t	j <u>y</u>ou	
i s<u>ee</u>	ɔi b<u>oil</u>	z dog<u>s</u>	
ɪ b<u>i</u>t	ʌu d<u>ow</u>n	ʒ mea<u>s</u>ure	
o b<u>o</u>ne		ŋ thi<u>ng</u>	

Table 2. Abbreviations. C common use (more than 7 people among those interviewed), F a few (4-6), U uncommon (1-3). Two capital letters show an informant's initials.

A	Arrowsmith	Ml	Murray 1999
D	Duff papers	Ma	Mackenzie
Di	Dixon & Green	Mc	MacGillivray
Do	Dorward	P	Poll Book, Stuart
E	Ewen 1996	Pe	Pennant
Fi	plan for Earl of Fife	R	Robertson
He	Henderson & Dickson	Rms	Thomson 1984
I	Invercauld map by Brown	Tw	Invercauld map 3
Im	Invercauld maps by others	Wa	Watson & Allan 1984
J	Jamieson	Wa88	Watson & Allan 1988
Jm	J McHardy	V	Victoria
M	Murray 1992		

IM noticed a few names in an unpublished 1800s poem by John Mackenzie of Glen Gairn and in a typescript by John Robertson of Ballachlaggan (Ma and R above).

Chapter 2. Extra information to add to names in Watson & Allan and the CCJ article

These were recorded by us since the CCJ article in 2011

Ath Mhagairle When searching old Invercauld papers, AW came across the name of a ford up Glen Derry, a name unknown to his informants. It was Avagerill and in another paper the Ford of Avagril. He inferred that the likely spelling in Gaelic was Ath Mhagairle, and gave the meaning as ford of ? testicles, adding a question mark to indicate doubt, because the suggested meaning seemed odd. When writing this section of the current booklet he came across a note by Mervyn Browne (below). This made him realise that it was likely to mean the ford of testicles or balls, in other words where the water comes up to a man's balls. Mervyn Browne, raised in Ireland and later a sheep-farmer at Ardeonaig on Loch Tay, remarked to AW about the name Bod an Deamhain (penis of the demon) for what is now named as the vaguer The Devil's Point. He mentioned that in Ireland a hill called Magairli an Deamhain, or balls of the demon, has the shape of two round hilltops of about equal height.

Craig Doin (OS), Watson & Allan (1984) decided that this was from Creag Doimhne, cliff of depth, but old spellings Craigdyne, Craig Daign, Diack's N grekan tong, and the common local pronunciation suggest other-wise; also, Doimhne in the east Highlands was pronounced like *don*. Watson & Allan stated that Diack's version 'was probably an error of location for An Creagan Domhain nearby on the other side of Dee', but in retrospect this is unlikely, as the eastern Gaelic pronun-ciation of Domhain is doːən, so some other derivation is required, maybe Dainn a barrier or rampart, which would fit this impressive hill with its long face of rocks.

Carn Seumas Mor na Pluice, Joe Dorward queried that the grid reference for this name in the 1984 book was the same as for Altanour Lodge. In fact it is the same. The cairn stood

The Captain's Road, an old military road, northwards on Corndavon moor the rounded hill of Cnoc Chalmac (hill of St Colm) rises above the green fields at centre, high hill beyond is Carn a' Bhacain (hill of the little bank) to the west of the road summit from Gairnshiel to Corgarff, April 2012 (Derek Pyper)

Eileen's Hoosie at the Quoich, where Eileen Scott was the last inhabitant, now abandoned, heather grows on the road to the cottage, 30 September 2011 (AW)

The Stuffer's Cottage east of Inverey, named after a former taxidermist at Mar Lodge, 21 August 2012 (AW)

close by the lodge, at the edge of the wood, facing up the glen. The late Ian Grant in 1974 told AW the location. The 1984 entry should have mentioned Gr for J. Grant's 1861 book *Legends of the Braes o' Mar* as the primary reference, the Ri for Michie's *The Records of Invercauld* (1901) being much later, and SGo (should have been Sg 1948) yet later. Seton Gordon retells the story in his pp 393 and 394, in a book still fairly accessible. The reference to him in the 1984 book after the pronunciation suggests that he gave the pronunciation, but he did not. In January 2013, IM found no trace of the cairn, but has since located a probable position.

Charter's Chest OS, noted as Charter House in John McHardy's diary (Murray 2010)

Coire an t-Slugain (OS in Glen Girnock, local pronunciation korn'lugən recorded by Wa, and earlier by A as kɔran'tlukan), spoken by John Robertson in July 2011 as ˌkorən'tlukən, quite like A's pronunciation

Ruins of the farm of Ach a' Mhadaidh (field of the wolf) in Glen Lui, Sgor Dubh (black peak) in shade on left, snow-covered Carn a' Mhaim distant further right, November 1983 (AW)

Connachat, recently AW heard several times ˈkɒnjəhat from an old resident, a pronunciation that fits with the Gaelic name Coinneachaig

Creag an Lochain, Watson & Allan suggested that the lochan was the high one towards Carn Creagach, but more likely Lochan Mor on the floor of Glen Ey, directly under Creag an Lochain

The Sgairneach Well, insert U, informants Charlie Wright and John Robertson

Sron of Corrie Chash, The Nose of Corhash (John Robertson), Watson & Allan had Sron of Corrie Chash, information as Stroin of Corhaash (I), but no

Derek Pyper, John Robertson and Cameron Murray (IM's son) – three generations stand at the ruins of former farm Rinasluic (Ruighe nan Sleac or cattle-run of the slabs), Glen Muick, 2 August 2013 (IM)

informant, Nose is translation of Sron, a hill-nose E of Corrie Chash

Wullie Wyllie's Wall (F), Scots Wall a well, was in Watson & Allan (1984) as Wullie Wylie's Well, but the inscription at the well has W. Wyllie 1873, and Wyllie is a common surname in Aberdeenshire, to older folk the Scots form Wullie Wyllie's Wall, to younger folk often the more Englished Willie Wyllie's Well

Errors in CCJ account on Invercauld map Im3

Amber Foord, 133912, a ford on Dee NNE of Dalgowan, a name overlooked earlier

Baddachubber, 096804 reference incorrect as noticed by Joe Dorward, correct grid reference 096903 for the centre of this copse, close to that for what is called the Maple-leaf Wuid since Canadians logged the hillside in the Second World War, the centre of the Maple-leaf Wuid being higher uphill than that of Baddachubber

the boat of Braiemarr, name overlooked earlier, same as the Boat of Inverchandlick in Wa

Ellen Begg, as shown on the map this was a small area of land on the N side of Dee, not an island as such, although it might have been an island in earlier times, and the river has changed course

Glac Begg, delete this entry, AW misread very poor printing on his photocopy of the original map

Other errors in the CCJ article

Informant Paul Becky should be Paul Beckier

The Mullach Fuird is pronounced ðˈmʌləxˈfjurd

Wuid o the Dams not at Gairnshiel, but on either side of public road N of the Brig o the Dam N of Bush above Crathie C, also The Wuid o the Dams (U)

Tigh na Cailliche Beathraiche or house of the wild witch, on Morrone, an unusual ridge of rock like gigantic masonry, in local legend the witch's house, July 1989 (AW)

Extra information about names in the CCJ article

The Doupin Stane, informant said later that it came from old ruined kirk of Crathie, so origin uncertain

George Mackay's Roadie, named after a former gamekeeper

Jock Milne's Stane and Jock Milne's Well are sometimes now Englished to John Milne's Stane and John Milne's Well (F)

The Laird's Face (JR), same as The Laird o Glen Muick, from the W, the rock resembled a man's face

The Mutton Larder (C), also Murray (1999, p.77), 256950, round building near Balmoral Castle, registered by Royal Commission on the Ancient and Historical Monuments of Scotland as Venison and Mutton Larder and Venison Larder, built in mid 1800s, still used as a venison larder but locally called the Mutton Larder

The New Walk or The Streak o Lichtnin, Murray (1999) reports this story about name-confusion, citing John Robertson, who also told us that The Corrie Chash Path (U) was same as the New Walk and the Streak o Lichtnin

The Sooth-rinnin Wallie is the only spring that runs south in that locality, unusual for the glen and its main burn face north

The name Ruighe

We decided to translate as cattle-run (Methods in *CCJ* article), because the word can have several meanings, e.g. from Dwelly, wrist, arm, outstretched part or base of a mountain, slope, summer residence for herdsmen and cattle, shieling. In Upper Deeside, many Ruighe names refer to ruins of shiels or shielings (Watson, Allan & Fraser 1984 in Chapter 5 below, note Ian Fraser's comment). However, a name such as Remicras in Glen Gairn indicates an original shieling of Micras, Micras being formerly a settlement of many farms near the River Dee east of Crathie. Later, however, it became an arable farm, and AW recalls it as such in the mid 1940s.

The Cobbler's Walk down to Dee, with the spire of Crathie Kirk peeping above the trees far left, below the wooded hill of Creag na Gaoithe (crag of the wind), and to the right of it the higher Creag a' Chlamhain (crag of the buzzard), the cobbler lived in a house above the suspension bridge over Dee below Crathie, 17 July 2012 (AW)

John Robertson and AW at the Eagle Hoose, Invergelder, built by Queen Victoria, where captive young golden eagles were kept in the late 1800s and early 1900s, 2005 (IM)

Above Gairnshiel, the River Gairn is frozen over, apart from a fast-flowing section at Sgeir an Deoch (rock of the drink), named from a piece of bedrock at the roadside, where horses and people paused to drink at a stone water trough, the trough in glen folklore was of granite and removed when the road became metalled and horses began to be less common. This photograph illustrates the variety of place names in a small area, the lone pine stands beside the farm ruins of Balnaan (probably Baile an Athain, stead of little ford) beside an old ford across Gairn, the Lang Haugh runs along the bank between Balnaan and the River Gairn and was once a favoured route by horse and sledge, the stark ruin of Easter Tulloch, formerly the Manse, on the slope to the right, the white spot in sunlight further away on the left being the farm ruins of Tullochmacarrick, and the far hill on the left is Carn Bad a' Challain (hill of clump of the noise), an eastward extension of Brown Cow Hill, 2 March 2010 (IM)

AW senior stands on Carn an 'Ic Duibhe with the high Beinn Bhrotain far beyond and Carn Cloich-mhuilinn the conical top on its left, both names as on OS maps are wrong, should be Carn an t-Uidhear (hill of the traveller) and Carn nan Clach-mhuilinn (hill of the millstones), January 1965 (AW)

Cairn Bannoch from Carn a' Bheannaich (hill of the point) is the little rocky point at far right under a cloud shadow, the Cairn of Gowal on left, viewed from Broad Cairn, the hollow below leads left into the Tap Gowal and the Burn of Gowal in Angus, Gowal a figurative name, from Scots the hollow between a person's legs, 27 February 1980 (AW)

Chapter 3. Unpublished names in upper Deeside, recorded since 2011

Heard or remembered or seen in notes by us since CCJ article in 2011

We heard almost all names from Gary Coutts, Alan Dennis, Joe Dorward, Bill Ewen, Peter Fraser, Peter Gillan, Ian Grant formerly of Tomidhu, Ann Keiller Greig, Simon Lenihan, Graham McCabe, Hugh Mackay, Geordie Main, Willie Meston, Robbie Mitchell, David Patterson, Derek Pyper, Tom Ritchie formerly of Torran, John Robertson, Ronnie Robertson, Bob Scott and Duncan Watt.

 Notable features are the high proportions of Scots and English names, and low proportion of Gaelic ones, compared with those in Watson & Allan (1984). Sadly, there are now markedly fewer indigenous folk left who know and use Gaelic names.

The Aberdeen Haugh (Michie diary 1884, F ˌebərˈdinˈhax), 188906 on south side of Dee, well known to Balmoral gamekeepers and fishing gillies for many years, same name applies to Invercauld Estate nearby just north of the east end of Invercauld bridge as noted by Wa

The Auld Brig Road (C Auld locally pronounced aˈl), name by Aberdeen climbers taking a short-cut from the bus at Crathie when going to Gelder Shiel, local name The Cobbler's Walk or The Souter's Road as in CCJ

The Auld Sheetin Lodge (U ˈaˈlˈʃitnˌlodʒ), Scots old shooting lodge, 307015, Tom Ritchie on a visit to the Torran with Ian Murray in October 2011 pointed out the stone remains of a former shooting lodge once owned by the Irvines of Drum in Lower Deeside.

The Aultonrea Corrie (U), 364908, towards Cairn Leuchan from Aultonrea

The Aultonrea Ridge (U), 360910, broad ridge with grouse butts above Aultonrea

The Balmenach Bog (U), 360976, boggy slope below Balmenach

The Bare Hill (U), S of Glenmuick House, so-called because of poor growth of vegetation

The Boar Hoose (F hus), S of 086900, a former small stone building near Claybokie, with a cobbled floor and stone-built high-walled yard, shown on the first OS 6-inch map (1866 survey), and was thought to have held livestock when Ronald MacDonald a former head deer-stalker on Mar, lived at Claybokie. In the late 1960s the factor Calum Macfarlane Barrow bought a young boar and sow from Aberdeen zoo. Fed on deer carcases that were unfit for selling, the two grew at a great rate. Occasionally they escaped, despite a high

Carn Aosda (OS), locally from Carn Aoise or hill of age, from the car park at Glenshee ski area, on a day when muirburn fires burned high into the alpine zone, April 2008 (AW)

fenced enclosure, and then caused havoc to gardens at Braemar, so they were sold to a Wiltshire zoo. The building and walled enclosure were demolished in the 1970s on the instruction of the then landowner Gerald Panchaud (R. Mitchell). The Earl of Fife introduced wild boars to Mar Lodge about 1790, but the introduction failed. A hair-covered boar's skull used to hang in the deer larder at Mar Lodge, perhaps from the Earl's introduction, and the Boar Hoose possibly also dated from that time

Bowman's Stane (F stin), at the riverside below Old Bridge of Dee, where Bowman accidentally hanged himself on a deer fence while collecting white heather for Queen Victoria

The Blue Rock Butts (U), 328857, grouse butts near the Blue Rock and above the Scoube

Breda's Isle (IM came across a name not heard by us, in notes shown to him by Ian Brown, written by his grandfather William Brown.), a place in Glenmuick Churchyard, probably meant Aisle, not Isle

The Bughts (U, bʌxts), dry-stone shelter pens for sheep in field near Torran

The Burma Road (U), 160872, steep zigzag track on to Sron Dubh in lower Glen Callater

The Burma Road (U), track along east side of Glen Gelder to the col towards Glen Muick

The Cairndoor Face (U), steep face of Cairndoor Hill above public road at the Shenval

The Canadian Falls (U, falz), a rapid in Dee at the former Canadian Brig just below the entry of Lui Water

The Chapel Loch (C lox), 362942, beside a derelict chapel for former Glenmuick House

The Chimney (U), NW of 282818, a steep narrow rocky gully on S side of Loch Muick

The Copper Mine (U), in a hollow W of Gairnshiel, now filled in, informant uncertain of exact location

The Cross Path Brig (F), 267834, across Glas Allt above the Falls, where Cross Path runs NE

The Delnabo Brig, see the Shakkin Briggie

The Deuk's Puil (U 'djuks'pil), Scots ducks' pool, former pond, now filled in, below the Stroup

Eileen's Cottage (U 'aelinz'kotədȝ), at the Quoich where Eileen Scott was the last inhabitant

The Faulds (U falz), Scots Fauld is outer land dunged by cattle, part of a field at Torran

The Gas Park (U), a former enclosed area at the Gasworks Loch

The Gasworks Loch (C), 357939 at a former gasworks for former Glenmuick House

The Gelder Shiel Brig (F), S of Gelder Shiel, carries road across to west side of Gelder Burn.

The Green Brig (C), same as the Balmoral Brig carrying the main road from Crathie to Balmoral, but in more common use

Ham's Hole (F), 166853, gravel borrow-pit excavated by former contractor Brian Ham for roadworks in Glen Callater

The High Drive (U), 187896, track along W slope of Glen Beg in Ballochbuie woods

The Inver Stane (F stin), alternative name to Donald Dinnie's Stane and the Lifting Stane as already published in Watson & Allan (1984) and the latter in Alexander (1952), a stone used for trials of strength at some Braemar Gatherings, had 256 lb cut into one side (see photo), IM heard the Gaelic *Cuid fir* associated with it, literally meaning some men (AW), the stone at Inver was also used for tethering horses many decades ago

The Lang Haugh (F 'laŋ'hax), flat ground between Balnaan and River Gairn

The Lang Ley (U 'laŋ'lɛi), 307012, a field at the Torran

Little Mammie (U), 318814, small top SE of Mammie

The Loup of Pollchynnich or Kenneth's Pool (Brown of Crathie) near Inchmarmnoc, Pollchynnich well known from Poll Choinnich, but we had not heard of the Loup, Scots for salmon leap

The Low Drive (U), 193898, track along foot of Glen Beg in Ballochbuie woods

The Mackenzie Chapel (F), 361944, former private chapel for family of Sir Allan Mackenzie, laird of former Glenmuick House, with tomb and graveyard beside it

Michie's Brig (U), 246934, footbridge over Gelder

The Mill Laivers (U 'mël'levərz), i.e. Scots levers, a pole pulled by horse to turn a mill, behind the steading at Torran in Glen Gairn

The Moss Road (U mos), 313036, cart track to peat-moss of Moine Allt Duisgan, folk of Torran and Richarkarie used it

The Parkin's Moss Trail, a signpost by the visitor centre at the Burn o Vat carries this name to a path and peat-moss named after Jim Parkin a former warden of the nature reserve

Raddie (U 'radi), Gaelic Radaidh is dark red, 351966, a fast-running fishing pool below Newton and W of the mouth of River Gairn, on south side of island, past reddish rocks

The Reid Sand Brae (U 'rid'san'bre), a small brae on the road about 312 856, named from the reddish colour of the gravel before the surface became tarmac

The Roebuck B(ridge), hand-written on the back of an old photo of a bridge, photo held by IM, site exactly the same as the later Edmund's Brig, but was a different bridge, photo from late 1800s or early 1900s

 The Ruch Gruip (JR 'rox'grĕp), Scots rough channel, NW of 283819, a rocky gully above Loch Muick

The Shakkin Briggie (U 'ʃakən'brɪgi), Scots Shakkin shaking, also the Delnabo Brig, 301010, over Gairn

The Slaughter Brae (JR 'slatər'bre), 293825, steep slope above Loch Muick, where red deer died in an avalanche about 1926, with many swept into the loch

The Spion Kop (U 'spaeən'kop), was wooden bothy immediately E of Ardoch at Crathie, noted with accompanying story (Murray 1999), named after well-known Boer War battle

The Stroup (U strup), Scots spout from a well, at the Torran in Gairn

The Stuffer's Cottage (C), pink wooden house E of Mealdarroch Cottage and near the Stuffer's Pool, was formerly inhabited by taxidermist at Mar Lodge

The Sunday Drive (C), 350953, old track through woods near Birkhall

The Tod Hillocks (U tod), Scots Tod a fox, Wa had Tod Hillock (OS) but no informant, and our informant said the name was The Tod Hillocks, between Black Hill of Mark and Murley SE of Loch Muick

The Tom Chuilein Road (U tam'hulən), 171836, a track from Glen Callater ending near Tom Chuilein

The Tuirc Road (U tʌrk), track to Carn an Tuirc from foot of Loch Callater

The White Ship (U hwɛit), big white boulder N of summit of Tom Meann above Abergairn

The Yalla Corrie (U 'jala), Scots yellow, 370916, wide corrie with much coarse grass due to continual ground-water springs, same place as the Corrie of Tom nam Buachaillean (Wa)

Current oldest gillies who know the local Dee fishing pools tell IM that the Key Pool is at Kate or Kate's Puil, not at Mitchell's Puil nearby, other references are vague in exact location but give the Key Pool from original Poll na h-Iuchrach (Alexander 1952, Watson & Allan 1984). Poll na h-Iuchrach/The Key Pool is in the same place as The Mitchell Puil, which is the next pool above Kate's Puil (I. Scott map 1959, reference in Watson & Allan 1984)

More names found by IM in John Michie diary (passed to IM indirectly and originally by Alison Innes)
Most of these we cannot locate exactly, although all were on Balmoral Estate. Invercauld Estate at one time included the Ballochbuie woods and Dallyfour near Invermuick but the diary was kept by John Michie Head Forester, Factor, and King's Commissioner at Balmoral, 1882–1919. The section seen by us is incomplete, but the names given are listed below.

The Aberdeen Haugh Plantation, Aberdeen Haugh on Balmoral towards Old Bridge of Dee

Ardinruach, Ard an Fhraoich, height of the heather, a smithy near Toldhu or maybe between there and Birkhall

The Ballochbuie Enclosure, would have been fenced for trees in lower Ballochbuie woods

Baltinsnach Smithy, maybe Bailean Sneachda, little stead of snow, location unknown

Black Park Woods near Genechal, note The Black Park a well-known name there

Bowman's Well, note Bowman's Moss a well-known name at Moine Chruinn near Connachat

Campbell's walk, near Balmoral Castle, possibly named after a Campbell who was minister at Crathie at the time (the name appeared in a diary entry of 1896), or after a Campbell a piper who was in service at Balmoral at the same year of entry in the diary

Clashlee Plantation, note there is a Clais Lighe in lower Glen Muick

The Coirebhruach Westwood road, obviously in upper Glen Tanar

AW skis on Meall Odhar below Glas Maol with its snow-corniced horseshoe corrie in exceptional snow cover, OS names wrong, should be Am Meall Odhar Mor and A' Ghlas-mheall, and the corrie further north, printed Coire Fionn on maps, is wrongly located and named, should be Am Fionn-choire and is the horseshoe corrie, 11 March 1972 (AW senior)

Craigmile's Mill, probably personal name, location unknown

The Exhibition chalet, erected between Balmoral Castle and the river, a little W of the castle

Garmaddie Bog

The Garmaddie Mill, was probably a sawmill

Greag Faechan, location unknown, suggests Creag Bheitheachain, rock of the little birch-place

Riddoch's Sawmill, Riddoch a saw-miller from Rothiemay had a portable engine and mill which he placed on the Water of Lui a mile above the confluence with the River Dee. He put it there to cut pines for building New Mar Lodge for the Duke of Fife. The Balmoral factor visited the mill, so maybe it also worked on Balmoral

The Smuggler's Walk, the lower section of the path leading to the Smugglers' Shank

Upper and Lower Dalyfour Haugh, flat fields at Dallyfour farm

Westwood road

Englished spellings of names of fishing pools on Mar

Joe Dorward found these spellings on Mar in a book by Augustus Grimble (1913), and kindly let us know. Most had already been named in Gaelic by Watson & Allan (1984), but not Tree Pool, Plaintain Pool and

Auchelie, a ruined farm in lower Glen Ey, OS misleadingly gave all Ach names in Aberdeenshire as Auch, second part of Auchelie also incorrect, from Ach a' Cheiridh or field of the waxy place or duskiness, 9 September 2011 (AW)

The Meikle Pap (OS), all OS Meikle names are pronounced Muckle in Aberdeenshire and should be spelled as such, Meikle being the form used in central Scotland (Derek Pyper)

Lower Geldie Pool. Watson & Allan gave far more than three Gaelic pool-names omitted by Grimble, so his Tree Pool and Plaintain Pool may have been Englished versions of names given in Gaelic by Wa. However, the Lower Geldie Pool was not named by Wa, either Englished or Gaelic. Presumably it lay near where Geldie Burn meets Bynack Burn, an area often called the Lower Geldie.

Three place names in lower Deeside
In May 2013, John Duff told AW a name on the Beltie Burn above Bogarn west of Banchory, known to the late Paddy Duncan as Lammie's Loup, Scots loup a jump or place for salmon to leap, ou pronounced as ow in English. John said Bogarn used to be a croft, and his mother bought milk there. Bogarn is from Gaelic Bog Fhearn, bog of alders. On 4 July 2013 AW met Paddy's brother Gordon, brought up with Paddy at Invercannie sawmill nearby. Gordon recalled Lammie's Loup, confirming it as a good place for catching fish. It is E of 650977. He added that it lay below Briggie's Dam, Briggie's being the nickname of the farmer at Bridgend upstream. We do not know the origin of Lammie's, maybe from a personal name, the surname Lamb in Deeside being called Lamm, with the addition as in Bert becoming Bertie, so Lammie. Another speculative possibility is the English word Lamb for a young sheep, again with Scots *ie* added.

Conachcraig (OS) should be Conachreag (high rocks or combination of rocks), view from Glen Muick with distant Cuidhe Crom of Lochnagar and Little Pap on left, much ice on River Muick in hard frost, February 1984 (AW)

Sgor an Lochain Uaine (OS) or peak of the green lochan, a good OS and Gaelic name Englished to the Angel's Peak by a former member of the Cairngorm Club, and unfortunately now added as (The Angel's Peak) after Sgor an Lochain Uaine on modern OS 1:25 000 maps, though not on earlier maps, a view from the Lairig Ghru, 15 April 1962 (AW)

Chapter 4. Incorrect Gaelic names on OS maps of Upper Deeside

The first name in each pair below is the OS form, the second the corrected form as based on evidence in *The Place names of Upper Deeside*, by Watson & Allan (1984).

Allt an Eas Bhig, Allt Easaidh Beag
Allt an Eas Mhoir, Allt Easaidh Mor
Allt Boruich, Allt Both-fhraoich
Allt Cac Dubh, Allt Cadhach Dubh
Allt Cailleach, Allt Chailleach
Allt Coire an Fhir Bhogha, Allt Coire Cadha an Fhir Bhogha
Allt Coire Bhearnaist, Allt Coire Bhearn-uisge
Allt Coire Cath nam Fionn, Allt Coire Cadha nam Fiann
Allt Coire Fhearneasg, Allt Coire Bhearn-uisge
Allt Coire Fionn, Allt Fionn-choire
Allt Coire nam Meanneasg, Allt Coire nam Mion-easga
Allt Connachty, Allt Chruinneachtaidh
Allt Dhaidh Beag, Allt Damhaidh Beag
Allt Dhaidh Mor, Allt Damhaidh Mor

Mike Taylor on Sgor Dubh looks at the cliffs of The Devil's Point (OS), an Englished euphemism from Bod an Deamhain or penis of the demon, February 1965 (AW)

Allt Domhain, An t-Alltan Domhain
Allt Garbh in Glen Dee, An Garbh-allt, note OS Coire Gharbh-uillt
Allt Glas, An Fheith Ghlas
Allt Glas-neulach, Allt Glas-leathad
Allt na Caillich, Allt Chailleach
Allt na Cloch, Allt na Cloiche
Allt na Lairig Ghru, Allt na Lairig Dhru
Allt Salach, Feith Salach
Allt Tom a' Bhealaidh, Allt Tom Bealaidh
Allt Vitch, Allt Mhaide
Alltcailleach, Allt Chailleach
Auchelie in Glen Ey, Ach Cheeree better Anglicised spelling, from Ach a' Cheiridh
Balhalach, Baile Chailleach
Beinn a' Bhuird, Beinn-bord
Beinn Iutharn Bheag & Mhor, Beinn Fhiubharainn Bheag & Mhor
Beinn Mheadhoin, Beinn-meadhon
Brackley, Braichlie a better Anglicised spelling
Cac Carn Beag, Cadha Chuirn Beag
Cac Carn Mor, Cadha Chuirn Mor

Creag nan Leachda (OS), locally Creag Leacach (rocky hill abounding in flat stones), a view from Dee at Ballochbuie, also shows The Y, a name for a snow-patch in a Y-shaped gully below the top, May 1984 (AW)

Cairn Hillock, Carn na h-Iolaire
Cairn of Claise, Carn na Glaiseath
Cairn Sawvie, Carn Saobhaidhe
Cairn Vallich, Carn Bhealaich
Carn an 'Ic Duibhe, Carn an Uidhir
Carn Aosda, Carn Aoise
Carn Chrionaidh, Carn a' Chronaidh
Carn Cloich-mhuilinn (Beinn Bhrotain), Carn nan Clach-mhuillin
Carn Leuchan, Carn Fhliuchan
Carn na Cuimhne, Carn na Coinnimh
Carn nan Sgliat, Carn nan Sgleat
Carn Tiekeiver, Carn Tigh Ic'Iomhair
Clais Rathadan, Clais Bhrodainn
Cnapan Nathraichean, Cnapan Fhearchair
Coire an Fheidh, Coire nam Fiadh
Coire an Fhir Bhogha, Coire Cadha an Fhir Bhogha
Coire Bhearnaist, Coire Bhearn-usige

Cairn of Claise (OS), Anglicised from Carn na Glaiseath or hill of the green grassy place, from Glas Maol, with Lochnagar beyond to the left, 1 July 1977 (AW)

The Tink, the name of the public bar at Invercauld Arms Hotel, Ballater, May 1984, hotel now converted to flats, wooded hill behind is Craig Coillich (rocky hill of witch or old woman), May 1984 (AW)

Coire Cath nam Fionn, Coire Cadha nam Fionn
Coire Fhearneasg, Coire Bhearn-uisge
Coire Fionn and also wrongly located, Am Fionn-choire
Coire Meacan, Coire Muilcinn
Coire na Cloiche on Derry Cairngorm, Coire nan Clach
Coire nam Freumh on Morrone, Coire nan Ragh
Coire nam Muc OS is Coire na Fuath-chlais, Coire nam Muc being further east at 136902
Coire na Saobhaidh in Derry, Coire na Saobhaidhe
Coire Poll Randaidh, Coire Poll Ranntaich
Coire Yaltie, Coire Ghealtaidh
Corn Arn, Coire an Eirbhein
Craig Coillich, Creag Cailliche
Craig Doin, Creag Dainn
Craig Leek, Creag Lice
Craig Nordie, Creag an Orduigh
Creag an Dail Bheag & Mhor, Creagan Dail Beag & Mor
Creag an Fhir-shaighde, Creag an Fhleisdeir
Creag an Lurachain, Creag Lurgainn
Creag Ghiubhais, A' Chreag Ghiubhas
Creag Leachdach, Creag Leacach
Creag Mulloch, Creag Mor-thulaich

The Feadans from Gaelic Na Feadan can mean bagpipe chanters or gullies where wind whistles, resemblance to chanters obvious in this photo, upper Glen Girnock, 2004 (IM)

Braeriach (OS), Anglicised from Am Braigh Riabhach, the brindled upland, a view from Ben Macdui across the Lairig Ghru pass, with Coire na Lairige or corrie of the Lairig to the right (was Coire Ruadh or red corrie to Mar stalkers), 22 May 1977 (AW)

Creag Ghiubhais (OS), locally from A' Chreag Giubhas (the pine rock), a view from Coilacriech pinewood in deep snow with Mount Keen peeping above the Glen Muick hills beyond, 28 November 1965 (AW)

Creag na Dearcaige, Creag nan Dearcag
Creag nan Leachda, Creag Leacach
Cuidhe Crom, A' Chuithe Chrom
Culardoch, Cul Ardach
The Devil's Point, Bod an Deamhain
Ear-choire Sneachdach, Ear-choire an t-Sneachda, burn Allt Coire an t-Sneachda OS
Feith na Sgor, Feith nan Sgor
Garbh Choire Dhaidh, Garbh Choire Dhe
Garbh Choire Mor, An Garbh-choire Mor
Garlot, Garbh-leathad
Glac Anthon, Glac Eanntoin
Glas Maol, A' Ghlas-mheall
Iar-choire Sneachdach, Iar-choire an t-Sneachda, see Ear etc above
Knockie Branar, Cnocaidh Branndair
Lairig an Laoigh, The Lairig Laoigh (i.e. Lairig of Lui)
Lairig Ghru, The Lairig Dhru (i.e. Lairig of Dru or Druie
Leabaidh an Daimh Bhuidhe marked as summit tor, which is Stob Easaidh Mor., Leabaidh etc unknown locally, maybe was grassy bank below tor
Lebhall, The Leth-bhaile
Loch Ullachie, Loch Iolachaidh
Loch Vrotachan, Loch Bhrot-choin
Meall an Lundain, Meall Lunndann
Meall Glasail Beag and Mor, Meall Glas-allt Beag and Mor (Wa by error put Bheag and Mhor, but Meall is a masculine noun)
Meall Odhar, Am Meall Odhar Mor

Moine Chruinn, A' Chruinne-mhoine

Pollagach Burn, The Pollach Burn (pron Poolach)

Poll Bhat, Poll Bhathaidh pron vaa

Rinasluic, Ruighe nan Sleac

Sgor na Cuileige, Sgor na Culath

Sron a' Bhruic, Sron nam Brac

Sron Gharbh (Glen Fenzie one), An Garbh-shron

Sron Riach, An t-Sron Riabhach

Stob Dubh an Eas Bhig, Stob Dubh Easaidh Beag

The Stuic, The Stuc or An Stuc

Tom a' Chatha, Tom a' Chadha

Tom a' Chuir, Tom a' Chairr

Tom Anthon, Tom Eanntoin

Tom Glady Wood, Tom Gleadaidh Wood

Tom na h-Ola, Tom na h-Olla

Tom Ullachie, Tom Iolachaidh

Torphantrick Wood, Ruighe Bhantraich Wood, new house Torphantrick perpetuates error

The March Burn (OS), Englished from Allt na Criche or burn of the boundary or march, before it plunges from the plateau into the Lairig Ghru, Sron na Lairige (hill-nose of the Lairig) beyond with the low ground of Speyside rightwards, 20 September 1998 (AW)

Beinn Mheadhoin (OS), locally Beinn-meadhon or middle-hill, from Cairn Gorm, Lochnagar distant to left, the tors on Beinn Mheadhoin are Sabhalan or barns of Beinn Mheadhoin.17 April 1981 (AW)

Lochnagar from Aberarder, old name Beinn Chiochan, hill of paps, or Beinn nan Ciochan, hill of the paps, an apt name as seen in this photo showing the Meikle Pap on left and the pap-like summit of Lochnagar well to the right of it and nearer, 4 October 2012 (IM)

The remains of a fresh autumn snowfall lie on 8 November 2014 beside Carn nan Tri Crioch or cairn of the three boundaries, erected long ago at a spot where Aberdeenshire, Banffshire and Inverness-shire meet at 1200 m altitude on the lofty plateau of Cairn Lochan south-west of Cairn Gorm. The dark bulk of Braeriach looms to the right, beyond the gulf along the pass of Lairig Ghru, with the head of Cairn Toul in the mists to the left. (Attila Kish)

Beinn a' Bhuird (OS), locally Beinn-bord or table-hill, from Cairn Gorm, with the White Mounth beyond Braemar on far right, 22 May 1977 (AW)

John Robertson on place-name trip, Glen Girnock, 15 May 1983 (Adam Christopher Watson)

Garbh Choire Mor, Garbh Choire Dhaidh and Coire Bhrochain from Ben Macdui, Garbh Choire Dhaidh (OS) is wrong, meaning rough corrie of David, should be Garbh-choire Dhe or rough corrie of Dee, named after the young Dee which plunges down its cliffs, and Brochan is 'literally gruel or porridge, but applied in place-names to anything broken up or comminuted, as Coire Bhrochain (Cairngorms), the corry of the broken stones' (W.F.H. Nicolaisen in Ordnance Survey 1973), 3 July 1983 (AW)

Fred Macaulay of the BBC's Gaelic section with Mrs Jean
Bain after he had recorded a radio broadcast with her at the
Ardoch, September 1976 (AW)

Mrs Bain feeds her poultry at the Ardoch, May 1980 (AW)

Mrs Jean Bain, last fluent speaker of the Aberdeenshire dialect of Gaelic, at the front door of the Ardoch, Crathie, May 1980 (AW)

Willie Grant, one of AW's two best Mar informants for his 1984 place-names book, bleeds a stag that he has just shot in upper Glen Derry, September 1948 (AW)

Willie Grant and Frank Scott, last watcher at Corrour Bothy in the early 1920s and in 1948 head stalker on the Forest of Mar, , have loaded a pony carrying the stag seen in the previous photo, September 1948 (AW)

Frank Scott leads a pony carrying the stag seen in the previous two photos, across the Derry Burn, September 1948 (AW)

Coilacriech Inn below the high pinewood on Geallaig Hill, often mispronounced, local pronunciation of Coil or Coyle in names being as in Kyle, May 1984 (AW)

The heathery flat at centre with old Scots pines is Eilean na Fiodhaige, the island or stream-side meadow of the bird cherry, no bird cherry since at least 1900, Glen Lui, 24 August 2012 (AW)

Derek Pyper looks at the ruins of the former habitation of Teetabootee (language and meaning doubtful) by the roadside in upper Glen Muick, once a sanctuary for many passing travellers and drovers, which bustled with activity as a busy pub until 1815, now passed by many thousands of tourists each year but unknown to most, 15 March 2013 (AW)

Sandy McDonald, Ian Grant, John Duff on a place-name trip to Glen Geldie, 4 October 1974 (AW)

Sergeant Arthur Davies' Grave, the pale stone projects above wind-clipped short heather, looking east down Glen Cristie to the hill of Morrone far right, December 1991 (AW)

Peter Gillan about to take a drink from a metal cup attached to a rock with a chain at Wullie Wyllie's Wall, water dripping from the cup, 1990s (IM)

AW at one of the two locations known as the Boars' Holes above Greystone, Crathie, a hiding-place with walls of stones and turf, 11 May 1996 (IM)

The Cuidhe Crom (should be A' Chuithe Chrom or the crooked wreath), on Lochnagar, viewed in a telephoto picture from Glen Muick, 27 April 2011 (IM)

Cairn Toul and Sgor an Lochain Uaine rise above mist, as skiers climb south-east of Ben Macdui, 10 January 2013 (IM)

AW senior at the Lifting Stane opposite Inver Inn, May 1984 (AW)

Clach Mhor Ruighe na Sroine, big stone of shiel of the hill-nose, in upper Glen Gairn, looking down to the green fields of ruined farm Daldownie by River Gairn, muirburn patches beyond on Brown Cow Hill, 1 September 2011 (IM)

Felagie cottage below Craig Leek, named after the Felagie Burn nearby (Feith Leigidh or slow bog-stream), beyond rise the Felagie Rocks, originally Am Mir Dubh or the black top, a name now forgotten in local speech, 1997 (IM)

Hillie's Brae in Ballater, with Craig Coillich beyond, 14 August 2012 (IM)

The Gauger's Lookoot in upper Glen Gairn, where an excise-man looked for illicit stills and carriers of illicit whisky, 24 March 2011 (IM)

John Robertson and Derk Pyper at the All-mhad Barn or wolf rock near Crathie, April 2014 (AW)

Punchbowl complete at lower Glen Quoich, July 1937 (AW sen)

Punchbowl worn away by decades of strongly flowing water, 12 February 2006 (IM)

AW senior at Meggie McAndrew's Cairn, Meggie died in a snowstorm while walking from Gairnshiel to Crathie, Blairglass fields beyond, Ben Avon on left, July 1981 (AW)

The Rockin Stane (left) above Pannanich near Ballater, 25 August 2010 (IM)

Adam Christopher Watson on Cnap a' Chleirich (knob of the clergyman), with the summit tor of Ben Avon beyond, August 1971 (AW)

Lady McQuarrie's Chair (language and meaning doubtful), formed by two boulders, the River Dee sparkles beyond, below a steep wooded slope at Micras east of Crathie, September 1983 (AW)

Chapter 5. A study of the place-names of Upper Deeside (from Nomina 8)

THE SIXTEENTH ANNUAL CONFERENCE OF THE COUNCIL   5
FOR NAME STUDIES IN GREAT BRITAIN AND IRELAND
1984

The Sixteenth Annual Conference was held at Crombie Hall, University of Aberdeen, from Friday, March 30th to Monday, April 2nd 1984 by kind invitation of visiting Professor W. F. H. Nicolaisen, who organised a fine programme. After a warm welcome from Professor Charles Chadwick, Dean of the Faculty of Arts and Social Sciences, University of Aberdeen, conference opened with a paper from Professor G. W. S. Barrow on 'Place-names and the Scottish medieval historian'. On the morning of March 31st, papers were read by Mrs Doreen Waugh on 'Caithness place-names', Professor Brian Ó Cuív on 'The family of Ó Gnímh in Ireland and Scotland: a look at the sources', Dr Alexander Rumble on 'The status of written forms in English onomastics', and Mr Arthur Owen on 'Topographical waifs and strays: how name studies and strayed medieval charters can help each other'. The afternoon was devoted to a series of talks on the Upper Deeside Project; speakers included Dr Adam Watson, Mrs Elizabeth Allan, Mr Donald MacAulay, Mr John S. Smith, Mr Derrick McClure, and Mr Ian Fraser. On Sunday morning Mr Peter Kitson spoke on 'The quantitative study of Old English charter boundaries' and Dr Gillian Fellows-Jensen on 'Place-names and settlements: some problems of dating'. In the following pages we are pleased to publish, in revised form, four of the papers and also a report on the Upper Deeside Project.

This was Council's first visit to Aberdeen and it proved a stimulating one, both in the quality of conference papers and in the bracing atmosphere - a combination of brisk Aberdonian climate, lively folk entertainment, and an invigorating Sunday afternoon excursion. Adam Watson and Elizabeth Allan took us by coach up Deeside towards Balmoral, and on the way introduced us to several of the Project's informants, who spoke to us about the land and its names. At Auld Brig of Dee we stopped to meet Mr Charlie Wright, until his recent retirement a deer-stalker on the Balmoral Estate. Thence we drove to a hostelry at Braemar where, after taking appropriate spirits and an excellent meal, we were entertained by a magnificent display of Scottish piping from Mr Wright. It was a memorable afternoon and evening to conclude a very successful conference.

PETER McCLURE

A STUDY OF THE PLACE-NAMES OF UPPER DEESIDE

Introduction

This paper presents a report on a study completed in summer 1983. The paper is in two parts. The first, by Adam Watson and Elizabeth Allan of the Institute of Terrestrial Ecology, reviews past publications on place-names in Upper Deeside, next concentrates on the methods used in the present study, and then discusses how the place-names illustrate the area's changing linguistic and social history. The second part provides a preliminary analysis of the main place-name elements from the Deeside list; it was written by Ian Fraser of the School of Scottish Studies, who gave advice to the study throughout.

The aim of the study was to make a comprehensive collection of place-names in Upper Deeside. This took ten years of spare-time work, leading to a book (Watson & Allan 1984). Few unpublished names had been expected, as more work had appeared on the place-names of Upper Deeside than on any comparable part of Scotland. However, the book gives about 7000 place-names, many of which are published there for the first time.

*   *   *

PART I

Past studies

The Ordnance Survey (OS) made the first major collection. Many names on the 1869 maps were incorrect, but subsequent editions revised some of these to make them correspond better with local forms.

Macdonald (1899) relied mainly on OS names, accepting most without checking locally, but querying others and sometimes giving local alternatives. He also searched some old documents, and from informants he collected a few unpublished names and noted some pronunciations. He died before completing the book. Alexander (1952) wrote, 'In regard to field-work he has had no equal in Scottish place-name study', but Alexander himself, along with MacKinnon (1887), MacBain (1922), and Watson (1904, 1926), is now considered to have made a better contribution.

On the other hand, Milne (1912) accepted all OS versions without checking locally, and noted no local pronunciations or old forms. He took Gaelicisation much too far with many names that were obviously lowland Scots, such as Gateside, which he translated as Gaothach Suidhe (windy seat). His (1908) article on place-names in upper Banffshire, which included names on the boundary of our area, showed the same uncritical approach.

Diack's (1944) book on standing stones included valuable collections of place-names from informants, with some pronunciations, and his unpublished manuscript on Glen Tanar contained a useful chapter on names. However, several published articles (reprinted in the 1944 book) made unwarranted assertions about linguistics. Other articles by him in Revue Celtique gave a few other names along with international phonetic symbols, but again with over-confident linguistic speculation.

Alexander (1952) collected many unpublished names from local people, and gave international phonetic symbols. However, he used his own anglicised spellings for many OS names, as in <u>Carn Taggart</u> for <u>Carn an t-Sagairt</u> and <u>Craigendall</u> for <u>Creag an Dail</u>. Although he cited maps by Roy, Robertson, and Thomson, he over-looked or ignored many names in them. Also, he gave no map references for locations, although these were widely in use even in the early 1940s. Nevertheless, he far surpassed Macdonald and Diack as a critical scholar, and his book remains one of the best studies so far published for a Scottish county. He also wrote two later articles, one of which included some material not in his book.

Macdonald, Milne and Alexander did not describe locations even approximately, let alone accurately. Many place-name locations which must have been familiar to them are thus now unknown. However, Diack's collections from Glen Ey, Corriemulzie, Morrone and the Sleach included some detailed descriptions, sufficient for us to locate many names during visits there. Only Diack and Alexander gave field-names, but emphasised them less than hills, streams and farms.

Macdonald and Milne published no informants' names, Alexander only one, and Diack virtually none. The books by Diack and Alexander appeared decades after their interviews with elderly informants, when most of these people must have died.

All four authors largely ignored Scots and English place-names. Alexander wrote, 'It has not been thought necessary to encumber the pages unduly with the frequent commonplace names of the Hillhead type', and 'Woodhill, in various parishes with Woodend, Woodside, etc.', and 'Bridgend, Glengairn etc'. He gave no cases of <u>Burn of -</u>, <u>Bridge of -</u>, or <u>Brig o -</u>, and no <u>Braehead</u> or <u>Littleton</u>.

A list of proper names in Dwelly (1901-11) included a few Gaelic names from the area, collected from local people by W. J. Watson. Watson (1916) published a good, short article, and Seton Gordon's various books on the area gave unpublished names heard from local people. Johnston's <u>Place-names of Scotland</u> (1934) included some names of Deeside villages, rivers and hills, but many of his derivations, such as <u>Bealaidh Tir</u> for <u>Ballater</u>, clash strongly with local pronunciations and so can be rejected. In 1931, Parker published a map of salmon pools, Scott (1959) a revised version, and Anonymous (1980) a third; all had a considerable number of errors in spelling and locations, did not cover the upper Dee near Braemar, and did not show all pool names. Stewart's (1974) booklet on Perthshire names, including some on the boundary of our area, took all its names from OS maps, with no pronunciations or old forms, gave some obviously incorrect meanings such as <u>Buchaille</u> (sic) <u>Bhreige</u> as 'the herd who tells lies', and transcribed many map names incorrectly, as in <u>Carn Geoidh</u> for OS <u>Carn a' Gheoidh</u>.

Some of these comments may seem over-critical, but they are intended to show readers wishing to search further how to make the best use of earlier works. The books by Macdonald, Diack and especially Alexander became constant companions during our study. In any case, in place-name study, as in other kinds of research, new contributions rest on the shoulders of those who studied before.

Methods

Important guidelines for studying place-names in Irish and Scottish Gaelic were published decades ago (Joyce 1869; Watson 1904, 1904-5; MacBain 1922), and their worth still stands. We followed them, along with the standard modern methods reviewed by Nicolaisen (1979). The basic approach was to emphasise pronunciations and other information from local informants, and to check locations in the field. We supplemented this with detailed surveys of published names and unpublished material in archive collections. As we had no experience of place-name study, we sought the help of professional workers from the beginning.

We had a few advantages, particularly our familiarity with the area, the people, and their speech. Both of us are native speakers of Aberdeenshire Scots and one (EA) was brought up in the study area. This made it easy to approach people informally and use tape recorders freely for noting pronunciations. Our close links with the people and our use of Scots speech for interviews were often important for getting authentic vernacular pronunciations. A few informants at first gave genteel versions of names, resembling the forms printed on maps and road signs, but when we questioned this, using Scots speech, they would admit that the vernacular forms were what they and their forebears had used.

However, as most place-names were obviously of Gaelic origin, a disadvantage was that we did not know Gaelic. We both learned Gaelic grammar to get a better basis for deriving Gaelic names.

We identified the exact locations of all but a few place-names, giving map references, and also visited every known location to check its position and possible derivation. Local people were asked for the name of every former habitation, field, pool, hillock, stream, and other major features. Periodically we looked for gaps where we had had few or no names, and then went to informants in these gap areas.

We spoke with 260 local informants, and visited some of them repeatedly. Their statements were checked with other local people, and we often took them out on to the ground in question. The study was wound up when the number of new names dropped below about one per two new informants. One of the most rewarding things in the study was meeting so many interesting people. Without them it would have been a mere desk job, sifting evidence of doubtful validity from extinct cultures. With their help, it was an exploration of a living culture, albeit one experiencing considerable change.

Nevertheless, spellings of names found in old documents were often important pointers to their derivation. We noted some early forms from published sources, but many more from unpublished papers and maps in estate offices and in other known archive collections on the area. Very few of these pre-date 1600, and most are from the late 1700s and the 1800s. Where we found unfamiliar place names in unpublished old papers, we went back to our informants to ask if they knew these names. Sometimes they did recollect hearing them, and occasionally even remembered locations.

These methods produced a fairly reliable base of map references, phonetic pronunciations and old spellings. Derivation of Celtic names was more subjective, and here we were greatly helped by comments on the manuscript by professional workers. If local informants pronounced a name as /alt 'beg/ and told us that this meant 'little stream', there was not much doubt that it came from the Gaelic name Allt Beag. With many names apparently Gaelic, however, local people did not know any meaning, and there were several possible derivations from Gaelic dictionaries; in such cases our suggested derivations are obviously more doubtful. In a few cases we could find no derivation from dictionaries, so that these were still more obscure. We ranked the reliability of Gaelic derivations on a scale from 1-6. This was useful in providing a standard, and also avoided the repeated use of such vague terms as 'probably', 'possibly', etc.

Unlike earlier authors in the area, we recorded all names that we found in whatever language, so it will be possible to assess the numbers of Gaelic, Scots and English names in different parts of the area now and in the future.

Language

The place-names reflect the area's unusual linguistic history. Gaelic gave way not to English, as elsewhere in the Highlands, but to Scots from lowland Aberdeenshire. This has been the main speech of the entire area in recent decades, and of the eastern end of it for centuries. Although most names are of Gaelic origin, and a few show clear evidence of Pictish influence, many are lowland Scots. Lowland Scots names are commonest on farmland at the east end of the area and fewest in the mountainous west end. The names of fishing pools illustrate this change well. In the eastern part of the area, most pool names in Dee are Scots, such as The Lang Puil, The Holly Buss Puil and The Brig Puil, whereas in the far west most are Gaelic such as Am Poll Buidhe, Poll nan Clachan Garbha and Poll na Drochaide. Some names are Scots or English translations from Gaelic names, and we commonly heard the Gaelic version from older people and the translation from younger ones. An example is Preas nam Meirleach in Glen Luibeg, now usually given locally as The Robbers' Copse. We also came across deliberate anglicisation of Gaelic names. In one such case, an English deer-stalking tenant found it hard to remember a corrie as Coire Bhearnuisge, so he decided to call it The Big Corrie and expected local stalkers and ghillies to do likewise.

In the course of the work we came across Mrs Jean Bain, the last speaker of Aberdeenshire Gaelic, and this led to a study of her Gaelic (Watson & Clement 1983). Unpublished Gaelic poems from Deeside, dating from the late 1700s, were discovered (Watson 1983a), and also the Earl of Fife's unpublished journal which gave useful information on social history and land use (Watson 1983b) as well as place-names. An Appendix to our book presents some more unpublished poems and rhymes which emphasise place-names and which are still known locally.

Social history

Many of the names illustrate the major changes that have occurred in the area's social history and land use. Communities far up the glens were at one time largely self-sufficient, with a great variety of trades such as turner, shoemaker, fuller, weaver, etc. which are illustrated by the place-names. Many names refer to the mosses where people formerly dug peat for fuel; virtually all are unused today. We found many names of shielings, where people once summered with their cattle in the higher glens; none are in use now. There has been a great decline in the number of inhabited farms and crofts, due to the massive voluntary depopulation of the more remote glens. This still continues, so that some glens are now completely empty of people, and only the ruins of former homes remain. The visitor coming across some interesting old ruin would have difficulty finding out its name from our long alphabetical list. We therefore list separately the former habitations in each individual glen, since many people are more interested in these human aspects than in the names of hillocks or other natural features.

Along with this depopulation, and with farm amalgamations, many field names have disappeared. Some have been replaced by the field numbers on large-scale, modern OS maps. Names in the hills are also vanishing. Many of today's gamekeepers and deer-stalkers were not brought up in the area, and are less inclined than

their predecessors to stay in one place for long. Also, the number of men employed
has greatly declined, so that each man (with a Land Rover) now has a very big area
to look after and cannot know the ground as intimately as the old-style stalker who
walked his smaller beat every day.

INSTITUTE OF TERRESTRIAL ECOLOGY
BANCHORY

*   *   *

PART II

One of the useful aspects of this collection from the point of view of the
professional onomastician, is the way in which <u>all</u> names have been investigated.
Although one comes to expect settlement names to be the subject of more intense
scrutiny in a survey such as this, topographic names, especially in mountainous
areas, are often allocated less attention. In this study, however, there has been a
particular effort devoted to the topographic element, in addition to settlement names,
and in an area like Deeside which displays a wide variety of landscapes, from valley
to high mountain zones, this has proved of inestimable importance.

<u>Settlement Names</u>

It is in the nature of mountainous areas that farms which are located in higher
ground where conditions are marginal will be often poor and therefore more liable to
abandonment at times of economic depression, social change or climatic deterioration.
This has been a prominent feature of the settlement pattern of Upper Deeside, and is
reflected in the large number of names which are either obsolete or which have reverted
to being applied to topographic features. This situation can be repeated in other,
similar, parts of Scotland, like upper Speyside, the Borders, and the Galloway hill
country.

The two most common Gaelic habitative elements which are found in the area are
<u>baile</u> 'farmstead' and <u>achadh</u> 'field'. There are some 50 examples of <u>baile</u>, such as
<u>Balintober</u>, <u>Balmenach</u>, and <u>Balintuim</u>. <u>Achadh</u> is less common in Aberdeenshire,
being a later settlement term. As its derivation implies, it is usually a smaller unit
of land, and tends to be located in less favourable agricultural conditions. Most of
the <u>achadh</u> names in Deeside apply to farm fields as such, although <u>Auchnerran</u> in
Cromar, <u>Auchallater</u> and <u>Auchtavan</u> were farm names in their own right. Many farms
with names containing <u>baile</u> and <u>achadh</u> are now deserted, such as <u>Baile a' Mhuillin</u>
near Inverey and <u>Ach an t-Sabhail</u> in Glen Gairn. We may also note <u>dail</u> 'meadow' as
being a common term. Many places so named are fields or water-meadows in existing
farms, but a substantial number have acquired the status of farms, such as <u>Dalnabo</u>,
<u>Dallyfour</u> (1599 Dalfour), <u>Dalvorar</u> and others. These are usually near major streams,
in relatively good land.

<u>Cill</u>, the term for 'church', is virtually absent in the study area, although a few
old church sites are referred to as such. Indeed, with the exception of more recent
names containing <u>kirk</u> and <u>chapel</u>, few place-names relating to church activity exist.
Gaelic <u>eaglais</u> 'church' occurs in a few instances.

The area was one noted for its shielings, transhumance being once an important aspect of agricultural life, so it is natural that we find a large number of terms relating to these. The usual eastern Gaelic word ruighe is found widely, some 50 examples being recorded, together with a substantial number of the Scots equivalent shiel, like Shiel of Back Coire Buidhe, and Shiels of Allt na Meadhonaidh.

Finally, we may note a number of Scots habitative names, like those in Mains (from demesne), about 10 examples, usually in the form 'Mains of . . .'. Names including -ton (Scots toun) are confined to examples like Newton (which are often referred to as 'The Newton'), Milton and Kirkton of Crathie.

Field-Names

Field-names in the area display the expected pattern, i.e. they contain both Gaelic and Scots terms. Some of the Gaelic field-names, however, are unusual, and it is surprising to find a few terms which are normally encountered in Argyll and the Southern Hebrides. The basic field-names, such as those containing achadh and dail, are of course found in some numbers, although it is difficult to be precise about the original extent of either, since there must have been a good deal of replacement in the eastern part of the area, if not throughout its entire length, by Scots terms. In addition, the word roinn 'portion' is found in at least 30 examples, and loinn 'enclosure' is also common (20+ examples) in such names as Loinn a' Choirce, which becomes Loinchork in Glen Girnock, and also occurs in simplex as The Loin. Other terms are ailean 'green, meadow' (Allanaquoich, Allanmore); cluan 'meadow' in Clunie; innis 'meadow, haugh', which becomes Scots inch; and the unusual claigionn 'hillock, in-field' in Claigionn na Caithriseachd near Abergeldie. This is a term found in Argyll and Lochaber, but in few other places, to my knowledge.

Some terms which are common further west in the Gaelic-speaking area are relatively rare here, such as lòn 'grassy meadow', although this does occasionally occur as a specific, like Rinloan and Baile an Loin, and there are a few examples of bàrd 'park'. The term eilean 'island' is also found here as a field-name, usually beside major rivers, and sometimes applied to islands cut off during changes in stream-beds. There are some 20 examples of these in generic forms, including 7 in simplex, a few hybrids such as The Eilean Park, and occasional farm-names like Baile an Eilein. It was interesting to find an example of losaid 'kneading-trough' (hence a very fertile field) at Invercauld. Normally this term is confined to Argyll.

Scots terms in this category are fairly predictable. They include haugh (and its diminutive haughie), howe 'flat ground' and frequent examples of park. Two examples of field-names containing the term waird, from Scots ward 'land enclosed by a dyke', were also recorded.

Hydronyms

Most water-names are Gaelic, but there has been a lot of anglicisation, and a few Scots hydronyms occur also. The standard Gaelic term abhainn 'river' occurs only as a specific in such names as Loinn na h-Aibhne (old form Loinahaun). Uisge 'water' is standard for the large streams such as the Dee, as Uisge Dé. The most common stream element is the term allt, with its diminutive alltan. For small streams, the term caochan is frequently used, and féith 'bog-stream' is very common. Other river or stream features include linne 'rocky pool', found mainly on the major streams and often Scotticised to linn, in the form 'Linn of . . .'. The term camas 'bend' or 'meander', found only on the larger rivers, becomes cambus in Scotticised

forms, like Cambus o' May. Wells are mostly denoted by fuaran, although tobar is
also found, while there are springs in hill country named from Gaelic sùil or Scots
swail 'eye', i.e. an eye-shaped green spot in otherwise dark or barren land.

Scots items in this category mostly involve the common stream term burn.
It is clear that this element has expanded into parts of the west of the area, although
it is naturally more common in the east. Again, 'Burn of . . .' is a usual formation.
One other Scots element, grain, is fairly common, applied to a series of small
rivulets which merge to form a larger stream. It produces occasional hybrids like
Grains o Allt Deas in Glen Tanar, but most grain- names are in the south-east of the
area, nearest lowland influence.

Mention should also be made of the Gaelic inbhir 'confluence', and its Scotticised
form inver, of which over 20 occur in the area. Again, we find formations like The
Inver of Bynack and The Inver of the Burn of Altdourie.

Other Toponyms

In an area where there is a great deal of topographic variety, mountain- and
hill-names form a very high percentage of the total. Although the Cairngorms were
not subjected to such a prolonged period of glaciation as the mountains in the west,
where there is much more obvious evidence of severe dissection and formation of
corries at much lower altitudes, they still present us with a large number of mountain
terms.

For the highest summits, beinn, the standard term for 'mountain', and its
Scotticised equivalent ben, are fairly numerous. The term monadh 'hill-range' also
occurs. In neighbouring Speyside, the Cairngorms were referred to as Am Monadh
Ruadh 'the red hill-range' to distinguish this from Am Monadh Liath 'the grey hill-
range' to the west, more familiar in its anglicised form as 'The Monadhliath
Mountains'.

By far the most common mountain term is càrn, with its Scotticised equivalent
cairn. This could be said to be the standard mountain term for the Grampians –
conical and round-topped rather than sharp-peaked. Sgor, of which more than 20
examples are found, indicates a stony or rocky surface, and is therefore a more
specialiased term than either càrn or beinn. Stùc 'projecting hill' is scarce, as one
might expect in this area, but there are 7 hill names containing stob 'peak'.

Lower summits are sometimes also labelled càrn, as well as those in the high-
summit category, but the term meall 'lump, hill' and its diminutive meallan occur
most numerously in the names of lower summits. Sidhean 'rounded hill' or 'fairy
hill', though extremely common in Inverness-shire and the north-west is less so
here, with only 4 examples with the generic, and occasional occurrences where the
term appears as a specific, like Tom an t-Sidhein. Torr(an) is also common, while
tulach and tom are frequent for hillocks. Cnoc is also found, becoming Scots knock
in forms like The Knock of Lawsie, while tulach becomes Tullich or Tulloch and is
the generic for innumerable farm-names throughout North-East Scotland.

Druim 'ridge', 'back' is another common topographic element, which is
anglicised to drum. Creag 'rock' becomes craig in Scots and is extremely common,
as is clach 'stone'.

Valley features of larger size are denoted by Gaelic gleann and srath, the latter
being usually the term for 'major river valley'. Both are common in the area, with

smaller valleys, gulleys and ravines having a variety of terms like clais, glac and lag. Hill-slopes of various kinds are found as bruach, leathad and leitir, and hill-promontaries as sròn 'nose'.

There are, in addition, numerous examples of coire 'corrie', or 'cwm', as is to be expected in a mountainous area, and the ravine-term, clais, is very common, often applied to former glacial melt-water channels.

The names of passes which were used as routeways include several interesting terms, such as bealach, a way between two peaks, and lairig, the term for a longer pass, as in Lairig Ghru. Cadha, referring to a way up a steep hill, is found in a number of names, such as Cadha an Fhir Bhogha 'the way of the archer' and Cadha Shios Feith Laoigh.

Scots terms are in general less common than Gaelic, and are either comparatively recent or confined to the east of the area. Moss and Muir are obvious examples, with formations like Muir of Tullich to denote moorland grazings pertaining to particular farm holdings. There are 12 examples of the term shank 'descending spur' or 'broad ridge', and a notch in the hills is often referred to as sneck, again a Scots term.

Conclusion

This survey of elements has, of necessity, been short. There is much variety, particularly of topographic names. On first sight, there is a relative lack of purely habitative names, but this is because a very large number of settlement names, usually of small farms, have toponymic origins. This may reflect the way in which man has exploited the area, often attempting to cultivate land at considerable altitudes in unpromising situations, and paying the penalties when marginal climatic change or a shift in economic conditions rendered occupation unprofitable.

The onomastic record of this collection, then, should not be viewed solely in a linguistic light. It is as much a record of economic and social change, and it is to be hoped that it will be regarded as a tool not only for onomasticians but for other scholars seeking further insights into the history of this fascinating and beautiful part of Scotland.

SCHOOL OF SCOTTISH STUDIES
EDINBURGH

*   *   *

REFERENCES

Alexander, W. M. (1952). The Place-Names of Aberdeenshire. Aberdeen.

Anonymous (1980 edn). Fisherman's Map of Salmon Pools on the Aberdeenshire Dee. Waverley Press, Aberdeen.

Diack, F. C. (1944). The Inscriptions of Pictland. Aberdeen.

Dwelly, E. (1901-11). The Illustrated Gaelic-English Dictionary. Reprinted 1971, Gairm Publications, Glasgow.

Johnston, J. B. (1934). Place-names of Scotland. London.

Joyce, P. W. (1869). Irish Names of Places. Dublin.

MacBain, A. (1922). Place Names: Highlands & Islands of Scotland. Stirling.

Macdonald, J. (1899). Place Names of West Aberdeenshire. Aberdeen.

MacKinnon, D. (1887). 'Place names and personal names in Argyll', The Scotsman. Edinburgh.

Milne, J. (1908). 'Kirkmichael (Banffshire) place names', Cairngorm Club Journal 5, 93-114.

Milne, J. (1912). Celtic Place-Names in Aberdeenshire. Aberdeen.

Nicolaisen, W. F. H. (1979). 'Field-collecting in onomastics', Names 27, 162-178.

Parker, M. (1931). Fisherman's Map of Salmon Pools on the River Dee.

Scott, I. (1959). Fishermans Map of Salmon Pools on the River Dee.

Stewart, T. F. (1974). Hill Names of Perthshire. Perth.

Watson, A. (1983a). 'Old Gaelic poems from Aberdeenshire', Scottish Gaelic Studies 14, 25-58.

Watson, A. (1983b). 'Eighteenth century deer numbers and pine regeneration near Braemar, Scotland', Biological Conservation 25, 289-305.

Watson, A. & Clement, R.D. (1983). 'Aberdeenshire Gaelic', Transactions of the Gaelic Society of Inverness 52, 373-404.

Watson, W. J. (1904). Place-Names of Ross and Cromarty. Inverness.

Watson, W. J. (1904-5). 'The study of Highland place-names', Celtic Review 1, 22-31.

Watson, W. J. (1916). 'Some place-names in the Cairngorm region', Cairngorm Club Journal 8, 133-136.

Watson, W. J. (1926). The History of the Celtic Place-Names of Scotland. Edinburgh.

Reference

Watson, A., Allan, E. & Fraser, I.A. (1984). A study of the place-names of Upper Deeside. Nomina 8, 6–14.

Chapter 6. Some place names from areas near Upper Deeside (Deeside Field, 1988)

This preliminary account by A. Watson & E. Allan includes some names from areas covered more comprehensively and with larger numbers of indigenous informants, especially in Strathdon and Strath Spey by Watson (2013), and also to a lesser extent in Chapter 8 below, which was complied in 2013 and 2014. If there is any difference in pronunciation or meaning between the 1988 account and Watson (2013), the latter should be taken as more reliable.

Some place names from areas near Upper Deeside

While interviewing local people for a study (Watson & Allan 1984) of place names in two parishes of Upper Deeside (Glenmuick, Tullich & Glengairn, and Crathie-Braemar), we were given some names incidentally from land adjacent to that area. In this article we publish these names, from Glen Tanar (Aboyne parish), Cromar and Deskry, Strathdon, Strath Spey, and upper Glen Clova, and also names from the Forest of Birse given by an Upper Deeside informant who had been brought up there. The Glen Tanar list includes names collected by the late F.C. Diack from informants in the glen, in his unpublished manuscript from the 1930s, and a few names from an unpublished document on the population of Glen Tanar (Harper 1928). The Cromar list includes a few names from Michie (1901).

The main method was to interview local people who had been brought up in the area and had lived there most or all of their lives. We recorded their vernacular pronunciations of the names, other relevant information such as legends or stories, and details about exact locations. Informants pointed out many places and often visited locations with us. This enabled us to give exact, six-figure grid references for most names. Actually seeing the locations was also valuable when it came to working out possible meanings of the names.

Some names given by informants were already on current Ordnance Survey (OS) maps, and for each entry we start with the OS version if there is one. Where local people use the definite article in Gaelic or English but the OS maps omits it, we add the article in brackets before the OS name. This does not affect the name's alphabetical position, e.g. (The) Galton comes under G.

The only reliable way of showing pronunciations is to use the methods designed for this (International Phonetic Association 1963). We give a brief, simple phonetic scheme below.

When deciding likely meanings of names, we used all information available: the OS names, the names given by Diack and other writers, the current vernacular pronunciations, and the appearance of the site. Names with doubtful meaning are shown by a question-mark, and in the more obscure cases we offer no suggested meaning. Most names are of Gaelic origin, and the spelling given follows classical Gaelic usage. Many names are obviously of lowland Scots origin, some are English, some have Pictish elements, and a few are of uncertain origin. Names with lowland Scots words are spelled according to the Scottish National Dictionary (Grant and Murison 1929-76).

This study could not have been done without the cooperation of many local people listed below. We thank them all. The Carnegie Trust for the Universities of Scotland gave a grant which covered some of the expenses of the study. Ian Fraser of the School of Scottish Studies gave useful comments.

Adam Watson & Elizabeth Allan

LIST OF INFORMANTS

Elizabeth J. Anderson	Deskry
Emily Anderson	Deskry
John Anderson	Deskry
Robert Anderson	Strathdon
Allan Brodie	Glen Tanar
Alex Esson	Cromar and Deskry
Robert Esson	Cromar and Deskry
William Gillanders	Cromar and Deskry
Douglas Glass	Forest of Birse, Glen Tanar
Ann Gordon	Cromar and Deskry
Seumas Grant	Speyside
William Ironside	Speyside
James C. Kellas	Cromar and Deskry
Ian A. Maclaren	Speyside
Dolina Macdonald	Speyside
Colin McGregor	Glen Tanar
Mary A. McGregor	Glen Tanar
Charles Milne	Glen Tanar
Brock Nethersole-Thompson	Speyside
Carrie Nethersole-Thompson	Speyside
James Niven	Strathdon
Mrs. Niven	Strathdon
John B. Robertson	Upper Glen Clova
Margaret Robertson	Upper Glen Clova
Leslie P. Simon	Cromar and Deskry
James Stewart	Cromar and Deskry
James Troup	Strathdon

PHONETIC SCHEME

(Aberdeenshire people speaking in English)

a	fat		dʒ	jet
e	take		ŋ	sing
ɛ	met		ʃ	shun
ë	her		tʃ	chin
ə	gardener		θ	thing
i	sheep		ð	this
ɪ	mid		ʒ	measure
o	bone		x	loch
ɔ	pot		j	you
u	root		hw	when
ʌ	sun			

ae	high
ɛi	height
ɔi	boy
oi	boy (when speaking in lowland Scots)
ʌu	around

ˈ (upper position) – strong stress on the following syllable

ˌ (lower position) – medium stress on the following syllable

ː long vowel, e.g. aː

· (upper position) – half-long vowel, e.g. a·

. (lower position) – a slight pause between two vowels

Glen Tanar
(Aboyne Parish)

Alehouse Croft (1638, Diack).
Allachfern Burn OS, Aldifern, often Allefern (Diack), ˌalaˈfern, Allt Fearn = burn of alder. A tributary of Allachy.
Alltan Roy OS, ˌaltanˈroi, Alltan Ruadh = red burnie. Runs into Allachy.
Allt Roy OS, altˈroi, Allt Ruadh = red burn, but probably was originally Alltan = burnie (see Alt Roy below). A burn south of Bridge o' Ess.
Alt Roy, Oldtownroy, that is Alltan roy, now Auldroy (Diack), Old Roy (Harper), Alltan Ruadh = red burnie. Two former houses (Harper) on south side of Tanar, below the burn Allt Roy OS.
Auldinchinnich, Allnachynnich (1638, Diack), Alltan Choinneach = burnie of mosses. Once a piece of shieling ground near the path to the moss of the Drum and west of this moss (Diack).
The Back o the Toun, ðɪˈbakɪˈtun, Scots Toun = farm-town, 461972. A field at Newton.
Back Sides, ˈbakˈseidz, 450971. A field near Newton.
The Badie Bush (Diack), Gaelic Bad = clump, and Bush in Upper Deeside is a translation of Preas = bush, thicket.
Bad na Muic OS, Badimuck (Diack), ˌbadiˈmʌk, Bad = clump, Muic = of pig. A hill.
Balgrennie (Diack), Balgrenie (Harper), Baile Greannach = rough farm-town. A former habitation with two houses (Harper) on north side of Tanar, probably uphill from Glen Tanar House.
Balnastroyne, Balnastrein (1600, 1717, Diack), Nether Bellastreen, more often simply Bellastreen (Diack), ˌbelaˈstrin, Baile na Sroine = farm-town of the hill nose. Bellastreen is the old local name for the site now carrying a house called Bastion, north-east of 476961. A former farm at the lower part of the present Home Farm buildings.
The Bank, ðɪˈbaŋk, 457971. A field on Newton.
The Bank, as above, 456971. A field on Waternadie next to the Bank on Newton.
Baudy Meg OS, ˌbadiˈmeg, Bad = clump, Meg perhaps from Mig = bog; Diack wrote that beg was also used, hence Beag = small. A hill, but Diack also recorded it as a hollow about a mile south of Birkenhillock.
Belrorie OS, bəlˈrore, Baile Ruairidh = Roderick's farm-town. Now a house north of Glen Tanar House.
(The) Belrorie Hill OS, ðɪˌbəlˈroreˈhël, named after the habitation Belrorie. Alexander was incorrect in stating that Bellrory was a hill.
Berry's Burn OS, Barrie's Burn (Diack), ðɪˈbareˈbʌrn. South-east of Millfield.
Big Donal, ˈbɪgˈdonəl, as in Scots pronunciation of Donald, 438970. A former field at Deecastle, triangular in shape, opposite Little Donal.
(The) Birken Burn OS, ðɪˈbërkənˈbʌrn, Scots Birken = birch. Tributary of Water of Gairney.
Birkenhillock (Diack, Harper). A former habitation with four houses on south side of Tanar, upstream from Craig of Borland.
(The) Black Craig OS, ðɪˈblakˈkreg. A hill south-west of Bridge o' Ess.
(The) Black Loch OS, ðɪˈblakˈlox. A peaty lochan north of Cock Cairn.
The Black Ship, ðɪˈblakˈʃëp, 468944. A building made of dark stone, in Glen Tanar.
The Bog, ðɪˈbog, 449970. A field near Newton.
Boginglack, Boganglaik (1717, Diack), ˌbogənˈglak, Bogan Glaice = little marsh of hollow, 467963. A former farm; 'the steading was in the glack between Craig na slic and Tom na crich' (Diack). Harper wrote that there were two houses there.
Boglewig (Diack), Bog Luig = marsh of hollow, north-east of 456977. A mossy place on west side of Netherton.
Bogs of Monrae (Diack), 470900. Peat bogs north-east of Cock Cairn.
The Boonie, the Boonyie (Diack), ðɪˈbuni, A' Bhuidheannaidh = at the yellow place, 455960. An area of hill ground with much grass, south-east of Deecastle.
The Boonyie road (Diack), the path from 446961 to the col at 452958, near above place.
Borland, Borlane, Boreland (Diack), sometimes Bordland meant 'land kept in the lord's own hand' (Diack). A former farm on south side of Tanar.
The Borland, ðɪˈborlən, 495962. This name is now used for the big wood on Craig of Boreland.

The Brae Ley, ðɪˌbreˈlɛi·, Scots = hillside pasture, 461975. A field at Newton.
Braeloine Cottage OS, Braelyne (1663, Diack), brəˈlein, Braigh Loinne = upper part of enclosure. A former farm on south side of Tanar. Formerly there were four houses here (Harper). The house of Braeline was on the site of the present chapel (Diack), i.e. St Lesmo's Church.
Bridgend (Diack). A former habitation with two houses on north side of Tanar, between Kildhu and East Millfield (Harper).
Bridgend. A former habitation with two houses (Harper) on north side of Tanar, upstream from West Millfield and probably near the present bridge at 480966. Diack wrote of 'the Bridgend', but we do not know which of the two Bridgends this was.
(The) Bridge o' Ess OS, was eʃ, less often aʃ (Diack), and later aʃ (Alexander), usually now ðɪˈbrigaˈes following the map spelling, Eas = waterfall often gives the sound ash in Scots (Alexander 1952). At the lower end of Glen Tanar.
(The) Bridge of Tanar OS, ðɪˈbrigaˈta·nar, often the Braeloine Brig, ðɪˌbrəˈleinˈbrɪg. North-east of Glen Tanar House.
Burn of Allnaharvy OS, Auldinhervie (1638, Diack), ˌaltnaˈhervi, Allt na h-Eirbhidh = burn of the stone dyke. Runs into Gairney.
(The) Burn of Boonie OS, ðɪˈbʌrnaˈbuni, for meaning see the Boonie. Runs into Tanar.
The Burn of Buller-Kye (Diack), 477894. Note Pullar Cuy OS, ˌpulərˈkae, is a hill on the Glen Esk side of the top of Allachy. Is Clachan Burn on OS, but not in current local use. Runs into Allachy.
(The) Burn of Counseltree OS, was Alt Costalty on Pont's map (Alexander), Corsaltrie (Diack), the Corseltree Burn (Alexander), ðɪˈbʌrnaˈkosəltri. Runs into Burn of Skinna.
(The) Burn of Duchery OS, ðɪˈbʌrnaˈdjuxre, for meaning see Hill of Duchery. Runs into Burn of Skinna.
(The) Burn of Monrae OS, ðɪˈbʌrnaˌmʌnˈre·. Runs into Allachy.
(The) Burn of Shield OS, ðɪˈbʌrnaˈʃil, probably Scots Shiel = summer hut or sheepcot. Runs into Allachy.
(The) Burn of Skinna OS, the Burn of Scan-aye (Diack), ðɪˈbʌrnaˈskɪnˈae. South of Glen Tanar House.
Burnroot OS, bʌrnˈrit, Scots Burnruit = Burn root. Houses and sawmill south-east of Dinnet.
Burnside OS, bʌrnˈseid. A house east of Dinnet Bridge.
The Buss o' Craig Neuk (Diack), the Buss (Alexander), Scots Buss = bush, ðɪˈbuʃ, 471952. The wood on Craig of Woodend, above Bush Cottage.
Cairn More OS, kernˈmo·r, Carn Mor = big cairn. South of Tillycairn.
The Canadian Road, ðɪˌkəˈnedjənˈrod, named after Canadian lumbermen who worked there during the Second World War, 498965. South-west of Bridge o' Ess.
Candycraig OS, ˌkjanaˈkreg, Ceann na Creige = end of the rocky hill. A habitation east of Tillycairn.
Clais an Uaraig, Clashen warrack (Diack), ˌklaʃənˈwarək, Clais = hollow, rest may be from Uar = water, 455969. A hollow with a well in it, south-west of Newton.
The Clais an Uaraig Burn, ðɪˌklaʃənˈwarəkˈbʌrn, east of 458970. Near Newton.
Clashanyant (Diack), Clais an Eant, Clais = hollow, rest probably from Eantag = nettles, south-east of 481958. On the Knockie, east of Glen Tanar House.
Cobbleheugh OS, ˌkobəlˈhjox, Scots Heugh = steep bank, Cobble should be Coble. A ferry-boat formerly crossed Dee here. A farm east of Dinnet Bridge.
Corntulloch OS, Contullich (1676, Diack), other Diack spellings Countlich, Contillich, Contulich, ˈkuntləx, Con-tulach = group of hillocks. A farm north-east of Deecastle.
(The) Corntulloch Burn OS, the burn of Coontlich (Diack), ðɪˈkuntləxˈbʌrn. Opposite Dinnet House.
The Corry of Little Tullich (Diack), 449960. Above Little Tulloch OS, south-east of Deecastle.
The Crag Heads, ðɪˈkragˈhedz, 462976 stretching to 465977. North-east of Newton.
Craigmahandle OS, Craigmahanle (Diack), ˌkregmaˈhanəl, Creag na h-Anaile = rocky hill of the breeze. A hill above Allachy.
Craig Neuk OS, Craignook (Diack), Creagan Fhiodhag = little rocky hill of bird-cherries (there are still some bird-cherry trees on this hill). A former croft at the foot of the Craig of Woodend up from Glen Tanar House. Harper wrote that there were two houses there.
Craig of Borland (Harper) A former habitation with four houses on the south side of Tanar, below a hill of that name (Craig of Boreland OS).
The Craig of Little Tullich (Diack), probably 444963, beside Little

Tulloch OS.

(The) Craig of Woodend OS, ðɪˈkregaˌwidˈen. Diack wrote that this ought to be called Craig Neuk (see Craig Neuk above). A hill south-west of Glen Tanar House.

Creagan Reamhar, Cragganrore (Diack), thick little rock, 452971. West of Newton.

Creag Damh OS, Craig Dav (Diack), kregˈda·, Creag Dhamh = rocky hill of stags. On north side of Tanar.

Creag na Slice OS, ˌkregnaˈslik, rocky hill of the slab. West of Glen Tanar House.

Crof of Braeline (1638, Diack). Presumably a former croft at Braeloine, north-east of Glen Tanar House.

The Crook, ðɪˈkruk, 454975. A field near Newton, possibly named because its north-west side is crooked.

Cul nam Bathaichean, ˌkolnaˈbexən, back of the byres, 456972. A field near Newton.

The Cunning Stones or Conning Stones (Diack), possibly Scots Cuning = rabbit. Standing stones on the Craig of Little Tulloch, east of Deecastle.

Dalwhing OS, Dalquhing (Diack), dalˈhwɪŋ, Dail Chuing = narrow haugh. A farm downstream from Bridge o' Ess.

(The) Dried Burn OS, ðɪˈdreiˈbʌrn. Runs into Gairney.

The Drum OS, ðɪˈdrʌm, An Druim = the ridge. A hill ridge south-east of Glen Tanar House.

Drumnabyle (Diack), ˌdrʌmnaˈbeil, Druim = ridge, 467969. A field east of Newton.

Duchery Beg OS, ˌdjuxreˈbeg, Dubh-chatharaidh Beag = little dark mossy ground. A hill south of Bridge o' Ess.

East Burn of Drum OS, the East Burn o the Drum, ðɪˈistˈbʌrnɪðɪˈdrʌm. Pairs with West Burn of Drum, which is further uphill but not further west. 'West' in Deeside names is often a relic of the Gaelic usage of Suas = upstream, which in Deeside usually was west (for further explanation, see Watson and Allan (1984), under Easter Auchallater). A burn north of Craigmahandle.

Easter croft of Braeline (Diack). A former habitation at Braeloine, north-east of Glen Tanar House.

The Easter Hole, ðɪˈistërˈhol, 464974. A hollow in a field near Newton.

East Millfield OS, Easter Millfield (Diack), ˈistˈmëlˌfild. A former farm on north side of Tanar; the land became part of the present Home Farm ground.

Everton (Harper), Scots Iver or Ever = upper. A former habitation with three houses on north side of Tanar, upstream from Bridgend west of Millfield.

Faichley (Diack). A former farm on the flat ground east of Burnside, west of Burnroot.

Fairlay Croft (Diack). A former habitation on the site of the present Netherton, south-west of Dinnet.

Fairy Loch OS, Lochie of the Glen or Fairy Lake (Diack), ðɪˈfe·reˈlek. On south side of Tanar, south of Millfield.

Fasnadarach OS, ˌfasənˈdarəx, Fas an Daraich = stance of the oak wood. 'I never heard Fasnadaroch in unsophisticated local speech' (Diack). A house south-east of Dinnet, below the oak wood.

The Finlet (Diack), Am Fionn-leathad = the white slope. Near top of Allt Roy, south of Bridge o' Ess.

The Fir Mounth, ðɪˈfërˌmʌnθ, Scots Fir = pine. The pass over to Glen Esk, by the Firmounth road.

(The) Firmounth Road OS, ðɪˈfërˌmʌnθˈrod. South of Glen Tanar House.

Foulbog, Fowl Bogg (Diack). A former farm, now a house called Craigendinnie. East of Bridge o' Ess.

The Front Park, ðɪˈfrʌntˈpark, 458977. A field near Newton.

Garthend (Diack), garθˈend, Scots Garth = enclosure. A former farm on north side of Tanar, first one up from Bridge o' Ess.

Gildiefay (Diack). A rocky place close to Drumnabyle, near Tillycairn.

The Gillineres (1663, Diack). A piece of land 'at the Bridgend,' downstream from Glen Tanar House.

Glen of Glentanar (Harper). A former settlement of four houses on south side of Tanar between Birkenhillock and Knockieside East.

Glen Tanar House OS, glənˈtanarˈhus. In the middle of Glen Tanar.

Goukstile (Diack), Scots Gowk = cuckoo or simpleton, Stile = gate. A former habitation.

Greencoat (Diack), probably Coat referring to Cot. A former habitation near Birkenhillock on south side of Tanar.

Greystone (Harper), greˈstin. A former farm on north side of Tanar, first down from Kildhu. There was also a Greystone Cottage (Harper), which is still there (current Electoral Register).

The Grip (Diack), Scots grip = to constrict, or Gruip = a groove,

---

probably 470975. A field on Tillycairn, below the house, in a glack (Diack).

The Hag Hillock (Diack), probably 477938. On east side of the Strone, south of Glen Tanar House.

The Hard Hillock, ðɪˈhardˈhëlək, 462974. A field at Newton.

Haugh of Braelyne (Diack), Scots Haugh = flat ground by a river. Probably beside Tanar near Braeloine Cottage.

Haughs of Allachy (Diack). Probably flat ground about 465940, beside Water of Allachy above its confluence with Water of Tanar.

The Heid Rigs, ðɪˈhidˈrɪgz, Scots = head ridges of ploughed land, south of 462973. Part of a field at Newton.

The Hermit's Well OS, ðɪˈhermɪtzˈwel, 447935 on OS map, but well no longer obvious. In upper Glen Tanar.

Hillhead OS, hëlˈhid. A habitation north-west of Glen Tanar House.

The Hillocks, ðɪˈhëləks, 465973. A field near Newton.

Hill of Cat OS, Peter Begg to Glen Tanar folk, and also commonly in Glen Esk, ˌpitërˈbeg. A hill on the march between Glen Tanar and Glen Esk.

(The) Hill of Duchery OS, ðɪˈhëlaˈduxri, Dubh-chatharaidh = black mossy ground. North-east of Craigmahandle.

(The) Hill of St Colm OS, ðˌˈhëlaˌsɪntˈkom. Above the top of Allachy.

The Hole (Diack), Hole (Harper). A former habitation on north side of Tanar, probably on upper fields west of Home Farm.

Holims, ˈholəmz, 459976. A field near Newton.

The Holms, ðɪˈhomz, Scots Howms = hollows, but this place is now usually called the Oak Wuid, Scots Wuid = wood, 461980.

The Horse Wall, ðɪˈhorsˈwa·l, Scots Wall = well, 457968. South-west of Newton.

The Hunt Road, ðɪˈhʌntˈrod, 483950. Older keepers in Glen Tanar called the grouse-shooting 'the Hunts', and the Hunt Road was a road to the grouse shooting. South-east of Glen Tanar House.

Jock Milne's Well, ˈdʒokˈmëlzˈwel, north of 484915, on east side of Water of Allachy. Named after a former gamekeeper. A well with an inscribed stone, up Allachy.

(The) Katrine Grain OS, ðɪˈketərənˈgren, ðɪˈkatərənˈgren, Scots Cateran = Highland marauder, Grain = small burn. At top of Allachy.

The Kaylie Butts, ðɪˈkeleˈbʌts, Scots Butts = small pieces of land, 464975. A field near Newton.

Kildhu OS, kəlˈdu, Cul dubh = black back. A former farm on north side of Tanar, now a house.

The Kingis fuird (1663, Diack), Scots = King's ford. On Tanar, west of Millfield.

(The) Knockie OS, the Knockie (1663, Diack), ðɪˈknoke, Scots = small hill. East of Glen Tanar House.

(The) Knockie Bridge OS, ðɪˈknokeˈbrɪg. South-east of Glen Tanar House.

Knockieside East (Harper). Two former houses on south side of Tanar between Braeloine and Glen of Glentanar.

Knockieside West (Harper). A former settlement of nine houses on south side of Tanar, upstream from Braeloine.

The Laird's Grave (Diack). On Candycraig.

The Lang Fauld, ðɪˈlaŋˈfa·ld, Scots = long fold, 457972. A field on Newton.

The Lang Land, ðɪˈlaŋˌlan, 459975. A field near Newton.

The Lang Loch (Diack). 'The Miltown' was on the north side of it (Diack); there is no longer a loch there. Probably was east of St Lesmo's Church.

The Lang Rigs, ðɪˈlaŋˈrɪgz, east of 463973. Part of a field at Newton.

The Lang Walk, ðɪˈlaŋˈwa·k, sometimes the Walk (Diack), 440971. Near Deecastle.

Lerny Mertin (Diack), possibly Leatharnaidh = place on the side of a slope, and mertin = Scots pronunciation of Martin or Gaelic Martain; this personal name 'survives, or did not long ago, in the neighbourhood' (Diack). A small field on Hillhead, south-east of Newton.

The Leys of Boonyie (Diack), 452959. A spot with 'evidence of old cultivation' (Diack), south-east of Deecastle.

The Lime Tree, ðɪˈleimˈtri, south-east of 470945. A planted tree south-west of Glen Tanar House.

Little Cockcairn OS. Not used locally now. A hill above Water of Gairney.

Little Donal, ˈlëtəlˈdonəl, 439972, pairs with Big Donal. A triangular field at Deecastle.

The Little Lewin (Diack), 496973. A hillock north of Garthend, west of Bridge o' Ess, pairs with the Muckle Lewin.

Little Tom Giubhais, ˈlëtəlˌtamˈdʒuz, 469926. A hill in lower

Allachy.

Little Tulloch OS, ˈlëtəlˈtʌləx, Tulach = hillock. A house east of Deecastle.

Logie Fechlie (Diack), ˌlogiˈfexle, Logaigh is an old form, meaning at hollow (Watson 1926), 454979. A pasture west of Dinnet Bridge, which was formerly cultivated (Diack).

Logie Fechlie's Wall, ˌlogiˈfexlezˈwa·l, Scots Wall = well, south-west of 455979. West of Dinnet Bridge.

Lordlie Bones, variant Lordni Bones (Diack), c. 451957. A flat at the top of the Boonyie road, south-east of Deecastle.

The Lord's Prop, ðɪˈlordzˈprop, often just the Prop, was My Lord's House (Diack), 442968. A big cairn with seats, east of Deecastle.

Lyannalie (1663, Diack), possibly Loinn Allaidh = wild enclosure. Was near the Kingis fuird, north of the Knockie.

The Mallachies (Diack), ðɪˈmalaxez, possibly an anglicized Na Malaichean = the hill-brows, 465975 and 468977. Two fields near Newton; each has an ascending ridge or hill-brow. Diack gave it as 'strips of rigs and baulks; a prehistoric road, now trenched out, went through them'.

The Mantick Howe, Scots Howe = hollow, ðɪˈmantəkˈhʌu·, 454971. Ruin of a former house near Newton.

The Mill Brig (Diack). It was near the Lang Loch, but no longer exists. Was south of Millfield.

Millfield OS, ˈmëlˌfild. A collective name (note East and West Millfield) for a group of houses on north side of Tanar.

Mill of Bellastroyne (Diack) was beside West and East Millfield, on north side of Tanar.

Mill of Borland (Diack). Presumably was on south side of Tanar, below Craig of Boreland.

Mill of Glen Tanar (Diack), otherwise known as Mill of Braeline. It was situated a little east of what is now St Lesmo's Church.

Milntoun of Glentanner (1638, Diack). The Miltown (1663) on the north side of the Lang Loch (Diack) was probably the same place, 'otherwise known as Mill of Braeline'.

Monrae OS, mʌnˈre·, Monadh Reidh = smooth hill. West of Allachy.

The Moss of Monawee (Diack), ðɪˈmosaˌmonaˈwi·, Moine a' Bhith = peat-moss of the resin, probably referring to pine roots in the peat, 504937. South of Bridge o' Ess.

The Moss o the Drum, Diack gave the moss of the Drum, and the Moss of the Drum, ðɪˈmosɪðɪˈdrʌm, 500925. A peat moss south-east of Glen Tanar House.

The Mounth Gate (1663, Diack), Scots Gate = road. Referred to part of Firmounth Road east of Glen Tanar House.

The Muckle Lewin (Diack), north-west of 498972. A hillock west of Bridge o' Ess.

Nather Waternadie (early 1600s, Diack). A former holding, paired with Over Waternadie. West of Newton.

Nether Bellastreen. See Balnastroyne.

(The) Netherton OS, ðɪˈneðərtən. A farm south-west of Dinnet Bridge.

The Netherton Brae, ðɪˈneðərtənˈbre·, 458980. A hill on the South Deeside Road west of Dinnet Bridge.

(The) Newton OS, ðɪˈnjutən. Also Waster or Wester Newton, Scots Waster = wester. A farm south of Dinnet Bridge.

The New Zealand Camp, ðɪˌnjuˈziləndˈkamp, 502969. A flat area near Bridge o' Ess, used by New Zealanders before the Second World War.

The Oak Wuid, see the Holms.

Old Miltown (1663, Diack).

Over Balnastroyne, Over or Upper Bellastreen (Diack). See Balnastroyne.

Over Waternadie (early 1600s Diack). A former holding, paired with Nather Waternadie. West of Newton.

Plough Thains, plʌuˈθenz, 455973. A field near Newton.

The Poisoned Well, ðɪˈpoizəndˈwel, south-east of 481951. Named after a case where a man at Glen Tanar House died after drinking from the well, but this was said to be mere coincidence, the well water being good. On the Firmounth Road, south-east of Glen Tanar House.

The Porphyry Brig, ðɪˈporfəreˈbrɪg, 461941. A bridge in mid Glen Tanar.

Portacraig (Diack), Port na Creige = passage of the rock, east of 453968. A gap between big rocks, west of Newton.

(The) Red Craig OS, ðɪˈredˈkreg. A hill south-west of Bridge o' Ess.

The Red Craig (Diack), 445958. A rocky slope south-east of Deecastle.

Rinnakylie, Rannakyllie (Diack), ˌrɪnaˈkɛili, Roinn na Cailliche = land portion of the old woman, 467972. A field near Newton.

Roadside, rodˈsɛid, 455976. A field near Newton.

Ronafloig (Diack). Roinn a' Phluic = land portion of the lump, 478975. A field near Candycraig.

The Ruch Bog, ðɪˈroxˈbog, 460924, Scots Ruch = rough. Up Gairney.

The Ruch Bog Well, ðɪˈroxˈbogˈwel, 457921, about 5m below the road. Up Gairney.

The Sands o Gannoch, ðɪˈsanzaˈgenəx, Gannoch from Gaineamhach = sandy, 486883. Alexander wrote of the hill as the Gennoch or the Gennel, and of the Sands of the Gennel, a bare sandy patch on this hill. At top of Allachy.

Slai na Gour OS, ˌslɪnaˈgʌu·ər, Sliabh nan Gabhar = moor of the goats. South-east of Deecastle.

The Smiddie Knowes, Scots = the smithy knolls, ðɪˈsmɪdiˈknʌuz, south of 440970. A brae on the public road near Deecastle.

The Smugglers' Gate, ðɪˈsmʌglërzˈget, north of 463880. A gate in a fence south-east of Cock Cairn.

The Smugglers' Road, ðɪˈsmʌglërzˈrod, 472881. A track near Cock Cairn.

St Colm's Well OS, sɪntˈkomzˈwel. Above top of Allachy.

The Stripes o' Argye (Diack), Scots Stripes = small burns, Argye possibly Ard Gaoithe = height of wind, 451942. In mid Glen Tanar.

The Strone OS, ðɪˈstron, An t-Stron = the nose. A hill nose south of Glen Tanar House.

Tappertootie (Diack), possibly Tiobar = well. East of and near to Hillhead. May refer to the well north-west of 472968, in front of Hillhead.

The Tath, ðɪˈtaθ, Scots Tathe = coarse grass growing on ground where cattle or sheep have been left to manure it, 464971. A field near Newton.

Tillycairn OS, older form was Tillycardine (Diack), Tulach Cardain = hillock of wood, ˌtëleˈkern. A farm south-east of Dinnet Bridge.

Tillydrenach (Diack), ˌtëleˈdrenax, Tulach Droighnich = hillock of thorns, 458978. A field near Newton, and also (Diack) a ridge or hillock there.

Tillyfunter, Tilliefounter (Diack), ˌtëleˈfʌntər, Tulach Phunndair = hillock of the one who confines straying cattle, 448972. A field near Newton. Also (Diack) a hillock north-west of 449972.

Tom chair (Diack), Tom a' Chairr = hillock of the rough ground, 492974. A sharp point west of Bridge o' Ess.

Tom Distick, Tomdistick (Diack), tamˈdɪstëk, Tom Disdeig = hillock of little rick, south of 456970. West of Newton.

Tom Giubhais OS, tamˈdʒuz, hillock of fir wood. A hill between Gairney and Allachy.

Tom Lair OS, tamˈle·r, Tom Laire = hillock of mare. A hill south-east of Deecastle.

Tom Mor, tamˈmo·r, big hillock, 461970. South of Newton.

Tom na Croiche OS, Tomnacrich (Diack), ˌtamnaˈkrix, Tom na Criche = hillock of the boundary. North-west of Glen Tanar House.

The Toris, the Torras (Diack), ðɪˈtorës, possibly An Dorus = the door, 457970. A hillock forming upper part of a field called the Bank at Newton.

The Tumlan Braes (Diack), possibly Scots Tummlin Braes = tumbling slopes, perhaps referring to broken rocks, 461942. South-west of Glen Tanar House.

The Twa an a Half Mile Quarry, ðɪˈtwa·ənaˈhafˈmeilˈkware, Scots Twa = two, c. 444937. A name hardly used now, when there are many small quarries for road gravel. In Glen Tanar.

The Walk. See the Lang Walk.

The Wall o' Remitshel (Diack), 443962, Scots Wall = well, Remitshel possibly Ruighe = shiel or cattle-run, and personal name Mitchell. South-east of Deecastle.

The Wast Bog, ðɪˈwastˈbog, Scots Wast = west, west of 459973. Near Newton.

Waternadie, Auchternadie alias Waternadie (Aberdeen Sasines 1658), ˌwatërˈnadi, ˌwatërˈnaldi, Uachdar = upper part, 453971. A former farm west of Newton.

Water of Allachy OS, the Allachy Burn, ðɪˈalaxeˈbʌrn, Aileachaidh = stony place. Runs into Tanar.

Weetfauld, Weetfold (Diack), Wetfauld (Harper). A former habitation on north side of Tanar, probably on upper fields west of Home Farm.

Welcomestyle (Diack), Scots Stile = gate. A former holding on Glen Tanar estate.

West Burn of Drum OS, the Wast Burn o the Drum, ðɪˈwastˈbʌrnɪðɪˈdrʌm, ðɪˈwestˈbʌrnɪðɪˈdrʌm, 495920. See also East Burn of Drum. North of Craigmahandle.

Wester Newton OS should be Easter Newton according to local people; it lies east of Newton OS.

West Millfield (OS, Harper), ˈwestˈmëlˌfild. A former farm on north side of Tanar; the land became part of the present Home Farm ground. Now a house.

(The) White Hill OS, ðɪˈhwɛitˈhël. On west side of Gairney.

Woodend (Diack, Harper); Alexander wrote Woodend (Glentanner House). A former farm on the site of Glen Tanar House.

(The) Wreaton OS, Wraton (Diack), ðɪˈretən, ðɪˈvretən. The similar Wraes at Kennethmont and Wrae at Turriff are pronounced vre·z and vre·. A farm west of Aboyne, north of Dee.

Cromar and Deskry

Allalogie OS, ˌalaˈlagi, Alltan or Allt Lagaigh (earlier form Logaigh (Watson 1926)) = burnie or burn at hollow. A former farm north-west of Loch Davan.

Allt Thumpack, Allathumpach (early OS), Thumpack Burn (Alexander), ˌaltaˈθʌmpək, Allt = burn, 393100. On Deskry.

Auchnahoy OS, ˌaxnaˈhoi, Achadh? na h-Oighe = field of the maiden. A former farm on Deskry, now afforested.

The Averin Flats, Everon Flats (Astor), ðɪˈevərənˈflats, Scots Averin = cloudberry, 385055. North-east of Morven.

Bad a' Chrasgaigh, badˈxraske, ˌbadnaˈxraske, clump of the crossing. Second pronunciation suggests Badan a' Chrasgaigh with Badan = clumps, 400084. Burn of Badnachraskie OS is nearby. An old right of way track from Deskry to Tillypronie.

The Bad nan Cleireach Burn, ðɪˌbednaˈklirəxˈbʌrn, Bad nan Cleireach = clump of the clergymen, 385088. At Chapelton on Deskry.

Balachailach OS, ˌbalaˈhɛilax, Baile Chailleach = old women's farm-town. A farm on Deskry.

Balgrennie OS, balˈgrene, Baile Greannach = rough farm-town. A farm north of Groddie.

Balronald OS, balˈronəld, Baile Raonuill = Ronald's farm-town. A former farm, now a house, west of Migvie.

The Barronry, the Barony (Alexander), ðɪˈbʌrənrə, Scots Barony or Barronry = an estate created by direct grant from the Crown. An old name for the lands of Pitellachie and Kinaldie.

(The) Belbo Burn OS, ðɪˈbëlbəˈbʌrn, see Bilbo. North-east of Groddie.

Bilbo, ˈbëlbə, old Scots Bilbie = a shelter or residence, 416060. A former farm north-west of Logie Coldstone.

(The) Birk Hill OS, ðɪˈbërkˈhël, Scots birk = birch. The OS map shows it as a hill south of Boultenstone, but locally the name usually refers to the hill pass carrying the public road from Logie Coldstone over to Deskry.

The Birk Hill Road, ðɪˈbërkˈhëlˈrod. The Birkhall Road (Michie, p. 92), The Birkhill Pass to Strathdon (Fraser). The road over the above pass.

Blelack (1772 spelling in Michie), ˈblelak, but pronounced blallak in Gaelic (Diack, in Alexander), Blath-lag = warm hollow. Blelack House OS is at 440036. An old estate south of Logie Coldstone.

The Blue Rock, ðɪˈbluˈrok, north-east of 372043. A patch of bluish-grey scree and rock on north side of Morven.

Bog of Rearie, bogarˈiri, possibly Gaelic Bogar = bog, rest obscure; was said to be the old name of Pitellachie.

Bottomend, Boddomend (1772 spellings in Michie). A pendicle of Easter Migvie.

The Braes of Coldstone, ðɪˈbrezaˈkolstən, 475063. Slopes beside Strath Don road north of Logie Coldstone.

Brankholm, ˈbraŋkʌm, 462054. A former farm north-west of Tarland.

Breemhill, brimˈhël, Scots Breem = broom, east of 436019. A former house on a hillock with broom, both house and broom demolished by ploughing in recent years. South of Logie Coldstone.

Bribery, ˈbrɛibəri, 429068. A former steep bit of road west of Migvie.

(The) Burn of Badanseaneach OS, ðɪˈbʌrnaˌbednaˈhenət, Bad na h-Annaid = clump of the church. On Deskry.

(The) Burn of Kinaldie OS, ðɪˌkinˈadiˈbʌrn. North-east of Groddie.

Cairnmore OS, kjarnˈmo·r, Carn Mor = big cairn. A house west of Migvie.

Cairn of Gilderoy OS, ˈkernaˌgɪldəˈroi, Gilderoy from Gille Ruadh = red-haired lad; Gilderoy was a well-known freebooter. A cairn on the upper Deskry.

Carrue OS, kaˈru·, same pronunciation as in Meikle Carewe Hill north-west of Stonehaven, Cadha Ruadh = red steep hill. A steep hillock south-east of Logie Coldstone.

(The) City Hillock OS, ðɪˈsiliˈhëlək, suggests Scots Seily = happy. Alexander gave a similar pronunciation and meaning. Beside Deskry

Water.

Clashnettie OS, klaʃˈniti, Alexander gave klaʃˈnete, Clais = hollow. A former farm on Deskry.

Collordon OS, kəlˈordən, Cul Ordain = back of little hill. A house north-east of Logie Coldstone.

(The) Corbies' Nest OS, ðɪˈkorbizˈnest, Scots Corbie = raven. A small crag on the upper Deskry.

Craig Glas OS, kregˈlas, was Craig Loishk on Invercauld map, suggesting Creag Loisgte = burnt rocky hill. West of Pronie Loch.

(The) Craig of Bunzeach OS, ðɪˈkrag, ðɪˌkragɪdɪˈbʌnjəx, Bunzeach from A' Bhuidheannach = the yellow place. A rocky hill, west of the farms on upper Deskry.

Craw Hillock, kraˈhëlək, Scots Craw = rook, crow. An old name for Groddie Cottage OS.

(The) Davan OS, ðɪˈda·wən. A farm north-east of Loch Davan.

(The) Davoch OS, West Davoch on OS 1:25000, ðɪˈdax, Scots Davach = a measure of land. Daach was spelling from c. 1540 in Michie, who wrote that it was the Davoch of Melgum. A farm north-west of Tarland.

Deskryside, ˌdeskreˈsɛid. Common name referring to places beside Deskry Water.

Drake's Mire, dreksˈmɛir, west of 426060. A former cottage north-west of Logie Coldstone.

Drummy OS, ˈdrʌme, ˈdrëme, from Druim = a ridge, 1772 spelling in Michie was Drummie. Places on a hill ridge south-west of Tarland.

East Burn of Dhuchrie OS, pronounced ˈdjoxre, Dubh-choire = black corrie. A tributary of Deskry; pairs with West Burn of Duchrie.

Easter Cairnmore (1772 spelling in Michie). A former farm near Migvie.

Easter Migvie (1772 spelling in Michie) Former name for the lands of Hopewell (Michie). South-east of Migvie.

Ennot Hillocks OS, ˈenətˈhëlək, probably from Annaid = church. Chapelton and Bad na h-Annaid were nearby. Ennot was probably Scots pronunciation of Annaid. On upper Deskry.

Etnach Hillock OS, ˈetnaxˈhëlək, Scots Etnach = juniper. On upper Deskry.

The Everton, ðɪˈevərtən, Scots Iver or Ever = upper, 438037. Was a ruin near Blelack House, now under a silage pit.

Fernyhowe OS, ˌferneˈhʌu·. Scots Howe = hollow. A former farm south-east of Logie Coldstone.

(The) Galton OS, ðɪˈga·ltən, perhaps from Scots Gal = bog myrtle. A farm north of Loch Davan.

The Glen Gate (Astor), ðɪˈglenˈget, 403065. West of Pronie Loch.

Groddie OS, ˈgrodi, from Grod = rotten, often referring to boggy ground. A farm west of Logie Coldstone.

(The) Heugh OS, ðɪˈhjox, Scots = the steep bank. A farm beside Loch Davan.

(The) Hill of Allamuc OS, ðɪˌhëla.alaˈmʌk, Allt nam Muc = burn of the pigs. A hill above Deskry.

Howe of Riegunachie OS, ðɪˈhʌu.arɪˈgunaxi, Ruighe Dhonnchaidh = Robertson's shiel. On upper Deskry.

The Iren-eer Walls, see Poldhu Wells.

Kinaldie OS, kɪnˈadi, possibly from Ceann Alltaidh = head of little burn. A farm north-west of Logie Coldstone, no burn there now but the farm land is drained.

The Kirkton, ðɪˈkërktən. 435044. The hamlet beside the church at Logie Coldstone.

Knappieround OS, the d at the end of the OS name is probably an anglicization, ˌknapeˈrun, ? A' Chnapaidh Chruinn = at the round little hillock. A house near Tarland.

Knock Hill OS, ðɪˈknoks, Scots the Knocks = the hills. A pair of hills east of Blelack.

Knocksoul OS, knokˈsʌul, Cnoc Sabhail = hill of barn. A farm west of Migvie, below a hill.

Ladies Well OS, ˈlediˈwel. North-east of Groddie.

Ladieswell Cottage OS, ˈlediˈwelˈkotədʒ. North-east of Groddie.

The Lang Craft, ðɪˈlaŋˈkraft, Scots = the long croft, was at the Ordie, on the west side, towards Greenhaugh OS.

The Left Corrie, ðɪˈleftˈkore, 385055. Pairs with the Richt Corrie. North-east of Morven.

Likely Cottage, ˈlëkleˈkotədʒ, Scots Likely = good-looking, 433053. A house north of Logie Coldstone.

(The) Loggie Burn OS, ðɪˈlogiˈbʌrn. Logaigh, later Lagaigh = at hollow (Watson 1926). Mains of Logie OS is nearby. North of Loch Davan.

MacRob's Cairn, məkˈrobzˈkjarn, 433035. Formerly was a cairn at a road junction south of Logie Coldstone. The cairn is no longer there due to road widening, and the name now refers to the road junction.

Mains of Pronie OS, 1772 spelling in Michie was Mains of Tillypronie. A farm east of Tillypronie.

Meggie Reid's Mossie, ˈmeɡiˈridzˈmose, north of 399072. A peat moss north-east of Morven.

Meikle Wife's Howe OS, ˈmʌkəlˈwɛifsˈhʌu·. OS Meikle is incorrect, local form in Aberdeenshire is always Muckle. West of Migvie.

Melgum OS, same spelling c. 1540 in Michie, ˈmelɡʌm. A farm north-west of Tarland.

The Mill of Westown (1793 spelling in Michie). In the Hopewell area, west of Tarland.

Miln of Auchterearn, and **Mill of Auchterairn** (1772 spellings in Michie) Uachdar? Earainn = upper part of land portion. Auchterearn was the same place as the modern Watererne. Alexander wrote that the spelling Waterairn replaced Auchtererne from about 1600 onwards. East of Migvie.

Monafrink, ˌmənaˈfrɪŋk, Manachrink Park (Invercauld map) was nearby, so possibly Moine Chruinn = round peat-moss. A former cottage at 427058, north-west of Logie Coldstone.

Morven OS, ˈmʌrvən, Mor-bheinn = big hill. The highest hill in the Cromar area.

Morven View OS, locally is usually Auld Groddie, ˈaːlˈɡrodi. South of Groddie.

(The) Mosstown OS, often called the Mosstown o Blelack, ðiˈmostənaˈblelak, to distinguish it from another Mosstown at 423048. Scots Moss = bog. A farm east of Logie Coldstone.

Muir of Kynoch (1838 spelling in Michie), Coynach OS is near here, Coinneach = moss. North-east of Logie Coldstone.

(The) Muirparks OS, ðiˈmirˈparks. Formerly was probably moory fields, now a wood, south of Logie Coldstone.

Mullachdubh OS, ˌmʌlaxˈduː, Mullach Dubh = black top. A hill on the upper Deskry.

Parkneuk OS, parkˈnjuk, Scots Neuk = corner. A habitation east of Logie Coldstone.

Pennystone Green OS, ˈpenəstənˈɡrin, probably from Scots Penny Stane, a former game using a quoit made of stone (Alexander). On the upper Deskry.

Pitellachie OS, pɪtˈelaxi, Peit Ealachaidh = land portion of rocky place. Old spellings in Michie were Pitellachie (Kinaldie), Pittalachie probably in 1690s, Pitalachie in 1709. A farm south-west of Migvie.

Pitellachie Castle, pɪtˈelaxiˈkastəl, formerly known as Bonlee Castle, bʌnˈliːˈkastəl, 419063. Bonn Liath = grey base. South-west of Migvie.

(The) Poldhu Wells OS, ðiˌpolˈduːˈwalz, Poll Dubh = black pool. Also called the Iren-eer Walls, ðiˈɛiranˈirˈwalz, Scots = the iron-ore wells. South of Logie Coldstone.

The Richt Corrie, ðiˈrëxtˈkore, Scots Richt = right, 367044. Pairs with the Left Corrie. North-west of Morven.

The Ruthven Hill, ðiˈrɪvənˈhël, Ruthven from Ruadh-mhaighin = red place (Watson 1926), 454031. North-east of Loch Davan.

Sandy Hillock OS, locally the Sandy Heugh, ðiˈsaneˈhjox, Scots Heugh = steep bank. South-east of Logie Coldstone.

The Seily Howe, ðiˈsiliˈhʌu·, Scots = the happy hollow, north-east of 442032. The fairies were supposed to stay there. The Seily Howe features in the old rhyme:

Dule, dule tae Blelack
An dule tae Blelack's heir
For drivin us fae the Seily Howe,
Tae the cauld Hill o Fare.

A former laird of Blelack was supposed to have driven the fairies away. A hollow on top of a hill near Blelack.

The Seily Wall, ðiˈsiliˈwaːl, Scots = happy well, 453033. Where three estates met - Blelack, Corrachree and Douneside - south-east of Logie Coldstone.

(The) Sloganbuidh Burn OS, ðiˌsloxanˈbuiˈbʌrn, Slugan Buidhe = yellow gullet. A tributary of Deskry.

Thornymuick, ˈθorneˈmʌk, Torr nam Muc = hill of the pigs. A former farm on Deskry.

Tillypronie OS, ˌtëlaˈprone, Tulach Pronnaich = hillock of dross or thing in small fragments; Prony on Gairn probably refers to screes (Watson and Allan 1984). North of Logie Coldstone.

Tillyreach Hillock OS, ˌtëleˈriəx, Tulach Riabhach = brindled hillock. East of Tillypronie.

Tom a' Char OS, ˌtamaˈxa·r, Tom a' Chairr = hillock of the bog. North-west of Logie Coldstone.

Tom Dubh OS, tamˈduː, black hillock. North of Pronie Loch.

(The) Tom na Wan Wood OS, ðiˌtamnaˈwanˈwid, Tom nan Uan = hillock of the lambs. On Deskryside.

Tulla Mutton, ˌtʌləˈmʌtən, Tulach? Meadhon = middle hillock, east

of 415047. Formerly there were three cottages here. East of Balgrennie.

Tulloch OS, same spelling from 1772 in Michie, Tulach = hillock. A farm east of Tillypronie.

Watererne OS, ˌwatərˈern, Auchterearn was 1772 spelling in Michie, for meaning see Miln of Auchterearn. A farm north-east of Migvie.

West Burn of Duchrie OS, Duchrie pronounced ˈdjoxre, Dubh-choire = black corrie. A tributary of Deskry; pairs with East Burn of Dhuchrie.

(The) White Cow's Mire OS, ðiˈhwɛitˈkuzˈmɛir. On upper Deskry.

(The) White Hill OS, ðiˈhwɛitˈhël, Whytehill was Michie's spelling from 1772. East of Logie Coldstone.

(The) White Hillock OS, ðiˈhwɛitˈhëlak. On the upper Deskry.

(The) White Hillocks OS, ðiˈhwɛitˈhëlaks. North-east of Morven.

Strathdon

Allt Bad Mhic Griogair OS, ˌaltˌbadmɪˈɡrɪɡar, burn of MacGregor's clump. Near Cock Bridge.

Allt Damh OS, alˈdʌu·, probably Allt Dhamh = burn of stags. South-west of Corgarff.

Allt Damh, as above, 272075. A former house beside above burn.

Allt na Ciste OS, ˌaltnaˈkist, burn of the chest. North-west of Corgarff.

Alltnaciste OS, as above. A house beside above burn.

Allt na Gaothain OS, ˌaldaˈhui, Allt a' Chuithe = burn of the snow-wreath. By the road to Gairn.

Allt nan Aighean OS, altˈnein, Alexander gave altənˈɛiən, burn of the deer. West of Delnadamph.

Allt Reppachie OS, altˈrëpəxə, MacDonald gave it as Rui-ippachie, Allt Ruighe Cheapachaidh = burn of cattle-run at tillage plot. West of Delnadamph.

Ardchattan OS, ˌardaˈhatən, Ard a' Chattain = height of the Cattanach. A former farm west of the foot of Glen Conrie, now afforested.

Badan Seilich, ˌbadənˈʃiləx, willow clumps, north of 268081. A former farm west of Corgarff.

Bad Leana OS, badˈlen, Bad Leathann = broad clump. By the road to Gairn.

Badnabein OS, ˌbadnaˈbin, Bad na Beinne = clump of the hill. A former farm west of Allargue.

Belniden OS, belˈnidən, Baile an Aodainn = farm-town of the hill face. A farm west of Lonach.

Birkford OS, bërkˈfjurd, Scots Birk = birch. A farm in Glen Carvie.

The Black Fauld, ðiˈblakˈfa·l, Scots Fauld = fold, north-east of 256090. A field near Cock Bridge.

Bogbuie OS, boɡˈbui, Bog Buidhe = yellow bog. At top of Glen Conrie.

Bogfoot, boɡˈfët, now Rowantree Cottage OS. A house east of Cock Bridge.

Boggach OS, ðiˈboɡəx, Am Bogach = the swamp. A former farm in Glen Conrie.

Bogheid, boɡˈhid, south of 261088. A former farm east of Cock Bridge, now afforested.

Boilhandy OS, belˈhandi, Baile Shandaidh = Sandy's farm-town. A house on the road to Gairn.

Boilmore OS, balˈmo·r, belˈmo·r, Baile Mor = big farm-town. A house west of Lonach.

The Brander Moss, ðiˈbrandërˈmos, Branndair = tangled roots in a peat moss (Diack), 306059. Above the road to Gairn.

Bressachoil OS, ˌbresaˈheil, Am Preas a' Chaoil = the osier bush, with Chaoil in an adjectival sense. A former farm in Glen Ernan.

Bruach Ruadh OS, broxˈroi, red bank. East of Delnadamph.

Buachaille Mor's Grave (site of) OS, ˈbuxəlˈmorzˈɡrev, Buachaille Mor = big herdsman, west of 273088. In a field north-west of Corgarff.

The Ca OS, ðiˈkaː, An Cadha = the pass. A hill south of Corgarff.

Cairn Culchavie OS, ˌkjarnˌkəlˈha·vi, Carn Cul? Chabhaidh = hill of back of the driven snow or snow-drift. West of Delnadamph.

Cairnlea Hill OS, kernˈli·, Carn Liath = grey hill. On west side of Glen Conrie.

(The) Camp OS, ðiˈkamp. A former army camp east of Cock Bridge.

Caochan Luachair OS = streamlet of rushes, locally the Muckle Torr Burn, ðiˌmʌkəlˈtorˈbʌrn, named after a nearby hillock, the Torr, Torr = hillock. South of Cock Bridge.

Caochan Raineach Mor OS, ˈmʌkəlˌkaxənˈranəx, big ferny

mound. A former farm near Colnabaichin.

Torran Breac, ˌtorənˈbrek, speckled hillock, 214089. A former farm west of Delnadamph.

Torranbuie OS, ˌtorənˈbui, Torran Buidhe = yellow hillock. A former farm at foot of Glen Conrie, now afforested.

Torran Deallaig OS, ˌtornəˈʃeltəx, Alexander gave tornəˈʃeltəg, Torr nan Dialtag, hillock of the bats. At Delnadamph.

The Torr Moss, ðɪˈtorˈmos, 242065. The Torr OS = the hill, is nearby. Peat-moss south-west of Cock Bridge.

The Torr Wuid, ðɪˈtorˈwid, 251071. South-west of Cock Bridge.

West Coire Buidhe OS, ðɪˌkorˈbui, An Coire Buidhe = the yellow corrie. South of Corgarff.

West Dunandhu OS, ˈwestˌdënënˈduˑ, Dunan Dubh = black hillock. A former farm north of Delnadamph.

Strath Spey

Achlean OS, axˈleˑn, Achadh Leathann = broad field. A farm in Glen Feshie.

Allt Druidh OS, altˈdruˑ, Allt Dhru = burn of the flow. Burn out of Lairig Ghru.

Allt na h-Airneis, altˈharnɪʃ, burn of the cattle. In Coire Buidhe, south-east of Loch an Eilein.

Allt Sgairnich OS, altˈskarnəx, burn of heap of loose stones. On Moine Mhor.

Aultnancaber OS, ˌaltnaˈgaˑpər, Allt nan Cabar = burn of the cabers or poles. A house east of Coylumbridge.

Badaguish OS, patˈjuˑɪʃ, Bad a' Ghiuthais = clump of the fir. A house north-west of Loch Morlich.

Ballintean OS, ˌbalənˈdʒiˑən, Baile an t-Sidhein = farm town of the fairy hillock. A habitation in Glen Feshie.

Balnespick OS, balnˈespɪk, Baile an Easbuig = farm-town of the bishop. A house near Loch Insh.

Balvattan OS, balˈvatən, Baile Bhadan = farm-town of clumps. Old fields near Whitewell.

Am Beanaidh OS, ðɪˈbene, 'it belongs to the large class of stream names with the ending (a)idh, common in the North and East of Scotland - that is, in Pictland - e.g., Tromie, Geldie, Divie, The root may be that of old Irish *ben-im*, I smite' (Watson 1916). River out of Glenn Einich.

Blackmill OS, blakˈmɪl, also known to old people as Am Muileann Dubh, mˌmulənˈdu, the black mill. A house in Glen Feshie.

Bond Street, bondˌstrit, 920895. A flat section of path up Eidart.

Bynack, as in Bynack More OS and other names, ˈbɛɪnək, Beidhneag, meaning unknown (see Watson and Allan 1984). Names of places north-east of Cairn Gorm.

Bynack Stable OS, pɪtˈʃjanəx, Bad Feannach = rough clump. At foot of Strath Nethy, below Bynack More.

(An) Cadha Beag OS, ðɪˌkaˈpek, the little steep hill. South-east of Loch an Eilein.

(An) Cadha Mor OS, ðɪˌkaˈmoˑr, the big steep hill. South-east of Loch an Eilein.

An Cagain OS, ðɪˈkaegən, An Caigeann = the rough mountain pass. A narrow place with screes in Glen Feshie.

The Caiplich, as in Water of Caiplich OS, ðɪˈkaplɪx, horse place, from Capall = horse. An area of upper glen north-east of Bynack More.

Cairn Gorm OS, nˌgarnˈgorom, ðɪˌkernˈgorm, An Carn Gorm = the blue stony hill. South of Loch Morlich.

Cam Sgriob OS, ðɪˈkʌumˌskrip, A' Cham-sgriob = the crooked scratch. A hill with long rocky channels, west of Grantown.

Carn Eilrig OS, karnˈelrɪg, Carn Eileirig = hill of deer trap. In lower Gleann Einich.

Carn Odhar OS, karnˈʌuˑ.ër, dun hill. West of Lairig Ghru.

Clach Bharraig OS, Clach-barraig (Forsyth) from barr = top, klaxˈvarɪk, Clach = stone. North of Cairn Gorm.

Coire an Lochain OS, ˌkoranˈloxən, corrie of the lochan. On Cairn Gorm.

Coire an t-Sneachda OS, ˌkoranˈdreaxk, corrie of the snow, or the Snowy Corrie, ðɪˈsnoeˈkore. On Cairn Gorm.

Coire Beanaidh OS, korˈbene, corrie of Beanaidh. The stream of Beanaidh Bheag runs out of it, into Gleann Einich.

The Coire Blair Stone, ðɪˈkoreˈblerˈston, 885927. On Mullach Clach a' Bhlair, so probably was Clach a' Bhlair = stone of the plain.

Coire Bogha-cloiche OS, ˌkorˌboˈklax, ˌkorˌboˈklɔix, corrie of stone arch. A corrie with screes on Braeriach.

(An) Coire Buidhe OS, ðɪˌkorˈbui, the yellow corrie. South-east of

Loch an Eilein.

Coire Cas OS, ˌkorəˈkas, suggests steep corrie. On Cairn Gorm.

Coire Creagach OS, korˈkrakax, rocky corrie. Also ˌkorˌkrakaxnamˈbo, Coire Creagach nam Bo = rocky corrie of the cows. In Gleann Einich.

Coire Dhondail OS, korˈgʌuntəl, Coire Ghunntail (Sinton), Coire Gamhandail (W.J. Watson, in Gordon 1925) = the corrie of stirkdale. East of Loch Einich.

Coire Eindart OS, korˈendʒart, korˈindʒart, Coire Inndeard = corrie of Eindart; Allt Eindart drains the corrie.

Coire Garbhlach OS, korˈgaˑlax, Coire Gabhalach = forked corrie. In Glen Feshie.

(An) Coire Gorm OS, ðɪˌkorˈgorom, the green corrie. On Sron na Lairige.

Coire Laogh Beag OS, ˌkorˌləˈpek, little corrie of calves. On Cairn Gorm.

Coire Laogh Mor OS, ˌkorˌləˈmoˑr, big corrie of calves. On Cairn Gorm.

Coire na Ciste OS, ˌkornaˈkiʃt, corrie of the chest (or box-shaped corrie). Also, ˌkoraˈhiˑʃt, suggesting Coire Chiste = corrie of chests. On Cairn Gorm.

Coire na Cloiche OS, ˌkornaˈklɔix, corrie of the stone. In Glen Feshie.

Coire nan Clach OS, ˌkornaˈklax, corrie of the stones. On Braeriach.

(An) Coire Odhar OS, ðɪˌkorˈʌuˑ.ër, the dun corrie. Above Loch Einich.

Coire Raibeirt OS, korˈrabërt, Robert's corrie. South of Cairn Gorm.

(An) Coire Ruadh OS, ðɪˌkorˈrua, the red corrie. On Braeriach.

Coylumbridge OS, ˈkoiljʌmˈbrɪdʒ, Coylum from A' Chuing-leum = the narrow leap, probably referring to the narrow rocky place at the bridge.

The Crags, ðɪˈkragz, 914089. Rocky outcrops above Whitewell.

Creagan a' Mhuilinn OS, ˌkreknaˈmulɪn, little rocky hill of the mill. North of Loch an Eilein.

Creag an Leth-choin OS, ˌkrekanˈlexən, rock of the half dog or lurcher, formerly was Lurcher's Rock locally (McConnochie). Above Lairig Ghru.

Creag Fhiaclach OS, krekˈiaxklax, toothed rocky hill. South of Loch an Eilein.

Creag Mhigeachaidh OS, krekˈmegaxe, rocky hill of the bog-field, with Mig = bog (Watson 1926). In lower Glen Feshie.

Creag nan Gall OS, ˌkreknaˈgal, rock of the lowlanders. East of Loch Morlich.

Creag Phitiulais OS, Pityoulish Hill, pɪtˈjulɪʃˈhɪl, used to be Creag a' Chaisteil, ˌkrekaˈxaʃtjəl, rocky hill of the castle. Creag Phitiulais is shown on OS at 929136. East of Loch Pityoulish.

(The) Croft OS, ðɪˈkroft. A former farm, now a house, south of Inverdruie.

Dorback as in Dorback Burn OS, ˈdorbak, Dorbag = little tadpole, minnow (Watson 1926), spelled as Doirbeag by Dwelly. An area south-east of Nethy Bridge.

The Drum OS, ðɪˈdrʌm, An Druim = the ridge. A field north-west of Loch an Eilein.

Earann Mhuireich, jaranˈvurix, Murdoch's share. A piece of land, now a wood, south of Blackpark near Inverdruie.

Eidart, as in River Eidart OS, ˈetʃart, Eideard, meaning unknown. In upper Glen Feshie.

Feith an Eireannaich OS, ˌfeanˈeranix, bog-stream of the Irishman. West of Lairig Ghru.

Feith Buidhe OS, ðɪˌfeˈpui, An Fheith Bhuidhe = the yellow bog-stream. West of Loch Avon.

Feshie, as in River Feshie OS, ˈfiʃi, Feithisidh = boggy haugh. South-east of Kincraig.

An Garbh-allt OS, the rough burn. Also the Rocky Burn, ðɪˈrokeˈbʌrn. Up Eidart.

Geal-charn OS, ðɪˈjalˌxərn, An Geal-charn = the white hill. South of Loch an Eilein.

Geal Charn OS, ðɪˈgjelˌxarn, An Geal-charn = the white hill. South-west of Tomintoul.

Gleann Einich OS, glənˈɛˑnix, Gleann Eanaich = glen of marsh. South of Rothiemurchus.

Guislich OS, ˈgjuˑsləx, Giuthaslach = fir place. A former house north-east of Coylumbridge.

Inchonie early 6-inch OS, inʃˈone, Inis = meadow, at 951103, on north side of Luineag. A former habitation below Loch Morlich.

Inshriach OS, inʃˈriax, Inis Riabhach = brindled meadow. A house west of Loch an Eilein. Inchriach OS is a flat area on south side of loch.

Invereshie OS, invër'ɪʃi, Inbhir Fheithisidh = mouth of Feshie. East of Kincraig.

The Irishmen's Corrie, ðɪ'ɛɪrɪʃmənz'kore, 945050. Feith an Eireannaich runs out of it; west of Lairig Ghru.

The Island, ðɪ'ɛilənd, 846935. A flat area almost surrounded by river and streams in Glen Feshie.

Kennapole Hill OS, 'kɛnepol'hɪl, Ceann-poll = head pool. Above Loch Gamhna, near Loch an Eilein.

Lochan Buidhe OS, ˌloxanfe'pui, Lochan Feith Buidhe = lochan of yellow bog-stream. South of Cairn Lochan.

Loch an Eilein OS, ˌloxan'elən, loch of the island. South of Aviemore.

Lochan na Beinne OS, ˌloxana'pin, lochan of the hill. North of Cairn Gorm.

Lochan nam Bo OS, ˌloxna'bo·, lochan of the cows. In Glen Feshie.

Lochan Odhar OS, ˌloxan'ʌu·ër, dun lochan. West of Lairig Ghru.

Loch an Spioraid OS, ˌloxan'spirit, loch of the spirit, ghost. In Abernethy Forest.

An Lochan Uaine OS, nˌloxan'uan, the green lochan. The water has a pale green colour. North-east of Loch Morlich.

Loch Einich OS, lox'ɛ·nix, Loch Eanaich = loch of marsh. West of Braeriach.

Loch Insh OS, lox'i·nʃ, lox'i·ʃ, Loch Inse = loch of meadow. Near Kincraig.

Loch Mhic Ghille-chaoil OS, ˌloxˌmɪgˌilə'xul. loch of the son of the thin lad. In Gleann Einich.

Loch Morlich OS, lox'mo·rlɪx, Loch Mor-thulaich = loch of big hillock. In Glen More.

Loch nan Cnapan OS, ˌloxna'kra·pan, loch of the knolls. South of Loch Einich.

Loch nan Geadas OS, ˌloxna'getəs, loch of the pikes (fish). West of Loch Morlich.

The Loist OS, ðɪ'loiʃt, An Losaid = the little hip, or An Loisgte = the burnt (place), 901107 and 899104. Big fields opposite Inverdruie House.

Lorgaidh, as in Allt Lorgaidh OS, ðɪ'lorgi, Lorgaidh = of the tracking. An area in the catchment of Allt Lorgaidh, in upper Feshie.

(An) Lurg OS, ðɪ'lʌrʌk, the shin. A farm south-east of Nethybridge.

Mam Suim OS, mam'suim, round hill of as much ground as will suffice four sheep. East of Loch Morlich.

Meall a' Bhuachaille OS, ˌmjala'vuaxəl, lump of the herdsman. North-east of Loch Morlich.

The Medicine Well, ðɪ'medəsin'wɛl, formerly was Fuaran Raoin Fhraoich (Gordon 1925), see under Rinraoich, 938101. A mineral well east of Coylumbridge.

Miadan, as in Miadan Creag an Leth-choin OS, ðɪ'miadan, Am Miadan = the meadow. A flat grassy area west of Cairn Gorm.

Moine Mhor OS, ðɪˌmən'mo·r, A' Mhoine Mhor = the big peat-moss. Also the Big Moss, ðɪ'bɪg'mos. South of Loch Einich.

Mointeach an Eighe, ˌmɔintjəxən'ei· (with e and i run together), peat-moss of the cry. A bog south of Inverdruie, west of the road to Blackpark.

Moormore OS, mur'mo·r. Sleavemore (Cairngorm Club map) indicates Sliabh Mor = big moor, so Moormore is only a partial translation. A former croft east of Coylumbridge.

Pairc Cruaidh, park'rui, hard field. At Lower Tullochgrue.

Pairc Mointich, park'mɔintjəx, field of peat-moss. At Lower Tullochgrue.

Pairc nan Clach, ˌparkna'klax, field of the stones. At Lower Tullochgrue.

A' Phocaid OS, ðɪ'pokɛt. the pocket. A corrie south-west of Loch Einich.

The Polchar OS, ðɪ'polxar, Am Pollachar = the pool place. A boggy area with pools south-west of Inverdruie.

Rathad nam Meirleach OS, ˌratna'mjarləx, Rathad nam Mearlach = road of the thieves, Mearlach is the local Speyside form of Meirleach. South of Loch an Eilein.

Rinraoich OS, rin're·ix, Raon Fhraoich = field of the heather. Nearby is Fuaran Raoin Fhraoich (Gordon 1925). A former croft east of Coylumbridge.

River Druie OS, ðɪ'drui, Druthaidh = flowing. Diack (1944) suggested Druth = fierce, violent. River at Inverdruie.

River Luineag OS, 'luinak, was said by local informant to mean rushing river, Luinneag = little impetuous one. River coming out of Loch Morlich.

River Nethy OS, 'neθe, Gaelic Neithich, meaning doubtful. At Nethybridge.

Ruigh-aiteachain OS, rui'etʃəxən, Ruighe Eiteachan = shiel of ? expansive place (see meaning under Coire Etchachan in Watson and Allan 1984). A hut on a wide flood plain in Glen Feshie.

Rynettin OS, rɪn'etɪn, Ruidh-naitinn (Forsyth), Ruighe an Aitinn = shiel of the juniper. A former farm in Abernethy.

Ryvoan OS, ri'voan, Ruighe Bhothain = shiel of the bothy. A former house north-east of Loch Morlich.

Seuman's, 'ʃemənz, Jimmy's, Seuman being an affectionate form of Seumas. A former house.

Sgoran Dubh Mor OS, ðɪˌskoran'du·, An Sgoran Dubh = the black little peak; this covers Sgoran Dubh Beag OS as well as Sgoran Dubh Mor. Sometimes ðɪ'skoran is used for the whole ridge including Sgoran Dubh and Sgor Gaoith.

Na Sidhean, ðɪ'ʃianz, the fairy hillocks, 954084 and 960086. South-west of Loch Morlich.

Sleac na Cailliche, ˌslaxkna'kaeləx, slab of the old woman, 893112. A rocky slabby bank south of Aviemore. Lag na Caillich OS, hollow of the old woman, is to the north.

Slochd Mor OS, ðɪ'sloxt, An Slochd = the den. A steep glen south-west of Glen Feshie.

Sron na Lairige OS, ˌstrona'la·rɪk, nose of the hill pass. A hill west of Lairig Ghru.

? Suidhe nan Gall, ˌʃuna'gal, level shelf of the lowlanders. A hollow east of Am Beanaidh opposite Whitewell.

Tollvah OS, tol'va·, Toll Bhathaidh = hole of the drowning. A former farm close beside River Feshie.

Uisdean ? Fhorsail, ˌuʃtjan'ɔrsəl, Uisdean was translated by a local person to AW as Hugh's, referring to a former known inhabitant of that name. The rest is possibly Fhorsail = prosperous (in the dative or genitive). A former thatched house south of Inverdruie.

Water of Ailnack OS, 'aelnak, Ailneag = little stony one (Watson 1926). A river in a rocky canyon near Tomintoul.

Upper Glen Clova

Altentersie Burn OS, alt'tarzən, Allt Tarsuinn = cross burn. South-west of Bachnagairn.

Corlowie OS, kor'lui, Coire Laoigh = corrie of calf. West of Clova hamlet.

Corrie of Bonhard OS, ˌkore.aˌbən'hard, Bonn na h-Airde = base of the height. East of Braedownie.

Craig o Buidhes, ˌkrega'buiz, Creag Bhuidhe = yellow rocky hill, 285789. A hillside north of Moulzie.

The Greens o Lepshiel, ðɪ'grinza lep'ʃil, 265793. OS gives Burn of Loupshiel nearby. Grassy glen bottom north-west of Moulzie.

Juanjorge on early and current OS, dʒɪn'dʒordʒ. A cliff east of Bachnagairn.

The Ought OS, ðɪ'oxt, An t-Uchd = the hill brow. North-west of Glendoll Lodge.

The Rives OS, ðɪ'raevz, Scots Rive = a severance. A split in a rocky hillside opposite Moulzie.

The Snub OS, the Snob o Loch Brandy, ðɪ'snobaˌlox'brandi, Scots Snob = protruding place. A hill nose above Clova hamlet.

Winter Corrie OS, ˌkore'wintër. On Driesh.

Forest of Birse

Allachrowan OS, ala'θron. Allt a' Chroithein = burn of the little fold. A burn north-east of Floors.

Arntillyhard OS, ˌarntɪle'ha·rd, ? Earann Tulach na h-Airde = portion of hillock of the high place, meaning Arntilly of the height; our informant had heard of Arntilly, which was a former farm lower down (Alexander). A ruined farm south-east of Ballogie.

Auchabrack OS, ˌaxa'brak, Achadh Breac = speckled field. A former farm east of Ballochan, also often called Easter Auchabrack.

Auchnashinn OS, ˌaxna'ʃën, Aghaidh na sine (Diack in Alexander) would mean hill-face of the storm. A hill well out on the moor south-west of Ballochan.

Auldgarney, Altgarnie in 1784 (Huntly Estate), al'garne, Alexander gave al'gerne. Allt = burn, garney from gairim = I cry (Watson 1926), south of 530905. A former house, named from the nearby burn, east of Ballochan.

The Auldgarney Haugh, ðɪˌal'garne'ha·x, 530904. A field beside above house.

The Auld Mill, ðɪˈaˑlˈmël, Scots Auld = old, north-east of 516902. A former mill west of Ballochan.

Ballochan OS, bəˈloxən, Baile Lochain = farm-town of lochan. There is no lochan there now, but in wet weather there are still pools in marshy spots, and quite a big one at the Howe. A farm below Birse Castle.

(The) Black Moss OS, ðɪˈblakˈmos. A peat-moss north-west of Birse Castle.

Blairfads OS, blerˈfadz, Blar Fada = long moor, with s an anglicized plural. A hill slope west of Birse Castle.

Bogmore OS, bogˈmoˑr, Bog Mor = big bog. A farm at Finzean.

Bogturk, bogˈtʌrk, Bog Tuirc = bog of boar, 554909. A flat area with rushes east of Burnfoot.

Brackenstake OS, ˌbrakənˈstek, Alexander gave brekənˈstek. A hill north of Birse Castle.

The Bruntland, Bruntland in 1784 (Huntly Estate), ðɪˈbrʌntlən, Scots = burnt land, 522902. A field at Ballochan.

Burnfoot OS, bʌrnˈfët. A house east of Ballochan.

(The) Burn of Allanstank OS, ˌalanˈstaŋk, Allt an Staing = burn of the stank or ditch. South-west of Ballochan.

(The) Burn of Auldgarney OS, alˈgarne, for meaning see Auldgarney.

(The) Burn of Bogturk OS, ðɪˈbʌrnaˌbogˈtʌrk, for meaning see Bogturk. East of Burnfoot.

(The) Burn of Cammie OS, ðɪˈkameˈbʌrn, Camaidh = curved one. A curving burn north-east of Mulnabracks.

(The) Burn of Corn OS, ðɪˈkornˈbʌrn, Corn = horn (referring to the burn's shape). West of Birse Castle.

(The) Burn of Kalfrush OS, ðɪˌkɪlˈθrʌʃˈbʌrn, possibly Cul Chrois = back place of crossings, as chr in Aberdeenshire often becomes fr. West of Auchabrack.

(The) Burn of Keirn OS, ðɪˈkernˈbʌrn, Scots Kirn = churn, or some feature resembling a churn in noise or motion, or a sloppy mess (as of mud). East of Gannoch.

(The) Burns of Allalees OS, ðɪˈbʌrnzaˌalaˈliz, Allt? Liath = grey burn, with s an anglicized plural. Burns on the drove road to Glen Esk.

Carnferg OS, ˌkermaˈferg, Diack (ms) recorded this m sound and also n, Carn na = hill of the, ferg ? Feurag from Feur = grass. A hill north of Ballochan.

The Castle Brae Park, ðɪˈkasəlˈbreˈpark, 520904. A field below Birse Castle.

The Claspit Stane, ðɪˈklaspətˈstin, Scots = the clasped stone, 595940. A large stone in two parts, held together by a metal clasp, at the roadside at the top of the Corsedarder.

(The) Cock Hill OS, ðɪˈkokˈhël. South-east of Ballochan.

Craigmahandle OS, ˌkragmaˈhanəl, Creag na h-Anaile = rocky hill of the breeze. A hill west of Birse Castle.

The Crannach, ðɪˈkranəx, An Crannach or A' Chrannach = the place of trees, 523902. A field south of Ballochan.

Dalbing, dalˈbɪŋ, Dail = haugh, north of 604922. A house at Finzean.

Dalsack OS, dalˈsak, Dail Saic = haugh of sack or measure of corn. A house at Finzean, formerly a farm.

The Drum, ðɪˈdrʌm, An Druim = the ridge, east of 604923. A short cut road at Finzean.

Easter Clune, ˈisterˈklin, Cluain = meadow, 612915. A farm at Finzean. An old rhyme goes 'Easter Clune, Wester Clune, Percie and Dalsack'.

Easter Floors, ˈisterˈflirz, Floors being 'A frequent name both in Scotland and England; the meaning is sites, ground' (Alexander). North-east of 530909. A former farm east of Floors.

Easter Floors Park, ˈisterˈflirzˈpark, 529909. A field at above place.

The Emmerty Braes, ðɪˈemërteˈbrez, Scots Emmert = ant, 520869. Hill slopes south of Ballochan.

(The) Emmerty Burn OS, ðɪˈemërteˈbʌrn. South of Ballochan.

The First Grip, ðɪˈfërstˈgrëp, Scots Grip = to constrict, or Gruip = a groove. There are several Deeside place names with Grip, where a road goes along a steep hillside above a river. In this case it is north-west of 562907, above the Water of Feugh, west of Woodend.

Gannoch OS, ˈgenax, ðɪˈgenax, Gaineamhach = sandy. Month gaiineach (Pont) and Month Ganiell (Gordon) indicate an original Monadh Gaineamhach = sandy hill. A hill south-west of Ballochan.

Garrolfoot, ˌgarəlˈfët, Garbh-allt = rough burn. A house at Finzean, at the foot of Garrol Burn OS.

The Gwaves OS, ðɪˈgwevz, Scots Quave = winding. A winding ravine north of Birse Castle.

The Gwaves Park, ðɪˈgwevzˈpark, 526906. A field at Ballochan.

The Hard Hillock, ðɪˈhardˈhëlək, 526903. A stony field at Ballochan.

The Haugh, ðɪˈhaˑx, Scots = the riverside meadow, 527905. A field east of Ballochan.

The Heid o the Forest, ðɪˈhidɪiˈforëst. Any place at the top of the Forest of Birse.

Hill of Duchery OS, ˈdjoxre, Dubh-chatharaidh = black mossy ground. North-west of Birse Castle.

The Howe, ðɪˈhauˑ, Scots = the hollow, south of 523904. A sheltered hollow near Ballochan.

(The) Knockie OS, ðɪˈknoke, Scots = small hill. A hill south of Ballochan.

Jock Ross's Cairn, ˈdʒokˈrosəzˈkern, c. 520891, but now demolished by a recent bulldozed track. A cairn by the track to Glen Esk, where a Jock Ross was found dead.

Lanchery OS, ˈlanxri, ? Lan-chatharaidh = full mossy ground. A hill north-east of Ballochan.

The Laundry, ðɪˈlandri, south-east of 527909. A building at Wester Floors.

The Mats, ðɪˈmats, possibly named after the nearby Burn of Auldmad OS, Allt Madaidh = burn of fox. Mill Croft OS in 1961. North-east of 516903. Ruins of a former farm west of Ballochan.

The Mats, ðɪˈmats, 517904 and 517902. Two fields beside the above ruins of the same name.

The Muckle Pot, ðɪˈmʌkəlˈpot, Scots Pot = deep pool, south-east of 522903. Where Burn of Corn joins Water of Feugh.

The Muckle Pot Haugh, ðɪˈmʌkəlˈpotˈhaˑx, 523903 on north side of river. A small field near the above pool.

Mudlee Bracks current OS, Mulnabracks on older OS, ˌmʌdliˈbraks ˌmʌlnaˈbraks from some old people in Glen Esk, Meall nam Breac = lump of speckled places, with s an anglicized plural. A hill on the Glen Esk march.

(The) Oxter Burn, OS, ðɪˈoksterˈbʌrn, Scots Oxter = armpit. East of Tampie.

Percie OS, ˈperse, probably Preasaidh = at copse place. A farm at Finzean.

Peter's Wallie, ˈpitërzˈwale, Scots Wallie = little well, south-west of 552911 on north side of road. A well with stonework erected and inscribed by a local man, Peter Brown. East of Burnfoot.

The Plumpin Puil, ðɪˈplʌmpɪnˈpil, north-east of 559907. A deep pool where sheep were plunged into the Feugh from a rock on the south side, in order to clean their fleeces before clipping. East of Burnfoot.

The Red Brae, ðɪˈredˈbre, north-east of 520893. A gravel bank on Feugh south-west of Ballochan.

The Sand Hole, ðɪˈsanˈhol, west of 526905. A sand quarry near Ballochan.

The School Park, ðɪˈskulˈpark, 534906. A field beside a former school, now a church, east of Ballochan.

The Scrattie, ðɪˈskrate, Scots Scrat = scratch, 531906. A field east of Ballochan.

The Second Grip, ðɪˈsekəndˈgrëp, south of 560908, see the First Grip for meaning. A steep narrow place west of Woodend.

The Sheep's Briggie, ðɪˈʃipsˈbrɪgi, south-east of 527905, and 522903. Two foot-bridges over Feugh near Ballochan.

(The) Slochd OS, ðɪˈslok, Scots Slock = hill pass. The top of the pass over to Glen Esk.

The Smugglers' Stane, ðɪˈsmʌglërzˈstin, north of 509900. A boulder south-west of Ballochan.

The Souchin Crags, ðɪˈsuxɪnˈkragz, Scots Souchin = making a moaning sound, as of the wind, 565908. Broken crags west of Woodend.

Tampie OS, ˈtampi. A hill on the Glen Esk march.

The Third Grip, ðɪˈθërdˈgrëp, 557909, for meaning see the First Grip. A steep narrow place west of Woodend.

The Three-neuked Park, ðɪˈθriˈnjukətˈpark, Scots = the three-cornered field, north-west of 532906. East of Ballochan.

The Three Springs, ðɪˈθriˈsprɪŋz, 504864, 506864, 505860. The sources of the Feugh, south of Ballochan.

Tounheid, tunˈhid, Scots = town head, west of 539900. A former farm near Auchabrack.

The Turbine House, ðɪˈtʌrbɪnˌhus, south-east of 527905. A former building for generating electricity, east of Ballochan.

Wester Auchabrack, Auchabrack on OS one-inch map, ˈwestërˌaxaˈbrak, 538903. A former farm south-west of Burnfoot.

Wester Clune OS, ˈwestërˈklin, Cluain = meadow. A farm at Finzean.

Wester Floors, Floors on OS one-inch map, ˈwestër ˈflirz, often called ðrˈflirz, south-east of 527909. A house, formerly a farm, north-east of Ballochan.

Wester Floors Park, westër flirzˈpark, 528909. A field beside the above house.

The Whisky Road, or **Roadie,** ðrˈhwëskiˈrod, 524900. A track where whisky used to be taken across the hill to Glen Esk.

(The) White Hill OS, ðrˈhwɛitˈhël. South-east of Ballochan.

Woodend OS, wɪdˈɛin, wɪdˈen. A farm at Finzean.

REFERENCES

Alexander, W.M. (1952). *The Place-names of Aberdeenshire.* Third Spalding Club, Aberdeen. Astor, G. (1971). *Tapestry of Tillypronie.* Privately published. Cairngorm Club (1895). Map of the Cairngorm Mountains. Based on OS 1 inch to 1 mile map, with annotations. Cairngorm Club Library, Aberdeen. Diack, F.C. (1930s). Unpublished typed MS on the history of Glen Tanar. Copy at Archives Dept., King's College Library, University of Aberdeen. Diack, F.C. (1944). *The Inscriptions of Pictland.* Third Spalding Club, Aberdeen. Dwelly, E. (1901-11). *The Illustrated Gaelic-English Dictionary.* Reprinted 1971, Gairm Publications, Glasgow. Forsyth, W. (1894). Place Names of Abernethy. *Inverness Scientific Society.* (1894), 372-379. Fraser, G.M. (1921). *The Old Deeside Road.* University Press, Aberdeen. Gordon, S. (1925). *The Cairngorm Hills of Scotland.* Cassell, London. Grant, W. & Murison, D.D. (1929-76). *The Scottish National Dictionary.* Scottish National Dictionary Association, Edinburgh. Harper, P. (1928). Old Glentanar. The population and the houses. Unpublished typed notes held by A. Watson. International Phonetic Association (1963). *The Principles of the International Phonetic Association.* University College, London. Invercauld Map (1807-9). Plans of the Estate of Invercauld in Aberdeen-shire. Surveyed and delineated by George Brown. At Invercauld House, copy at Register House, Edinburgh (RHP 3897). Michie, J.G. (1901). *The Records of Invercauld.* New Spalding Club, Aberdeen. Watson, A. & Allan, E. (1984). *The Place Names of Upper Deeside.* Aberdeen University Press, Aberdeen. Watson, W.J. (1916). Some place-names in the Cairngorm region. *Cairngorm Club J.* 8, 133-136. Watson, W.J. (1926). *The History of the Celtic Place-names of Scotland.* Blackwood, Edinburgh.

Chapter 7. Some incorrect Gaelic names on OS maps outside Upper Deeside

Allt Garbhlach, All Gabhalach

Bridge of Brown, Anglicised from Scots Brig o Broon, Glen Brown likewise, originally from Gaelic Bruthainn (nothing to do with brown)

Caderg, Anglicised from Cadha Dearg

Caenlochan, Anglicised from Cadha an Lochain

Canness, Anglicised from Cadha an Easa

Carn Ait (Glen Shee), Carn Eite

Coire an t-Sneachda (Cairn Gorm), Coire an t-Sneachdaidh

Coire Dhondail, Coire Gamhandail

Coire Eindart and Allt Eindart, second word Inndeard (MacBain)

Coire Garbhlach, Coire Gabhlach

Coire Raibeirt (Cairn Gorm), Coire Robaidh

Eidart, Anglicised from Eideard (MacBain)

Glas Tulaichean, Glas-thulchan

Gleann Einich, Gleann Eanaich

Glen Feshie, Anglicised from Gleann Feithisidh

Loch Einich, Loch Eanaich

Loch Insh, Loch Inse

Monadhliath Mountains, Am Monadh Liath

Monamenach, Anglicised from Monadh Meadhonach

Sgor Gaoith, Sgor Gaoithe

Sron a' Cha-no, Sron a' Chadha Nodha

Vinegar Hill, Anglicised from A' Mhin-choiseachd (see Chapter 8)

Chapter 8. Some names and other information outside Upper Deeside

This chapter rests upon names heard by AW over many decades, supplemented by information in old maps, current maps, and published books and papers. It includes a few references to names in several estate maps of uppermost Banffshire held at Register House in Edinburgh. In his 2013 book, AW listed all of these names. The present chapter did not involve searches of estate maps elsewhere, and likewise did not entail the 2013 book's coverage of general Scottish historical documents such as the Register of the Great Seal, Register of the Privy Seal, the Retours, Register of Sasines, Valuation Rolls and others. This chapter should therefore be regarded primarily as a record of many place names used by local folk, and how they pronounced them, along with some analysis of what they are likely to mean in English. Full searches of estate plans and other written sources can come at any time, for the data are safe. Without the pronunciations heard from the lips of local folk, however, they are of little worth on their own. This chapter preserves the first essential step of local pronunciations. In a substantial proportion of these, the data were not safe and in many cases might well have gone with the deaths of older informants.

Back to 1947, AW heard some names spoken by folk in Sutherland from Jean Balfour, Donnie Campbell, Hughie Campbell, Robert and Chris Carrick, Davie and Isabel Duncan (also Inverness and Perth), Frank Gillan, Philip Glazier (also Ross), George Holden (also Ross), Marcus Kimball, Attila Kish, Robert MacAulay, Alex Macdonald, Donnie Macdonald, Donnie Macleod, Philip Macrae (also Ross, Inverness, Perth and Argyll), Gavin Maxwell (also Ross and Inverness), D. G. Moncrieff, Donald Morrison, Ian Pennie, James Robertson-Justice (also Ross), Bruce Sandison, Billy and Cathy and John Scobie, Bill Simpson (also Ross and Inverness); in Ross back to 1947 from Derry Argue (also Banff), Dick Balharry, Sir John Brooke, Lord Burton (also Inverness), Malcolm Douglas (also Inverness), Mr and Mrs Fleming of Monar Lodge and Duncan Fraser (all three also Inverness), Willie Grant (also Perth), Jim Lockie, Tom Longstaff, Dan and Catriona McCowan, Mr Mackay of the Forestry Commission at Craig, John Mackenzie, Rev Lachlan Maclean Watt, Duncan Maclennan (also Inverness), Maimie Nethersole-Thompson, Frank Scott, the shepherd at Loch Rosque in 1947, an old lady at Killilan in 1948, and the stalker at Patt in 1949, and since 1960 also by Calum Anton, Reay Clarke (also Sutherland), John Hay, Hamish Leslie-Melville, Lea McNally, Alex Murray and John Pottie (last three also Inverness), Raymond Simpson, Mark Stewart and Paul van Vlissingen; in Inverness back to 1941 by Davie Adams, Archie Anderson and Mrs Anderson and her brother from Newtonmore, Murdoch Bell, John Berry (also Perth), Hugh Blakeney, MacCalum Cameron, Mrs Campbell the Grantown fishmonger (also Moray), Bob Cattanach, M. Cattanach the Newtonmore confectioner, John Clark, Billy and Jim Collie, Marina and Roy Dennis, Basil Dunlop (also Moray), Donald Emslie-Smith, Duncan Fraser, Simon Fraser, Mrs Garrow, J.P. Grant and John Grant, Charles and Willie Grant, William Ironside, Mrs Lorimer of Aviemore, Jimmy McArtney, Donald McDonald, Archie Macdonald, Derek McGinn, Mrs Mackay of Craiglynne Hotel (also Moray), Ewan MacPherson, Hamish and May and Willie Marshall (all three also Moray and Banff), Donald Milton, Carrie and Brock and Myrtle and Desmond Nethersole-Thompson (the last also Sutherland), Ewan and Cameron Ormiston, Richard Perry, Dave Pullan, Mrs Ross of Grantown's Ben Mhor Hotel (also Moray), Louis Stewart (also Ross and Perth), Alick Sutherland, Bob Sutherland (also Perth), Rev and Mrs Wood of Newtonmore, and the stalker at Coignafearn Lodge in 1947, and since 1961 also Neil Baxter, Keith Bryers, Tony Cardwell, Bob Clyde, Ian Crichton, Mr Davidson head stalker at Glen Feshie, Akie Dempster senior and junior and Douglas Dempster, Ronnie Douglas, Bill and Rhoda Drummond, Charles Fraser, Iain Glen, Dave Gowans, Seumas Grannd, Fred Harper, Eric Langmuir, Alex and Mrs Main, Dolina Macdonald, Pat McLean, Lea Macnally, Peter Moore, Alex Murray, Roger O' Donovan, Neil Ormiston (also Argyll), Ruaridh Ormiston, George Oswald, Tom Paul, Donny Ross, Neil Sutherland, Ian Sykes, Sandy Walker, Tim Walker, Pat Wells, and the farmer at Achnahannet in the late 1970s; in Argyll back to 1947 from Bob Black, Morton Boyd, MacCalum Cameron, Andrew Campbell, Bruce Campbell, Sandy Carr, Martin Charleton, Frank Darling (also Inverness),

The house of Airdachuillin at Loch Stack, September 1960 (AW)

John Scobie at Loch Stack, below Ben Stack, Sutherland, September 1960 (AW)

Alwyne Farquharson, Mike Gregory, Robin Horn, Jim Hunter, Sam Macdonald, Calum Macfarlane-Barrow, Hamish Macinnes. Peter McLellan, Sunny MacPhail, Charlie Palmar, Philip Rankin, Peter Weir, and the Ballachulish ferrymen in 1947; in Perth back to 1945 from Bill Bain, Mervyn Browne, James Duncan (also Inverness and Moray), Charles Grant, Ian Grant, Willie Grant, Ronnie Hepburn, Donald and Nell and Sandy Macdonald, Ian McIvor, Mr McNaughton of Glen Tarken, Sir George Nairn, Bob Scott, David Stephen, and the stalker at Coire Bhachdaidh Lodge in 1949, and since 1961 Niall Campbell, Davie and Isabel Duncan, Mr Ferguson at Atholl, Ron Greer, Ronnie Hepburn, Eleanor Howie, Donnie and Mrs Kennedy, Ron MacGregor, George and Elizabeth Macleod, Alastair Munro, Alex Murray, Michael Nairn, John Robertson, and Ian de Sales la Terriere; in Moray back to 1945 from Alexander Laing, Hugh Blakeney, Jim Craib, Ronnie Douglas, Sir William Gordon-Cumming, Robert Grant (also Inverness and Banff), Ian Lawson, Hector MacBean, Sandy McConnochie, Mr and Mrs McDougall of Upper Craggan, Lady Pauline Ogilvie-Grant, Roland Richter, Patrick J. Sellar (also Inverness and Banff), and Sandy Walker (also Inverness); and in upper Banff back to 1943 from Robert Anderson, Rob Bain, James Beattie of Glen Livet, Alan and Calum Campbell, Walter Coutts, Jim Craib, John Edelsten, Sir John Forbes, Victor Gaffney, Miss George of Glen Livet, Rodney Heslop, Raymond Hewson, Veronica Lankester, Jimmie McIntosh, John McDonald, Mrs Marr of Coynachie, Peter Menzies, James and Mrs Niven, George and Jimmy Oswald, Sir Edward Peck, Mrs Ross near the Whisky Castle at Tomintoul, Edward Stuart, and James Troup.

Four men who had outstanding experience of the Highlands and excellent memories, and came to know scores of local shepherds, deerstalkers, gamekeepers and others, were Seton Gordon, Tom Weir, Pat Sandeman, and Leslie Brown. They told AW many local pronunciations from all counties in the lists below, heard in SG's case as far back as the first two decades of the 1900s and in the others back to the 1930s.

Some place names that AW heard were from people whose names he knew at the time, but omitted to record and has since forgotten. One general snag that he has noticed is that residents in the earlier decades were more reliable in the sense that they had learned the names from their local communities through oral tradition and conversation. This is still the case with selected old indigenous residents, but for many local persons since the 1970s there has been a dilution due to emigration of indigenous folk and immigration by outsiders. Increasingly, the outsiders who have become deerstalkers and gamekeepers and others such as temporary hydro-electric workers and ski workers tend to be shifting and mobile, not staying for long. When asked about names, they rely more often on the OS map and give pronunciations that are more likely to be erroneous.

AW tried to allow for this by checking pronunciations with genuine very old indigenous folk, but this cannot be certain in areas where such folk have died or become too ill to interview. This affects the section on Perthshire names particularly. Here, AW in several cases has given pronunciations that he judged tended to follow the spelling of the OS map, especially if informants were not Gaelic speakers. This leaves the matter open for further research in future, using early forms of the names in old maps and estate papers, which in some such cases may be more reliable than current pronunciations on the lips of those who are not natives to the area.

Since 1990, AW heard some names at Cairn Gorm, used by skiers but not on OS maps, from Nic Bullivant, Bob Clyde, Mark Diggins, Bob Kinnaird, Attila Kish, Tom Paul, Ruari Macdonald, Eric Pirie, Jo and Mollie Porter, George Reid, and Helen Rennie. Special thanks are due to Davie Duncan, who in the last two years told AW many names in Inverness and Perth, including some by Donald Milton of Feshiebridge. IM saw a name from Glen More in a book (Loader 1952). Seumas Grannd made valuable comment on a few Inverness names.

Of the numerous names listed below, nearly all are on OS maps, but many not. Local pronunciations are shown, as well as recently Englished names in the Glen More area. Davie Duncan gave some Badenoch names from local informants at Feshie, and (additional to the Inverness-shire names heard by AW) many Feshie names from estate papers where he did not hear the names from residents. Davie told AW the pronunciations by telephone, and likewise IM heard an unpublished name at Arisaig and gave AW the pronunciation. He tape-recorded a Perthshire name in an interview with Nell Macdonald in the 1990s.

Ben Stack at sunset, September 1958 (AW)

AW heard many more names in all the counties listed,.and especially in his homeward counties of Perth, Moray and Banff, but those given are an interesting selection, with special emphasis on Badenoch and north Atholl. Even there, the coverage is fair only for Glen Feshie, the north side of Glen Banchor, and part of Tarf, but the only old estate papers seen were a very few that Davie Duncan fortunately copied years ago. A comprehensive study of the place names of Badenoch or of Atholl or of upper Banffshire, including old maps and estate papers, would run into thousands of names for each region, about the same for each potential book as the 7000 or so in *The place names of Upper Deeside.*

In the lists below, the first form given is from current OS maps. If this is preceded by parentheses enclosing the definite article The or the Gaelic equivalents A', Am, or An, it follows that people heard by AW used the definite article but the OS omitted it in their maps. If 'not on OS' is given, this means not on current OS 1:25000 maps. OS 6 inch means the first OS 6 inch to the mile map from the late 1800s.

Watson & Allan (1988) presented a more comprehensive set of information in areas around Upper Deeside, from many informants additional to those above. In addition, Watson (2013) included a long list of names heard from the late Donnie Smith of Lurg near Nethybridge in eastern Inverness-shire, the last fluent speaker of the Strathspey dialect of Gaelic. Also he included a shorter list from Bobbie Macleod of Kinlochbervie, former deerstalker at Gualin in Strath Dionard near Durness and a speaker of the north-west Sutherland dialect of Gaelic. In addition, Watson (2013) presented large numbers of names that he did not hear and were previously unpublished, from estate plans held at Register House in Edinburgh. The lists below present a selection of interesting names, far from a comprehensive account of all names heard, especially in AW's homeward counties of Perth, Moray, and Banff.

Sutherland

Achfary (and also Achadh Fairidh OS), axˈfaˑri, Achadh Fairidh, field of watching

Airdachuilinn, ardˈxuˈlən, Aird Chuilinn, land-point of the holly

Arkle, ˈarkəl, in Gaelic Airceil, Norse Ark-fjall is ark-hill, a likely derivation in view of the hill's shape (MacBain, Watson 2002)

Bad na Baighe, ˌbadnaˈbeˑ, there is a birch wood, so maybe Bad na Beithe, clump of the birch, but Macfarlane had Badnabagh

Balnakeil, ˌbalnaˈkil, Baile na Cille, stead of the church

Beinn Ceannabeinne, binˈkjanabin, hill of end-hill, above Durness

Beinn Spionnaidh, binˈspiano, hill of strength, the pronunciation in the Gaelic chapter of Bearhop is different and dubious, given the lack of checking of local pronunciations, Ben-Spionnue (Scrope) was nearer the mark

Ben Dreavie, binˈdriˑvi, AW did not hear an English meaning

Ben Griam, binˈgriam, Beinn Griam, Grim's hill (Watson 2002), Grim a Norseman

Ben Hope, binˈoˑp, Beinn Ob, Hope from Norse hop a bay, thence Gaelic Ob (Watson 2002)

Ben Horn, binˈhorn, Beinn Horn, Norse horn means a horn

Ben Klibreck, binˈkliˈbrək, in Gaelic was Beinn Clibric (Watson 2002), Cli maybe from Norse klif or cliff, last part Norse brekka a slope (Watson 2002)

Ben Loyal, AW did not ask for a pronunciation by a NW Sutherland dialect speaker, but binˈlaiəl to local Sutherland folk at Kinloch, in Gaelic was Beinn Laghal, Laghal suggesting Norse laga-fjall or law hill, or laga-völlr law-field (W.J. Watson's 'Some Sutherland names of places' 1905–06, in Watson 2002), would have been vøllr, in Norse, in modern Norwegian voll is a meadow, Watson (1926) later gave Laghail, but he did not write 'legal hill' (Bearhop) or 'legal mountain' (Drummond), Binleyoll (Macfarlane)

Ben Screavie, binˈskrivi, Beinn Sgribheiche, rugged hill

Ben Stack, binˈstak, in Gaelic Beinn Staca, Gaelic Stac is from Norse precipitous hill or cliff or skerry (MacBain), Stakka a stump in Old Norse (Agnarsson et al.), in modern Norwegian stakk, in Gaelic means precipice or conical hill, both fitting Ben Stack

Cape Wrath, in Gaelic Am Parph (MacBain, Watson 2002) from Norse hvarf a turning-point, also the name The Parph (OS), pronounced parf, is commonly used for the whole peninsula

The Cape Side, a common name for land on the Cape Wrath side W of Kyle of Durness

Carn a' Mhadaidh, karn'vado, stony hill of the wolf, note local pronunciation of Mhadaidh

Cashel Dhu, ˌkaʃəl'duˑ, Caiseal Dubh, dark bulwark or mound, at top of Loch Hope

(The) Clo Mor, klo'moːr, from An Clo Mor, AW did not hear an English translation, but Clo is a nail, pin, or peg, so maybe the big peg, a cliff E of Cape Wrath, joined in the west by another Clo name, Stac Clo Kearvaig

Cnoc Carn an Leime, ˌknɔkˌkarnˌn'leˑm, round hill of stony hill of the jump, steep cliffs in a corrie on seaward side

Cnoc Madaidh, knɔk'mado, round hill of wolf, note also Carn a' Mhadaidh

Coldbackie, 'kalbake, in Gaelic Callbacaidh (Watson 2002), from Norse kald-bakki or cold bank, Caltabacky (Pont), OS form Anglicised, presumably on erroneous assumption that Cal was Scots for English Cold, a settlement near Tongue

(The) Conival, 'kɔnəvjal, An Con-mheall, the combination of lumps or the high lump, hill by Ben More Assynt

Cranstackie, karn'stake, Cranstackie (Thomson), this local pronunciation by reliable informants shows that the Anglicised OS spelling is incorrect, should be Carn Stacaidh, hill of little rocky point

Creag Riabhach, krek'riˑavax, bh pronounced locally, whereas in the Cairngorms region it lengthens the preceding diphthong but is not pronounced, brindled crag, in the Parph

Creag Riabhach, krek'riˑavax, as above, W of Kinloch

Cul Beag, kul'bek, little back, hill N of Ullapool

Cul Mor, kul'moːr, big back, hill N of Ullapool, near Cul Beag

Durness, 'dʌrnəs, Gaelic Diuranais, from Norse dyra-nes, deer-cape (Watson 2002), modern Norwegian Dyrnes similar meaning but Dyr means any animal or beast, and this was the case with old Norse (Agnarsson et al.)

Erribol, 'erəbol, in Gaelic Eiribol, from Norse eyrr-bol or gravel-beach stead (Watson 2002)

Faraid Head, 'farət, Anlicised to Farout Head in early OS maps, now Faraid Head, in Gaelic was Rudha na Farai(r)d or projecting cape (Watson 2002)

Farrmheall, 'faravel, Far-mheall suggested from Norse Faer or sheep (MacBain, Watson 2002) but the latter wrote more probably is pure Gaelic from Farrmheall or projecting lump, which describes it well, Drummond gave it from Gaelic Faire a skyline or horizon, which is possible, but he adduced no evidence on pronunciation and did not mention MacBain or Watson

Fashven, 'faʃvin, Gaelic Faisbheinn from Norse hvass or pointed (Watson 2002), so Hvass-bheinn

The Flows, flʌuz, not on OS, almost always mispronounced by incomers as floz, has nothing to do with the English term flows, is a Scots word for boggy ground, widespread in Caithness as well as Sutherland, occurring in Inverness-shire, in Galloway as the Silver Flowe, and in Orkney as Scapa Flow, all locally flʌu, and in Caithness and Sutherland there is also the adjective 'flʌui, meaning ground prone to be boggy; the fanciful phrase The Flow Country, invented by scientists visiting the region, is not used by indigenous local folk though widely by outsiders, some Flows are named from nearby places, such as the Strathy Flows south of Strathy hamlet

Foinaven, 'fɔijəvin, Foinne-bheinn, wart-hill, Feinnbhinn (Macfarlane)

Forsinard, ˌforsən'ard, fors Norse for a waterfall, the rest Gaelic meaning upper (Watson 2002), presumably Fors an Aird or waterfall of the height

Gobernuisgach, ˌgobər'nuiʃkix, in Gaelic was Gob an Uisgich, beak of the water-place (Watson 1926), now often called just Gober for short, three big streams converge near it

(The) Gualin, 'gualan, from A' Ghualann, the shoulder (here, of a hill), the Gualin (Scrope)

Handa, 'handa, from Norse Sand-ey or sand-island, Sandey in standard Norse spelling, with S aspirated in Gaelic (Watson 2992), and hence to become Shanda, pronounced as Handa

Inshore, ˌinə'ʃoˑr, Inis Fheoir, meadow of the grass

AW and English setter Harra on Ceann Garbh (rough head) of Foinaven, with Ben Stack and far Quinag southwards, September 1959 (AW sen)

The cliffs of Creag Riabhach or brindled rock, one of the most remote spots in Scotland, rise above Loch na Creige Riabhaich, south-west of the Kyle of Durness, September 1958 (AW)

Kearvaig, 'kɛrveg, in Gaelic Cearbhaig, Anglicised to Kerwick, from Norse Karfavi or galley bay (MacBain), Karfavi not confirmed by Agnarsson et al., but they gave Karfi as a galley or swiftly-moving ship, note that Vik in Old Norse and modern Norwegian is a narrow inlet or creek, can be a small bay

Kildonan, kɪl'dɔnən, Cill Donnan (Watson 1926), church of Donnan a saint, MacBain wrote that this was corrupted from an earlier version Kil-domhnach or Lord's kirk

Kinloch, kɪn'lox, Keand Loch (Pont), Ceann Locha, head of loch, near Tongue

Kirkibol, 'kɪrkəbol, Norse kirkja-bol or church stead, Kirkjabol in standard Norse spelling, settlement with church, below Tongue

Laid, 'leəd, An Leathad (Dwelly), the hillside

Laxford, 'laksfərd, Gaelic Lusard (Watson 2002), from Norse Laks-fjorður or salmon fjord, spelling Laks not confirmed by Agnarsson et al. but Lax given instead, Lax-fjorðr in standard Old Norse spelling, Loch of Lussord (Macfarlane) referred to the sea-loch

Loch an Dherue, ˌloxan'dʒiri, Loch an Dithreibh, loch of the wild land

Loch Choire Lodge, lox'kɔˑr, Loch Corr (Scrope), the lack of aspiration of Choire in the local pronunciation and in Scrope suggests maybe Loch Coire, loch at corrie rather than loch of the corrie

Loch More, lox'moːr, Anglicised, in classical Gaelic form Loch Mhor, big loch

Meallan Liath, ˌmjalan'lia, grey little lump-hill, near Tongue

Melness, 'mɛlnəs, Norse mel-nes, bent-grass cape (Watson 2002), Melr is old Norse for bent-grass (Agnarsson et al.), a settlement on Kyle of Tongue

Melvich, 'mɛlvəx, in Gaelic Mealbhaig (Watson 2002), A' Mhealbhaich (Ainmean-Aite na h-Alba), from Norse Mel-vik, bent-grass inlet, see above name, settlement on N coast

A' Mhoine, ə'voˑinə, the peat-moss, a great expanse W of Kyle of Tongue, geologists named the Moine schist bedrock that covers most of the Highlands after it

(The) Plat Reidh, 'plat're, Am Plat Reidh, the smooth flat, which it is

Quinag, ə'xunjak, A' Chuinneag, the water-pitcher or churn, a hill S of Kylesku

Reay, reˑ, a name in Sutherland with the Reay deer-forest and also in NE Sutherland and NW Caithness where it appears in the name of the Dounreay nuclear station, in Gaelic was Rath or fort, with the name Magh Rath for plain of fort, and Dounreay from Dun Rath or hill of fort

Rhiconich, usually rɪ'koˑnɪx, but to best native Gaelic speakers ri'koˑənax, suggests Ruighe Coinneach, cattle-run or shiel at moss

Sandwood, from Norse Sand-vatn or sand-water (Watson 2002)

Sgribhis-bheinn, 'skriˑʃvin, maybe Norse Sgrioda, scree, Gaelic Bheinn, hill (Watson 2002), Skryshbhinn (Macfarlane), Sgrioda not confirmed by Agnarsson et al. but Skrida is to creep or slide

Smoo, smuˑ, from Norse smuga a narrow cleft (MacBain), confirmed Smuga in Agnarsson et al., a cave and inlet E of Durness

Strabeg, stra'bek, from Srath Beag, little strath or valley, Strabeg (Macfarlane)

Strath Chailleach, stra'xalax, Srath Chailleach, strath of old women

Strath More, stra'moːr, Srath Mor, big strath, above Loch Hope

Strath Shinary, stra'ʃɛnare Srath Sean-airigh, strath of old shiel

Suilven, 'suləvin, in Gaelic Sulabheinn, from Norse Sula-fjall or pillar-hill (Watson 2002)

Sula Sgeir, 'suləskər, often mispronounced, from Sulair-sgeir, gannet-rock, many gannets breed there, N of Sutherland

Sutherland, from Norse Suðurland, south land

Tongue, tʌŋ, sometimes tending to tuŋ, from Norse Tunga, a tongue of land (MacBain), a narrow tongue of land lying below Tongue village almost divides the Kyle of Tongue

Whiten Head, 'hwɪtən'hed, The Whittenhead (Macfarlane), this spectacular high cliff is pale in colour, so probably from Norse Hvit, white, as in Whitby, white town, and the en may be a definite article as in modern Norwegian, thus white one

A couple of interesting names in nearby Caithness

Morven, 'morvən, Gaelic Mor-bheinn or big hill

Scaraben, 'skaraben, likely Norse Skara to jut out, a fitting description, along with Gaelic for a hill, Beinn, so Skara-bheinn

Ross

In Ross names below with Gaelic Beinn, ň resembles that in piňon pine, and in other counties this is also the case to some extent, though tending towards ŋ in Inverness, Perth and Banff. For names and Gaelic in wester Ross, especially the area around Gairloch and Loch Maree, the recent studies by Roy Wentworth are notable, such as his *Place names of the Beinn Eighe NNR* (1999), published by Scottish Natural Heritage, and his *Rannsachadh air fon-eolas dualchainnt Ghaidlig Ghearrloch, Siorrachd Rois* (2003), University of Aberdeen, see also the website Gaidhlig Ghearrloch.

Achnashellach, ˌaxna"ʃelax, Achadh nan Seileach, field of the willows, a settlement, Achanashillach (Macfarlane)

Anancaun, ˌaˈnaˈgjʌun, ath-nan-ceann, ford of the heads (Watson 1904), Achanacand (Macfarlane), buildings near river

Aonach air Chrith, in Gaelic was Aoineadh air chrith or shaking precipice because it is so sharply pointed (Watson 1904), ˌøːinagerˈxriˑ, g throaty, literally steep promontory or precipice on the shake, Aoineadh air Chrith, but Watson on this was ignored in recent books (Bearhop, Bennet, Broadhead et al., Drummond)

Applecross, 'apəlkros, was Aporcrosan in 673, and Watson (1904) took this as estuary of Crosan and heard the name of the river at the village as Abhainn Crosan, Apor like Aber

Bealach na Ba, should be Bealach nam Bo, pass of the kine, reported also as just Am Bealach, the pass (Watson 1904), Bealach nam Bo (Gordon 1934), heard by me as, ˌbjalaxnamˈboː, Bealach nam Bo (website of Applecross Heritage Society 2014), OS map spelling clearly incorrect, but John Murray (2014) repeats Bealach na Ba without referring to Watson (1904) and the other references above, again exemplifying the flaws of place-name study without checking pronunciations by indigenous local people

Beinn Airigh Charr, 'biňˌareˌaˈxaˑr, Watson (1904) recorded Binn Airigh a' Charr, hill of shieling of the projecting rock or rock-shelf, pronounced quickly, stressing first and last syllables and the accent on the A of Airigh (i.e. a long A), but he has been ignored in several recent books (Bearhop, Drummond, Milne & Brown), note also that the authors of the Gaelic chapter in Bearhop give the pronunciation of Ben and Beinn in all counties as bYn, which in their own invented phonetic scheme is equivalent to IPA baen, a form that regrettably appears to be unique to them, as well as to Drummond who also uses it, and John Murray in his 2014 book invented his own phonetic scheme which differed considerably from that in the SMC books by Bearhop and Drummond, but Murray gives byn, and also pays no attention to local pronunciations, so that we have the Gaelic for Derry Cairngorm, Carn Gorm an Doire, given the clumsy caarn Gawrom un DAWruh

Beinn Alligin, biňˈalikən, Watson (1904) gave Beinn Alligin as Beinn Ailiginn or Ben of Alligin, and there is also the township of Alligin and Inver Alligin the settlement at the stream mouth, so Beinn Alligin OS means hill of Ailiginn (stream), a point ignored in recent books (Bennet, Broadhead et al., Drummond), who gave it as possibly jewelled mountain (Bennet), mountain of beauty or of the jewel (Broadhead et al.), and 'the usual translation is jewelled mountain or mountain of beauty' but also on a different page 'darling peak?' (Drummond). Bearhop was near the mark by stating that it is derived from the River Alligin, a name either from ailleag a jewel or from ail a rock, the OS name for the river is Amhainn Alligin, and Alligin Shuas is a coastal settlement nearby. Drummond wrote 'The nearest word in Gaelic dictionaries to this name is ailleagan a jewel or a darling, and the usual translation (but omitting any references) is jewelled mountain or mountain of beauty'. Watson (1904) also pointed out that jewel or pretty woman was a possibility, but that the short l in Ailiginn as he heard it went against this. However, the short l in Ail would seem to fit (AW comment)

(The) Beinn Bhan, A' Bhinn Bhan (Watson 1904), the fair hill, əˌviňˈvaːn, at Applecross

Beinn Dearg, biňˈdʒerək, red hill, SE of Ullapool

Cul Mor (left) and Stac Pollaidh (right), November 1956 (AW senior)

Ben Loyal from above Kinloch, April 1959 (AW)

Beinn Eighe, biň'e:, hill of file, called 'from the serrated outline as seen from Kinlochewe' (Watson 1904), the teeth of the file being upstanding rocks recorded by Watson (1904) as Bodaich Dhubh Binn Eighe or the black carls of Beinn Eighe, and in 1948 AW heard the Black Carls commonly used in and around Kinlochewe

(The) Beinn Fhada, biň'ata, often has been Anglicised to Ben Attow, from A' Bheinn Fhada, the long hill

Beinn Fhionnlaidh, biň'junle, hill of Finlay, a past stalking tenant could not pronounce it and decided it would be Benula, and likewise a former shooting lodge (Benula Lodge OS) on the N side of Loch Mullardoch until a dam for a hydro-electric scheme raised the water above the lodge

Beinn Lair, biň'la:rə, hill of mare, not hill of the mare as in Broadhead et al., should be spelled Beinn Laire, often mispronounced as, ben'ler,'To be taken in connection with Ardlair; there are two rocks near this promontory in L. Maree called an Lair, the mare, and an searrach, the foal. The meaning is thus Mare-hill, and Mare-promontory'.

Beinn na Muice, ‚biňna'muixkə, hill of the pig, above E end of Loch Monar

Ben Wyvis, Ben Ouish (Roy), Ben-weavis (Scrope), from Beinn Uais, biň'u:əʃ, high hill

Bidean an Eoin Deirg, ‚bidʒanjo:ən'dʒerɛk, pinnacle of the red bird, in Gaelic often a name for the red grouse, a striking peak above Loch Monar, Rev A.E. Robertson heard it locally called The Spidean (Drummond 2007), a name that is elsewhere in west Ross on Liathach and has the same meaning of pinnacle, Watson & Allan recorded two Deeside places called Spiodagan or little sharp-topped place, each a sharp hillock

Bidein a' Choire Sheasgaich, ‚bidʒanaˌxɔrə'hɛskəx, pinnacle of the barren or reedy corrie, Seasgach can also mean fallow cattle, at west Monar, should be spelled Bidean

The Black Carls, see Beinn Eighe

Carn Eige (OS), recent editions of the Scottish Mountaineering Club's Hillwalkers' Guide *North-west Highlands*

Sunset on the Strathy Flows of Sutherland, late June 1988 (AW)

(Broadhead et al. 2004), the SMC book *The Munros* (Ed. by D. Bennet 1999), both published by Scottish Mountaineering Trust), and the SMC book *Munro's Tables* (Ed by Bearhop 1997, SMT) name this hill Carn Eighe and the books translate as file peak or file hill. This is fanciful invention, adduced with no evidence from fieldwork by interviewing local residents, and hence ignoring the literature on place names and accepted good practice in research on place names. Watson (1904) clearly showed it as Carn-eite, and presented a local rhyme involving it and Mam Sodhail. Ronald Burn recorded it as Carn Eite. My local informants called it Carn Eite. karnˈjetʃə, similar sound to Gleann Eite (Anglicised Glen Etive), and Buachaille Eite Mor (Anglicised Buachaille Etive More), note also Lochan Mathair Eite (OS) on Rannoch Moor for a lochan near the start of the River Etive, meaning lochan of mother of Etive, see Watson (1904) for other names similar including Eiteachain, and Watson & Allan (1984) for Coire Etchachan and other Etchachan names in upper Deeside, maybe Carn Eite or hill of extending, see old rhyme about Carn Eite by Watson (1904) under Mam Sodhail

A' Chioch, əˈxiˈəx, a local name which Tom Weir heard and told to me (see A' Chioch in Weir 1948), not on OS 1:25000, often Anglicised by climbers to The Cioch, means the pap, a striking rocky promontory at the end of a ridge from Sgurr a' Chaorachain at Applecross, with the Cioch Nose up the edge of it a notable rock-climb

Coire nan Arr, ˌkɔrənanˈaˈrag, Coire nan aradh with dh hardened to g, ladder corry, where a set of stone steps allowed access up and over the top, before the road was made across Bealach nam Bo (Watson 1904), Corry-na-narig (Thomson) and Cor-nan-a-rag (Scrope) fit with Coire nan Aradh, note not the Coire nam Faradh of

Dick Balharry on Loch Maree, June 2012 (Mrs Balharry)

John Murray (2014), which does not fit the pronunciation and has no supporting evidence adduced

Coire nan Con, ˌkɔrnaˈgɔn, corrie of the dogs, on Ben Wyvis

Coire na Sleaghaich, ˌkɔrənaˈʃleˈgax, corrie of the Slioch or spear-like place

Coire Mhic Fhearchair, ˌkɔrəˌvixkˈɛrəxər, corrie of the son of Farquhar, on Beinn Eighe

(The) Dirrie Mor, An Diridh Mor, the great ascent (Watson 1926, Gordon 1934), nˌdʒiriˈmoːr

(The) Dubh Loch, ˈduːlox, An Dubh Loch (Watson 1904), the black loch

Am Faochagach, ˈføxak, from Faochag (Burn and AW's informants), whelk, perhaps referring to shape, a hill above Strath Vaich, Drummond after speculating about heather and berries decided that 'shell-likeness is indeed the true meaning', but he had ignored Burn and did not check with local informants, nevertheless decided that the OS form means the place abounding in whelks, which is how the OS form would be translated if one were to accept its validity, but the Gaelic chapter in Bearhop states bluntly 'but properly Am Fraochagach....the heathery place', and even giving an invented pronunciation based on this, while Bennet and Broadhead et al. have Am Faochagach as on OS maps, but translate it as the heathery place, which is incorrect, and Broadhead et al. continue the inventions by stating that Faochaig in Glen Elchaig means the whelk or little heathery hill, while the authors of the Gaelic chapter in Bearhop invented, 'but properly, little heathery hill' along with an invented pronunciation based on the first invention, examples that exemplify the pitfalls of using a map and dictionary without checking earlier sources or local pronunciations

(The) Fionn Bheinn, ˈfjunaviň, from Am Fionn-bheinn, the white hill, near Achnasheen

(Am) Fionn Loch, mˈfjunlox, Am Fionn Loch (Watson 1904), in classical Gaelic should be spelled Am Fionn-loch

Freevater, friˈvaˈtər, from the Gaelic name Fridh Bhaltair or deer-forest of Walter, see Watson (1926) for an account of Walter

(Am) Fuar Loch Beag, mˈfuarloxˈbek, from Am Fuar-loch Beag, the little cold loch

(Am) Fuar Loch Mor, mˈfuarloxˈmoːr, from Am Fuar-loch Mor, the big cold loch

(Am) Fuar Tholl, mˈfuarʌul, Am Fuar-tholl, the cold hole, a hill prominent from Loch Carron

(Am) Fuar Tholl Mor, mˈfuarʌulˈmoːr, Am Fuar-tholl Mor, the big cold hole, a N-facing corrie on Maoile Lunndaidh

(Am) Fuar Tholl Mor, mˈfuarʌulˈʹmoːr, Am Fuar-tholl Mor, the big cold hole, a N-facing corrie NW of Sgurr a' Choire Ghlais

(An) Glas Leathad Mor, nˈglasˌleəˈtmoːr, big green slope, the long big grassy slope W of the plateau of of Ben Wyvis

(An) Gorm Loch Beag, nˈgorəmloxˈbek, the little green loch, green because of grassy banks

(An) Gorm Loch Mor, nˈgorəmloxˈmoːr, the big green loch, see above

Gruinard, ˈgruiˈnjard, some informants gave a sound almost like Greenyard in English, Gaelic Gruineard, from Norse grunnfjörður or shallow firth (Watson 1904), fjord a better word than firth

Kinlochewe, ˌkinˌloxˈjuˈ, Cinn Loch Iu, at head of Loch Ewe, spelling Iu from Watson (1904), who wrote that the River Ewe coming out of the loch was Abhainn Iu to natives, he suggested that Iu might be yew (i,e, tree) as in Irish eo and Welsh yw, and stated that Loch Maree was formerly called Loch Ewe from the facts of the River Ewe issuing from the loch, from Kinlochewe at the loch's head, and Letterewe on the E side of the loch, Loch Ew and the 'fresch' Loch of Ew were distinguished from the salt Lochew and Inner Ew (i.e. Inbhir Iu) at the mouth of the river Ewe near Gairloch, and the present Loch Maree was clearly described in detail with its length as being Loch Ew (Pont), who also had Clachan-kean Lochew, i.e. Clachan Cinn Loch Iu or settlement of Kinlochewe, also spelled as Can Loch Ew, and the Kinlochewe River as Avon Con, so Abhainn Con, perhaps dog-river, Pont wrote of 'Lochew, by sum it is cald Loch Mulruy' (i.e. Maree)

Kishorn, ˈkiʃɔrn, Gaelic Cis-orn from Norse keis-horn or bulky cape (Watson 1904)

Liathach, ˈliaˌgax, g throaty, grey or hoary place, 'pronounced Liathghach, the gh developing naturally' (Watson 1904), Leagach (Thomson), a steep hill at Torridon, often mispronounced with t instead of g

Loch Beinn a' Mheadhoin, ˌloxˌbiňaˈveˈən, loch of hill of the middle, in Glen Affric

Beinn Bhan beyond the cliffs of Sgurr a' Chaorachain, Applecross, September 1958 (AW)

Looking up Coire nan Arr to the Cioch Nose, a steep climb up the right edge of the cliffs of Sgurr a' Chaorachain, September 1958 (AW)

Beinn Damh and Maol Chean-dearg from Loch Coultrie, September 1958 (AW)

Shieldaig Island with its ancient pines, September 1958 (AW)

Raasay from Shore Street at Applecross village, September 1958 (AW)

AW senior on Liathach looks down Loch Torridon, April 1961 (AW)

An Riabhachan and Sgurr na Lapaich from helicopter, Loch Mullardoch left, November 1988 (AW)

Sgurr a' Choire Ghlais and Sgurr na Ruaidhe from helicopter, Slioch beyond, with snowier and higher Fannich hills nearer to the right, November 1988 (AW)

A wild morning looking west from Beinn na Muice above the wood that shelters Monar Lodge, up Loch Monar to Bidean an Eoin Deirg on right, the cliffs of Bidein a' Choire Sheasgaich to left, and Lurh Mhor slightly nearer and further left, before the dam was built that raised the loch well above the wood and lodge, 8 April 1949 (AW)

Loch Clair, lox'kla:ər, loch of level place

Loch Coulin, lox'ku:lən, in Gaelic was Culainn with u strongly nasal, a locative of con-lann meaning high enclosures or collection of enclosures (Watson 1904), so Loch Conn-lann, loch at high enclosures or at collection of enclosures

Loch Lundie, lox'lundi, Loch Lunndaidh (Watson 1904), Loch Loundie (Scrope), loch of wet place

Loch Maree, ˌlox̧ˌma'ri, in Gaelic Loch-ma-rui(bh), Loch of St Malruba (Watson 1904), see Kinlochewe also, the Anglicised Malruba is better expressed as Maol Rubha (Watson 1926)

Lurg Mhor, ˌlurək'vo:r, big ridge, a hill in west Monar

Mam Sodhail, Mam Sabhal, mam'sɔ:l, rounded hill of barns (Watson 1904), pronunciation given is by AW's informants, classical Gaelic form would be Mam Shabhal for rounded hill of barns, Mam Sabhail for rounded hill of barn (shape), latter fits pronunciation better, Watson (1904) wrote of it, 'noted for grass', and it still has much grass: he gave a fine old Gaelic rhyme with good rhythm, Carn-eite nan gobhar, 's Mam-sabhal an fheoir, or Carn-eite of goats, and Mam-sabhal of grass'

Maoile Lunndaidh, møil'lundi, brow of wet place, above Loch Monar

Maol Chean-dearg, ˌmøla'xjʌunˌdʒɛrək, Maol cheann-dearg, red-headed brow (Watson 1904), so literally brow of the red-head, not bald red head as in Bearhop, Bennet, Broadhead et al., Drummond, last hyphenated

Alick Sutherland at Gaick Lodge, Sgor Dearg on right and snowy Sron Bhuirich distant left, on AW's first visit to Alick, in 1948, his sister-in-law and two nieces were there on holiday, and on 5 July AW's diary runs, 'Was entertained with Gaelic songs from one of the two young girls', 14 April 1951 (AW)

The bare gravelly flats at Gaick Lodge in a snowy spring, with Sron Bhuirich behind, 14 April 1951 (AW)

Loch an t-Seilich, looking towards Sgor Dearg, with Coire Madagan Mor to right, 14 April 1951 (AW)

part is compound, so should be spelled Maol Cheann-dearg, Watson (1904) pointing out that the hill was composed of the red Torridonian sandstone

Meall a' Ghiubhais, ˌmjʌulˈyuːʃ, lump-hill of the pine, above Loch Maree

(Am) Meall Gorm, ˌmˌmjʌulˈgɔrʌm, the blue lump-hill, at Applecross

A' Mhaighdean, əˈvaˑitʃən, the maiden, a prominent hill N of Loch Maree

An Riabhachan, nˈriːaxan, the brindled place (MacBain), part of the 'shootings of Riochan' (MacBain), a hill S of upper Loch Monar

Seana-bhraigh, ˈʃʌunavraˑi, old upland, a hill near Beinn Dearg

Sgorr Ruadh, skurˈruag, gh throaty, recorded as Sgurr Ruadh, red peak, from the red Torridonian sandstone (Watson 1904)

Sgurr a' Chaorachain at Applecross, ˌskuraˈxøraxən, 'Based on "caoir" a blaze of fire, with the secondary meaning of torrent. The mountain is extremely steep on the Kishorn side' (Watson (1904), but recent books confuse by speculations, with peak of the little sheep (Milne & Brown 2002), and peak of the rowan-berried place (Drummond 2007), though Broadhead et al. are closer to Watson with peak of the torrent, note the

Upper Glen Feshie in extreme snow, with Leathad an Taobhain on right and river completely unseen, 14 April 1951 (AW)

later references are unreliable (see under Carn Eige above)

Sgurr a' Choinnich, ˌskuraˈxɔːnjix, peak of the moss, and likewise Sgurr a' Choinnich Beag and Mor above Glen Spean, not mossy peak as in Bearhop, Broadhead et al., Bennet, and Drummond, in west Monar.

Sgurr a' Choire Ghlais, ˌskuraˌxɔrəˈglaʃ, peak of the green corrie

Sgurr Ban, skurˈbaːn, white peak, named after the white quartzite screes on this sharp top on Beinn Eighe

Sgurr Mor, skurˈmoːr, big peak, a high peak NW of Garve

Sgurr na Fearstaig, ˌskurnaˈfjerstək, Watson (1904) gave the one above Strath Carron as Sgurr nam Feartaig, peak of the sea-pinks, which grow there, in west Ross the usual word for sea-pink or sea thrift is Feartag, feminine (Dwelly), so should be Sgurr nam Feartaig

Sgurr na Fearstaig, ˌskurnaˈfjerstək, as name above, W of Sgurr a' Choire Ghlais

Sgurr na Lapaich at Mullardoch, peak of the bog, ˌskurnaˈlaːxpix, note the strong local aspiration in 'laːxpix

Sgurr nan Ceathramhnan, ˌskurnanˈkeranan, sometimes ˌskurnaˈgeranan, peak of the quarters, high peak W of Affric

Sgurr nan Conbhairean, ˌskurnaˈgonvaran, peak of the dog-men (i.e. handlers), a prominent high peak N of Cluanie

Sgurr na Ruaidhe, ˌskurnaˈruˈi, peak of the redness

Shieldaig, ˈʃildeg, Gaelic Sildeag from Norse Sild Vik or herring bay (Watson 1904)

Shore Street (C, Applecross Heritage Society website), street with houses at village

Slioch, ˈʃlegax, from Sleaghach an adjective but here a noun, the root Sleagh meaning a spear (Watson 1904), so maybe just means spear-like place or hill, Burn recorded the local Gaelic pronunciation as sluggich (Allan 1995)

Allt Garbhlach of Glen Feshie in spring thaw, April 1969 (AW)

An Socach, n'sɔ:xkax, the projecting hill, at Ben Wyvis

Srath a' Bhathaich, stra'va:ix, strath of the shelter, E of Loch Damh

Strath Kanaird, stra'kanjard, last word in Gaelic is Cainneart from Norse kann-fjorður or Can firth, Can in the name refers to a broch (Watson 1904)

Strath Vaich, stra'va:ix, Srath Bhathaich, strath of the shelter, NW of Garve

Strome, strom, Norse straumr a current (Watson 2002), modern Norwegian stromm

An Teallach, n'tjalax, the forge, a high rocky peak with several pointed tops, SW of Ullapool

Inverness

Achlean, ax'leən, Achadh Leathann, broad field, a farm in Glen Feshie, was Achleanmore (Roy) with Achleanbeg to the N, Achleathain more (Thomson) with Achleathain beag to the N, so Achadh Leathann Mor and Beag

Achnagonalin, ˌaxna'gɔnələn, Achnconnalon (Roy), Auchnagonalan (Thomson), Achadh nan Coinnlean, field of the barley stalks, former farm, now an industrial estate S of Grantown

Achnahannet, ˌaxna'hanət, Achadh na h-Annaide (Watson 1926), field of the chapel, a farm NE of Duthil

Achnahatnich, ˌaxna'haxtnix, Achadh na h-Aitionnaich, field of the juniper place, farm NE of Coylumbridge

Allt a' Bhreac-choire, alt'vreaxˌxər , burn of the speckled corrie, runs into uppermost Feshie

Allt a' Chagain, alt'xa'gən, burn of the narrow pass, in upper Feshie

Allt a' Chaorainn, ˌalt'xurən, burn of the rowan, up Glen Banchor

Allt a' Chrom-alltain, alt'xrɔmˌaltən, burn of the crooked burnie, runs into lower Feshie

Allt a' Mharcaidh, alt'varke, burn of the horse-place

Allt an Daimh, ˌaltan'dae, burn of the stag, runs into uppermost Feshie

The former farm of Achleum on east side of Feshie, below the big snow patch on left at Ciste Mhearad, June 1983 (AW)

Allt an Lagain Odhair, ˌaltanˌlakənˈʌuˈr, burn of the little dun hollow, W of Coire Bhlair

Allt an Lochain, ˌaltanˈloxən, burn of the lochan, runs out of Loch Ghiuthsaichan

Allt an t-Seilich, ˌaltanˈtʃelix, burn of the willow, in Monadh Liath

Allt Bhran, altˈvraˈn, runs into Tromie, Bhran indicates turbulence, signifies 'raven' (MacBain)

Allt Buidheannach, altˈbuːənjax, should be Allt Buidheannaich, burn of the yellow place, on Braeriach

Allt Bruthach an Easain, ˌaltˌbruaxanˈjɛsən, burn little waterfall, up Glen Banchor

Allt Chomhraig, altˈxɔˈrək, burn of the confluence

Allt Coire Chaoil, ˌaltˌkɔrˈkuˈl, OS form ungrammatical, should be Allt Coire Caol, burn of narrow corrie

Allt Coire Dhomhain, ˌaltˌkɔrˈdoːən, OS form ungrammatical, should be Allt Coire Domhain, burn of deep corrie

Allt Coire Follais, ˌaltˌkɔrˈfɔləʃ, burn of prominent corrie

Allt Coire na Cloiche, ˌaltˌkɔrnaˈkloix, burn of corrie of the stone, runs into Allt Ruadh

Allt Creag na h-Iolaire, ˌaltˌkrakanaˈhilər, burn of rocky hill of the eagle, up Glen Banchor

Allt Creagach, altˈkrakax, Alt Cragach (Thomson), craggy burn, runs into Allt Bhran

Allt Cuil na Caillich, ˌaltˌkulnaˈkalix, burn of nook of A' Chailleach, possibly Cul or back

Allt Fhearnagan, altˈarnagən, Fearn is alder, so burn of the little alder place

Allt Fhearnasdail, altˈarnstəl, burn of the alder-haugh, runs into Feshie below Tolvah

Allt Garbh, altˈgara, rough burn, a burn with steep eroded banks, in Monadh Liath

Allt Garbh Ghaig, altˈgaraˌgaək, burn of rough Gaick, should be Allt Garbh-ghaig

Allt Garbhlach, drains Coire Garbhlach into Feshie, Alt Gheallach (Thomson), recorded as Allt Gabhlach (MacBain) and heard by AW in 1940s from many in Kingussie and Kincraig areas as The Allt Gabhlach,

The pass of An Cagan in Glen Feshie, scarred by a collapsed bulldozed track, June 1983

alt'ga'lax, so from An t-Allt Gabhlach or the forked burn, see Coire Garbhlach

Allt Lorgaidh, alt'lɔrəki, burn of track, referring to Lorgaidh as a district with a pass through to top part of Feshie next to Atholl

Allt Luineag, given as Allt Linneach (Gordon 1925), alt'linjax, burn of pools, above Moine Mhor, but note foord of Luinaig in old papers at end of Inverness-shire section, Luinaig would be from Luinneag or tempestuous one, as in River Luineag in Glen More

Allt Madagain, alt'matakən, burn of little wolf (see MacBain), in Glen Banchor

Allt Mor, alt moːr, big burn, runs into Allt Fhearnasdail

Allt na Leuma, ˌaltna'lem, in classical Gaelic form is Allt na Leim, burn of the jump, in a narrow gorge up Feshie

Allt nam Bo, ˌaltna'boˑ, burn of the cows, runs into Feshie

Allt nam Meann, ˌaltna'mjʌuŋ, burn of the kids, runs into Feshie

Allt nam Meur, ˌaltna'meˑr, burn of the fingers (streams)

Allt nan Clachan, ˌaltna'glaxan, burn of the stones, in upper Feshie

Allt nan Soithichean, ˌaltna'sɔiˑəxan, burn of the dishes, in upper Feshie

Allt na Sumaig, ˌaltna'sumək, burn of the saddle-cloth, in upper Feshie

(The) Allt Ruadh, alt'rua, red burn, at Inshriach, often Englished to The Red Burn now, from An t-Allt Ruadh, the red burn

Allt Sgairnich, alt'skaˑrnix, burn of stony place, Alt na Scornich (Thomson), on Carn Ban Mor

Allt Shios Glas-choire, alt'hiˑs'glasxɔr, burn of down or east green corrie, up Glen Banchor

Allt Shuas Glas-choire, alt'huas'glasxɔr, burn of up or west green corrie, up Glen Banchor

Creag na Sroine on west side of lower Glen Feshie, June 1983 (AW)

New Year's Day 1952 at Glenballoch Cottage in Glen Banchor, shepherd Archie Anderson bald-headed on left, his brother from Newtonmore far left, AW in middle, then Archie's sister in law, and Archie's wife on right, Archie's son in front. T. Weir carries the dinner goose after bringing a bottle of whisky (Tom Weir)

Arisaig, 'arəsek, in Gaelic Arasaig, Norse ar-oss a river-mouth and vik an inlet (MacBain), Arryseig, Arrisaig (Macfarlane)

Ardnish, ard'niʃ, Ard is Gaelic high, nish from Norse Nes a cape, near Arisaig

Aviemore, ˌavi'moːr, often mispronounced by incomers with stress on Av, from Agaidh-mhor (MacBain), maybe big cleft, Agaidh Mhor ˌaki'voːr (Diack), in full An Agaidh Mhor

(The) Badan Dubh, ˌbatan'duˑ, from Am Badan Dubh, the black little clump, NW of Tolvah

(The) Badan Mosach, ˌbatan'mɔsax, from Am Badan Mosach, the insignificant little clump, SE of Achlean

Baileguish, bal'gjuˑiʃ, Baile Giubhais, farm-stead of pine wood, former farm up All Fhearnasdail

Balachroick, ˌbala'xroək, Baile a' Chroic, farm-stead of the antler

Creag Meagaidh with the gap of Uinneag Coire Ardair on right and the basin of Poite Coire Ardair below it, March 1949 (AW)

Ballintean, ˌbalən'dʒiən, Baile an t-Sidhein, farm-stead of the fairy hillock

Balnain, bəl'naːn, Beal an Athain (MacBain), mouth of the little ford, 872052, originally a farm, then later was thought (Donald Milton to Davie Duncan) to have been built to house woodcutters, with a fence to enclose horses used for logging

Balnascriten, ˌbalna'skritən, MacBain, brought up in Glen Feshie, gave Balanscrittan, and Sgriodan usually masculine, so Baile an Sgriodain, farm-stead of the gravel, in Glen Feshie

Balnespick, bal'nɛspək, Baile an Easbuig, farm-stead of the bishop, near Loch Insh

(The) Bealach Dubh, ˌbjalax'duˑ, Am Bealach Dubh, the dark pass, at Ben Alder

Beinn a' Bha'ach Ard, ˌbiňˌva'ix'aˑrd, from Beinn a' Bhathaich Ard, hill of the high sheltered place, a hill of striking shape with several points, prominent from low ground around Inverness and Beauly Firth

Beinn a' Bhric, ˌbiň'vrixk, Beinn Bhreic (Thomson), Benevrich or Ben-y-vricht or Ben Vreek (Grimble), a hill famed for quality of pasture and deer (Grimble), masculine noun Breac means trout, rarely badger or wolf (Dwelly), AW heard no translation from an indigenous resident

Beinn a' Chlachair, ˌbiňa'xlaxər, hill of the stonemason, a hill S of Loch Laggan

Near the edge of Coire Ardair of Creag Meagaidh, looking past the crags of Coire a' Choille-rais to the distant massive cliffs of Beinn a' Chaorainn, March 1949 (AW)

Beinn Bheoil, biň'vjɔːəl, sometimes translated literally as hill of the mouth, as in SMC guide books, but Drummond was closer to the mark by suggesting perhaps fore mountain, locally the meaning in late 1940s and 1950s given to me was hill in front, which it is, as viewed from Loch Ericht being the hill in front of Ben Alder

Beinn Bhuidhe, biň'vui, yellow hill, N of Newtonmore

Beinn Eibhinn, biň'je·vən, pleasant hill

Beinn na Lap, ˌbina'laːp, Binni Lapp (Gordon), Beinnnanlaup (Thomson) suggests plural Beinn nan Lap, Ben-na-lapt (Scrope), hill of the bog, W of Loch Ossian, the a in bina is throaty, almost an aspirated laxp, though not as strongly aspirated as AW heard with Sgurr na Lapaich in Ross, the Gaelic chapter in Bearhop gives it as dappled hill, impossible because Lap is a noun, not an adjective, Lap in Dwelly is a defective spot in colour painting and dyeing, and has a short a, whereas the a in the Lap of Beinn na Lap is long and accented, as in the Lapach or bog in Sgurr na Lapaich of Ross, hence the dappled in Bearhop is invention,

Drummond states that the Lap in Beinn na Lap 'is said to mean' (without giving any reference, but presumably Bearhop) 'dappled, since lap refers to a defective colour spot, in textiles', but bog fits Beinn na Lap well, because it rises from one of the biggest bogs in Scotland at Rannoch Moor, and it seems likely that Beinn na Lap may have been Beinn na Lapaich, but the last syllable dropped out of pronunciation as occurs frequently in Perthshire and Deeside and Strathspey dialects of Gaelic, with a good example noted by Watson (1926) in Loch Garry, Gaelic Garaidh, becoming Gar in Perthshire Gaelic speech

Beinn na Sgiath, ˌbiňna'skia, hill of the wing (shape), above Laggan

Beinn Udlaman, biň'udlaman, in SMC guides the meaning is given with no evidence as gloomy hill, but Drummond mentions the more likely possibility by MacBain that it may be from Gaelic Udalan, a swivel, note Allt Udlaman runs off the hill into Loch Ericht, Ben-utman (Scobie)

Ben Alder, biň'jalar, Bin-Aillhoyr (Pont), was Beinn Allair, later Beinn Eallair pronounced Yallar (MacBain), hill of rocky place

A' Bhuideanaich, on the Monadh Liath, ə'vuːənjax, from A' Bhuideannach, the yellow place, a grassy stretch

Biallaid, 'bialətʃ, in Gaelic Bialaid, from Bial a mouth in Badenoch Gaelic, the rest being suffix (MacBain), a farm where the River Calder runs into a plain W of Newtonmore

(Am) Binnein Mor, mˌbiňjən'moːr, the big pinnacle, highest peak in the Mamores

Cliffs of Coire Ardair from frozen Lochan a' Choire, Easy Gully the straight snowy gully, January 1951 (AW)

Binnein Shios, ˌbiňjən'hi·s, lower (eastern) pinnacle, at Loch Laggan

Binnein Shuas, ˌbiňjən'huas, upper (western) pinnacle, at Loch Laggan

Blackmill, of Feshie, was Am Muileann Dubh, mˌmulən'du·, the black mill

Blackwater Reservoir, was Uisedu or Blackwater (Thomson), so obviously Uisge Dubh, level greatly raised by a dam, but formerly according to old maps was a long set of connected lochs with islets

Boat Bay (Mearns), not on OS, near outlet of Loch an Eilein, a beach for launching and landing a boat

Am Bodach, m'pɔtax, the old man, a small hill near larger hill A' Chailleach in Glen Banchor

Bogha-cloiche, 'boˌklɔx, stone-bow, a hill at Gaick

Brae of Feshie not on OS but on Roy, pronounced Brae as in Scots, upper hills above River Feshie in its upper parts

Am Breac-choire, m'breaxˌxər, the speckled corrie, W of Carn an Fhidhleir

Bruthach an Easain, ˌbruaxan'jɛsən, brae of the little waterfall, up Glen Banchor

Bruthach an Sguilein, ˌbruaxan'sgu:lən, brae of the basket (shape), at Gaick

The Buideannach, not on OS, 'vu:ənjax, so from A' Bhuideannach, the yellow place, a grassy shelf at 935003 on Braeriach, the burn below, running into Gleann Einich, is Allt Buidheannach (OS)

Bulroy, bul'roi, from Bhuaile-ruaidhe (MacBain), a form that presumably came from A' Bhuaile-ruaidhe or the red fold, Bulruaidh (Thomson), former croft at 846995

The Burma Road, not on OS, track from Lynwilg up An Gleannan on to Monadh Liath

An Cagan, 'ka·gan, the narrow pass, a narrow bend in Glen Feshie

Cairn Gorm, nˌkarn'gɔrəm, from An Carn Gorm, the blue hill, often mispronounced by incomers with stress on Cairn and omission of r, like Kain Gom, note two syllables in pronouncing second word, an extra vowel to ease pronunciation, another instance in Strath Spey being Tullochgorum W of Dulnain Bridge, where the OS name retains gorum

(The) Cam Sgriob, ðr'kʌu:mˌskrip, so would have come from A' Cham-sgriob, the curved furrow, note that there is a curved rocky melt-water channel on the summit

Camalup, 'kamalup, Camadh Luib, curve of the bend, former farm NW of Tolvah

Caochan an Duine, ˌkuxanan'dun, hidden burn of the man, runs into uppermost Feshie

(The) Caochan Ban, ˌkuxan'ba:n, An Caochan Ban, the white hidden burn, W of Eidart in upper Feshie

(The) Caochan Dubh, ˌkuxan'du·, An Caochan Dubh, the black hidden burn, black because of thick peat, on Moine Mhor

(The) Caochan Dubh, ˌkuxan'du·, An Caochan Dubh, the black hidden burn, black because of thick peat, in upper Feshie

Caochan Mhic Ghille Feitil, ˌkuxanˌvixkˌyili'fetəl, hidden burn of the son of the ?treasure lad, Feitil maybe Feudail, treasure or booty, should be spelled Caochan Mhic Ghille-feitil or feudail, runs into Eidart

Caochan na Laire Fiadhaiche, ˌkuxanaˌla·r'fɪ·əx, hidden burn of the wild mare, runs into uppermost Feshie

Caochan Tarsuinn, ˌkuxan'tarsən, athwart hidden burn, runs into Allt Lorgaidh

Carn a' Bhothain Mholaich, ˌkarnˌvo'hən'volix, hill of the rough bothy, up Glen Banchor

Carn an Fhidhleir Lorgaidh, ˌkarnˌjilər'lɔrəki, Cairn Iular Loragy (Thomson), Lorgie hill of the fiddler, distinguishing it from the higher Carn an Fhidhleir on the Aberdeenshire march, see Allt Lorgaidh, and other Lorgaidh names are Meall Tionail Lorgaidh and Glas-leathad Lorgaidh

Carn an Leth-choin, ˌkarnan'ljexən, OS name means hill of the lurcher, but because of the sloping shelves of rock that are the hill's main feature, one wonders if it like Creag an Leth-choin in Strathspey, may be not crag of the lurcher but Creagan Leacainn, crags of the sloping shelved hillside, hence Carn nan Leacann, hill of the sloping shelved hillsides, up Glen Banchor

Carn Ballach, karn'balax, hill of Ballach, see Gleann Ballach

(The) Carn Ban, karn'ba:n, An Carn Ban, the fair or white hill, a snowy hill on Monadh Liath

Carn Ban Beag, ˌkarnˌban'bek, little fair hill, in Glen Feshie

Carn Ban Mor, ˌkarnˌban'mo:r, big fair hill, in Glen Feshie

(The) Carn Dearg, karn'dʒɛrək, An Carn Dearg, the red hill, on Monadh Liath

Carn Dearg Beag, ˌkarnˌdʒɛrək'bek, small red hill, Carn dearg beag (Thomson), W of Feshie

Carn Dearg Mor, ˌkarnˌdʒɛrək'moːr, big red hill, Carn dearg mhor (Thomson), W of Feshie

Carn Liath, karn'lia, grey hill, above Loch Laggan

Carn Macoul, karn'muxkəl, Cairn Machoul (Thomson), maybe Carn Muc-cuil, hill of pig-nook, see Muccoul in MacBain which was more likely to have been a habitation at NE end of Loch Laggan (Macoul in Thomson), a hill up Glen Banchor

Carn na Caim, ˌkarna'kaəm, hill of the curve, at Drumochter

Carn na Criche, ˌkarna'krix, hill of the boundary, on the Monadh Liath

Carn Sgulain, karn'skuːlən, hill of basket (shape), in Glen Banchor

Carnachuin, ˌkarna'xuin, CarnaChuineadh (Thomson), so from Carn na Coinnimh, cairn or stony spot of the assembly, as in Carn na Cuimhne in upper Deeside, often said to mean cairn of the remembrance, but old forms of the name show it to be Carn na Coinnimh or cairn of the assembly (Watson & Allan 1984) as in Glen Feshie, house and former croft in Glen Feshie, the monument nearby being to servicemen who died in the second world war

The Carnachuin Bridge (Watson 1992), not on OS, across Feshie below Carnachuin

A' Chailleach, ə'xaljax, the old woman, pairs with Am Bodach in Glen Banchor

A' Chioch, ə'xiˑɔx, the pap, a rock outcrop near Gaick

Chno Dearg, nˌkroxk'dʒɛrək, from An Cnoc Dearg, the red hill, Chno Dearg meaning red nut is an OS error, Cnoc Dearg (Burn in Allan 1995), hill SW of Loch Laggan towards Loch Treig

Ciste Mhearad of Feshie, should be Ciste Mearaid, kiʃt'merət. Margaret's hollow

The Clach Bharraig Bothy, not on OS, hut on W side of Allt Mor at S edge of woods in Glen More at 984073, used by climbers and skiers in 40s and early 50s, later demolished

Clach Bhlair, klax'vlaˑər, also commonly now the Blair Stone, a big stone E of the summit cairn, stone of the Blair or flat ground at Mullach Clach a' Bhlair, see Coire Bhlair

Clais Bheag, klaʃ'vek, little hollow, near uppermost Feshie

Clais Damh, klaʃ'damf, hollow of deer, not on OS, 835844, in upper Feshie, top of Allt Clais Damh OS

Clais Luineag, maybe is Clais Linneach, klaʃ'linjax, hollow of pools, but see Allt Luineag

Cluas na Creige, ˌkluasna'krek, ear of the crag, around Coire Mharconaich

Cnap nan Laogh, ˌkrapnan'løˑg, hill of the calves, up Eidart

Cnapan Alasdair Mhoir (Gordon 1948), not on OS, 922962, a rocky spur E of Loch nan Cnapan on Moine Mhor, little hilltop of big Alasdair, ˌkraxpanˌaləstər'voːər

Cnapan Eachan, ˌkraxpan'exan, little hill of horses, up Eidart

Cnoc na Daimh, misprint, should be Cnoc an Daimh, round hill of the stag, ˌkroxkan'dae, note nearby Allt Cnoc an Daimh OS, in upper Feshie

Cnoc Fraing, kroxk'fraŋk, round hill of Frenchman, Jamie Williamson the laird of Alvie tells DD that when his family bought the estate around the late 1920s the shepherds and gamekeepers called it the Frenchman's hill, and AW heard the above pronunciation from Brock Nethersole-Thompson around 1980 when he was a gamekeeper there, a hill above Dulnain

Cockstreet (early OS), kok, a row of houses ENE of Dalnavert, near present Tombain OS

Coille an Torr, ˌkɔilən'dɔˑr, wood of the hillock, in Glen Feshie

Coire a' Bhealaich, kor'vjalix, corrie of the pass, Coire Bhealaich (Thomson), E of Corrour Shooting Lodge, it and Coire Creagach and Coire na Cloiche (Perth list) were mentioned in Scrope (in Anglicised form) as fine deer-stalking haunts

Coire a' Chriochairein, kɔr'xriˑxərən, corrie of the boundary keeper, authors of the Gaelic chapter in Bearhop give the meaning as stonechat in the name Sron Coire a' Chriochairein, but this was confused with Cloichearan the stonechat, and a stonechat is unlikely to be on alpine land anyway, high above Loch Laggan

Coire Allt a'.Mharcaidh, ˌkɔrˌalt'varke, corrie of burn of the horse-place

On perfect packed powder, Jim Kerr does an elegant ski-turn on Carn Liath, looking south past the shimmering Loch Laggan to Binnein Shuas, Beinn a' Chlachair beyond, and Chno Dearg rising on right distance, January 1952 (Tom Weir)

Coire an Daimh Ruaidh, ˌkɔrnˌdaeˈrui, corrie of the red stag, in uppermost Feshie

Coire Arcain, kɔrˈarkən, corrie of sow, above Achlean

Coire Ardair, kɔrˈaːrdər, Coire Ardobhair pronounced Ardair (Watson 1926), corrie of high water, above Loch Laggan

Coire Beul an Sporain, ˌkɔrˌbialənˈsporən, corrie of mouth of the pouch (shape), at Drumochter, Beul in Badenoch Gaelic is Bial (MacBain), the corrie gives its name to the Balsporran Cottages at the railway line below

Coire Bhathaich, kɔrˈvaːix, corrie of the shelter, at Drumochter

Coire Bhlair, kɔrˈvlaˈər, corrie of the Blair or flat ground at Mullach Clach a' Bhlair

Coire Bhran, kɔrˈvraˈn, corrie of the Bran, see Allt Bhran, one in Glen Feshie, one in Glen Tromie

Coire Bog, kɔrˈbɔk, corrie of bog, a peaty corrie with mires and pools, NW of A' Chailleach

Coire Bogha-cloiche, kɔrˈboˌklɔx, corrie of stone-bow, on Braeriach

(The) Coire Breac, kɔrˈbrexk, An Coire Breac, the speckled corrie, in upper Feshie, marked by OS on a ridge, should be in corrie to the W

Coire Cam, kɔrˈkam, curved corrie, at Drumochter

(The) Coire Caol, kɔrˈkuˈl, An Coire Caol, the narrow corrie, in Glen Feshie

Coire Chais, kɔrˈxaʃ, corrie of the difficult or steep place, Corry Chaash (Thomson), at Drumochter

Coire Cheap, kɔrˈxep, corrie of stumps, near Ben Alder

Coire Chrion-alltain, kɔrˈxriˈnˌaltan, corrie of the parched little burn, N of Carnachuin

Coire Chuirn, kɔrˈxuərn, corrie of the stony place, at Drumochter

(The) Coire Creagach, kɔrˈkrakax, An Coire Creagach, the rocky corrie, in upper Feshie

Coire Dhondail should be Coire Gamhandail, corrie of stirk-dale (W.J. Watson in Gordon 1925), or maybe stirk-haugh would be better and less Englished than dale, kɔrˈgʌuntəl

(The) Coire Domhain, kɔrˈdoːən, An Coire Domhain, the deep corrie, in Glen Feshie

(The) Coire Dubh, kɔrˈduˈ, An Coire Dubh, the dark corrie, on A' Chailleach

Coire Eindart should be Coire Inndeard (MacBain), kɔrˈindʒard, meaning unknown, W of Eidart

The Red Bothy below A' Chailleach of the Monadh Liath, January 2013 (Cameron McNeish)

Coire Fhar, kɔrˈaːr, corrie of the horizon, at Drumochter

Coire Follais, kɔrˈfɔləʃ, prominent corrie, beside Creag Follais

Coire Garbhlach heard by AW in 1940s and 1950s as The Coire Gallach, kɔrˈgaˈlax, so from An Coire Gabhlach or the forked corrie, which describes it well, see also Allt Garbhlach, John Clark of Achlean told David Duncan in July 2013 that he, his father and his grandfather all called the corrie Cor Galloch, and Seumas Grannd confirms to AW that he always heard it like Kor Galax, note that Roy mapped it as Corygalach

(The) Coire Gorm, kɔrˈgɔrəm, An Coire Gorm, the green corrie, on Meall Dubhag

Coire Gorm a' Chrom-alltain, green corrie of the crooked burnie, AW heard just The Coire Gorm, kɔrˈgɔrəm, from An Coire Gorm, the green corrie

Coire Madagan Beag, ˌkɔrˌmatakanˈbek, Madagan a diminutive of wolf or dog (MacBain), so little corrie of Madagan, at Gaick, see name below

Coire Madagan Mor, ˌkɔrˌmatakanˈmoːr, big corrie of Matagan at Gaick, see name above and MacBain, mapped by Roy as Corry Vattican, which suggests an original Coire Mhadagain, maybe a collective name for the two corries

Coire Mharconaich, kɔrˈvarkonix, corrie of the horse-place, up Eidart

Coire na Caillich, ˌkɔrnaˈkalix, a craggy corrie below the top of A' Chailleach

Coire na Ciche, ˌkɔrnaˈkix, corrie of the pap, above Allt Bhran

Coire na Cisteachan, ˌkɔrnaˈgiʃtjaxən, should be Coire nan Cisteachan, with pronunciation g after nan as in Coire nan Clach in next name, Corrynaghistichan (Roy), corrie of the chests, upper Feshie

Coire nam Meur, ˌkɔrnaˈmer, corrie of the fingers (streams), up E side of Feshie

Coire nan Cisteachan, as above, at Drumochter

Coire na Cloiche, ˌkɔrnaˈkloix, corrie of the stone, above Allt Ruadh

Coire nan Clach, kɔrnaˈglax, on Braeriach, corrie of the stones

Coire nan Laogh, ˌkɔrnanˈløˈg, corrie of the calves, up Gleann Lochain in Monadh Liath

Coire Odhar Beag, ˌkɔrˌʌuərˈbek, little dun corrie, E of Corrour Station

Coire Odhar Mor, ˌkɔrˌʌuərˈmoˈr, big dun corrie, E of Corrour Station

(The) Coire Ruadh, kɔrˈrua, An Coire Ruadh, the red corrie, in Glen Feshie, another on Braeriach facing Gleann Einich

Coire Uilleim, kɔrˈuljəm, corrie of William, at Drumochter

Con-tuil-aid, MacBain who wrote that Ballintean was 'called of old Countelawe (1603) and Cuntelait (1699)' and explained as Cunntadh-lait....Perhaps, like Contin, it is from Con-tuil-aid, the meeting of the waters, that is, here Feshie and Fernsdale', Coundilaid (Roy), Contalait (Moll) and Countelait (Thomson), all with no Ballintean shown, AW never heard Con-tuil-aid locally

Corarnstilbeg, ˌkɔrˈarnstəlˈbek, Coire Fhearnasdail Beag, corrie of the small alder-haugh, former farm

Corarnstilmore, ˌkɔrˈarnstəlˈmoːr, Coire Fhearnasdail Mor, corrie of the big alder-haugh, former farm

Corrie Yairack, kɔrˈjarək, from Coire Earrag in Gaelic (MacBain), maybe from Gearrag, short one, applied to a stream, so Coire Ghearrag, corrie of the short-one

Corrour, kɔrˈʌuər, from Coire Odhar or dun corrie, name of shooting lodge at top of Loch Ossian, name of deer-forest there and of Corrour Station at summit of railway from Glasgow to Fort William, named from Coire Odhar Mor and Coire Odhar Beag, big and little, two shallow corries E of the station

Corrieyairack Pass, a Wade Military Road

Coylumbridge, locally just Coylum, pronounced, ˈkoiljəm, probably Comh-leum (Diack with Grant) or together-leap, Cuing Leum or narrow leap (MacBain), Cuingleum or gorge leap (Watson 1926)

Craggan of Clune, ˌkraganaˈklun, was ˌkrakanˈklun, from Creagan little rocky place, Cluain meadow-land (MacBain), Craggen (Thomson), Craggan and Strone were holdings of Clan Chattan and held much farmland, now an upper part of Newtonmore

Crathie, ˈkraθe, in Gaelic Craichidh (MacBain), same word as in Deeside Crathie (see Watson & Allan 1984), in Irish Gaelic meant a quaking bog (Joyce), also connotations of shaking (Watson 1926), note the change from Crachy (Blaeu) to Crachymoir (Moll) representing Craichidh Mor or big Crathie, to Crathimor (Roy) and Crathy more (Thomson), now just Crathie, but there were two farms

Creag an Fhir-eoin, ˌkrakanˈirjɔˈən, rock of the man-bird or eagle,

Creag an Loin, ˌkrakanˈlɔˈin, rocky hill of the marsh, up Glen Banchor

Creag Bheag, krakˈvek, little crag, up Feshie

Creag Bheag, as above, behind Kingussie

Creag Bheag, as above, in Glen Banchor

(The) Creag Dhubh, usually now krakˈduˈ or kregˈdu, but was əˌxrakˈduˈ, from A' Chreag Dhubh, the dark rocky hill, at Newtonmore, Craigow (Thomson) followed the old pronunciation

Creag Dhubh, as above, between Feshie and Tromie

Creag Fhiaclach, krakˈiaxklax, toothed rocky hill

Creag Follais, krakˈfɔləʃ, conspicuous rocky hill

Creag Ghiuthsachan, krakˈjuˈsaxən, rocky hill of the little pinewood, classic Gaelic form would be Creag Ghiuthsachain

Creag Leathan, krakˈleˈən, broad rocky hill, should be spelled Leathann

(The) Creag Liath, əˌxrakˈlia, from A' Chreag Liath, the grey rocky hill, in Glen Banchor

Creag Meagaidh, krakˈmɛke, rocky hill of bog

Creag Mhigeachaidh, krakˈvigaxe, rocky hill of the bog-place

Creag na Caillich, ˌkraknaˈkaləx, crag of the old woman, up Feshie

Creag na Goibhre, ˌkraknaˈgɔir, crag of the goat, in upper Glen Feshie

Creag na h-Iolaire, ˌkraknaˈhilər, rocky hill of the eagle, up Glen Banchor

Creag na Sroine, ˌkraknaˈstrɔin, crag of the hill-nose, on W side of Feshie

Creag Pitridh, krakˈpitri, from Pit a hollow (MacBain), so rocky hill of hollow place, note Coire Pitridh nearby, a hill S of Loch Laggan

The) Crion-alltan, ˈkriˈˌn̩altan, from An Crion-alltan, the little burnie, N of Carnachuin

Croft Drealan, not on OS but on Thomson, croft upstream from Glenbanchor croft, in 1832 on old register (Hamish Marshall), maybe Croit Dreallain, croft of little blaze

Croftroy, kroftˈroi, was a croft, now an upper part of Newtonmore, maybe from Croit Ruadh or red croft, or Croit Roy, Roy's croft

Croidh-la, ˈkroila, same in Gaelic (MacBain), Creyla (Roy), Croila (Thomson), possibly from Cruadhlach or rocky declivity a locative Cruadhlaigh (MacBain), meaning at rocky declivity

Cromran (early OS), ˈkrɔməran, Donald Milton pronounced it as ˈkrɔmnan, saying it was a plot where his father cultivated corn and tatties, E of Cockstreet, MacBain gives Cromaran possibly for Crom-raon or crooked field, note Na Crom-raon or the crooked fields was just outside Braemar, and Cromeran in Glen Muick (Watson & Allan 1984).

(The) Cruaidh-alltan, ˈkruˈiˌaltan, An Cruaidh-alltan, the hard burnie, in upper Feshie

Cruban Beag, ˌkrubanˈbek, in Irish Cruibin a little hoof (Joyce), a rocky hill that gives its name to former farm Crubenbeg, in Badenoch Gaelic the Cruben in Crubenmore was Crubinn (MacBain), little hooflet

Cruban More, ˌkrubanˈmoːr, see above name, big hooflet

Culra Lodge, ˈkulrə, named after nearby Allt a' Chaoil-reidhe, burn of the narrow meadow, below Ben Alder

Dail a' Chaorainn not on OS 1:25000 but Sidhean Mor Dail a' Chaorainn shown on a prominent hillock above, dalˈxuarən, former crofts in lower Glen Banchor, was Dalhuaran more (Thomson), with Dalhuaran beg up the burn to the N on its E side, so Dail a' Chaorainn Mor and Beag, big haugh and small haugh, in 1951, Ewan MacPherson told me that his grandfather had farmed at the bigger of the haughs, which Ewan pointed out to me during a ski tour

Dail na Seilg, Dalnashalig (Roy), Dalnashalg (Thomson), Dalnashallag (1832 register seen by Hamish Marshall), so Dail nan Sealg, haugh of the hunts, former croft at top of Glen Banchor, heard by me as ˌdalnaˈʃalag

Dalballoch, was Dalvalloch (Hamish Marshall), dal'valax, former farm at foot of Gleann Ballach, so Dail Bhallach, haugh of Ballach, Ballach meaning walled (MacBain)

Dalnahaitnach, ˌdalnaˈhaxtnix, Dail na h-Aitionnaich, haugh of the juniper place, former farm on Dulnain

Dead Man's Corrie, a name used by recent stalkers on Glen Feshie Estate for a corrie by Allt Luineag E of Tom Dubh, where they tell that a stalker Urquhart from Mar shot himself by accident when finishing off a wounded stag that had moved from Mar

Diollaid Coire Eindart, ˌdialtʃˌkɔrˈindʒard, saddle of corrie of Eindart, see Allt Eindart and Coire Eindart

Donn Street, not on OS, consisted of a few houses along the road between Feshiebridge and the road to the Iosal, Donald Milton was unsure whether it was Don or Donn, but pronounced as in River Don by local folk dɔn, and unsure whether it came from Gaelic Donn for brown or was English

Dot's Croft, not on OS, Dott's Croft (Loader) had wrong name, location and description. Seumas Grannd thinks it would have been Dot Cameron a former gardener/handyman at Glenmore Lodge, see also comments below, towards end of the Inverness-shire section, by Dolina Macdonald, who said that gardener Mr Cameron and his wife lived in a cottage nearby to Glenmore Lodge

Drake's Bothy, dreks, named after Major Tom Drake of Inshriach, 883056 at foot of Allt Coire Follais, mentioned in Watson (1975)

Druimanlochain, there were formerly two Druimanlochains, West Druimanlochain being renamed Drumcluan and East Druimanlochain being the current Druimanlochain (OS)

Druimcaillich, Drumnacallich (Roy), Druimchaiellach (Thomson), ˌdruimnaˈkaləx, ridge of the old woman, former house in Glen Feshie

Druim nam Bo, ˌdruimnamˈboˑ, ridge of the cows, up Feshie

Druim Rath, ˌdrʌmˈraˑ, not on OS, Druim Rath ridge of fortress, or Druim Raimh ridge of woodland are likely, a broad ridge SW of Loch Gamhna, running up to the Rothiemurchus march dyke and now part of the Inshriach woodland of the Forestry Commission

Drumochter, drʌmˈoxtər, Drumouchker (Roy), was Druim Uachdair, druimˈuaxkər, ridge of upper ground

(The) Dubh-ghlaic, ˈduˈglak, from An Dubh-ghlaic, the dark hollow, a steep-sided glacial melt-water channel N of Newtonmore

The Duchess of Bedford's, not on OS, a name used by Feshie deerstalkers to refer to the ruins of a former shooting lodge at the foot of Allt Lorgaidh

Dun da-lamh, ˌdundaˈlaeˑ, classical Gaelic form Dun Da Lamh without hyphen, in Badenoch Gaelic Dun Da Laimh (Diack with Grant), fort of two hands, perhaps referring to good views of the two main approaches to Badenoch from the west (Diack with Grant), a wooded peak with a large ancient fort on top, at Laggan

Eag a' Chait, ɛkˈhatʃ, gap of the cat, a rocky melt-water channel south of Loch Morlich

Eidart is from Eideart (MacBain), ˈetʃart, many local informants on Spey and Dee to me

The Eilean, ˈelan, not on OS 1:25000, from An t-Eilean, the stream-side meadow, where Newtonmore Games are held

An Eileirg, ðrˈelrək, Niulrig (Thomson) is near the old Gaelic pronunciation of An Eileirg, the deer-trap, in upper Feshie

An Eileirg, ðrˈelrək, An Eilerig, the deer-trap, E of Allt Coire Bhran

(The) Elrick Burn, ˈelrək, Elrick Anglicised from Eileirg or deer-trap, the Strath Spey pronunciation of the Eilrig in Carn Eilrig near Aviemore is in Diack with Grant, The Elrick Burn runs into upper Findhorn

English Charlie's, a hollow near the road to Loch an Eilein and SE of The Polchar, where an English tramp named Charles often stayed, the spot called English Charlie's by local folk, later, Douglas Weir built a new house there and named it English Charlie's following the tradition, but after he moved the new owner gave it a new name

Fassfern in Lochaber, ˈfasefɛrn, Gaelic Fasaidh-fearn (MacBain), abode or stead of the alders, Am Fasadh Fearna, alderwood stance (Watson 1934)

Feith Mhor, feˈmoːr, big bog-stream, up Gleann Chomhraig

Feith na Craoibhe Chaorainn, ˌfenaˌkruˈiˈxuˈrn, bog-stream of the rowan tree, W of Sron na Ban-righ

(The) Feithlinn, feˈlin, broad bog-stream (MacBain), so Feith Leathann, a boggy burn that runs into Dulnain

Fersit, ˈfɛrsət, from Fearsaid, an estuary or sand-bank, a good description of the site (MacBain), a settlement at N end of Loch Treig, Thomson marked Fersit mor (big Fersit) on the W side of the lower loch, and on the E side a dwelling Fersit riach or Fearsaid Riabhach, brindled sand-bank, Ferseden (Pont) obviously a plural, presumably Fersaidean

Feshieside, originally a croft there called Croftbeag, from Croit Beag or little croft, and Feshieside (not on OS) is commonly a name for anywhere around the River Feshie

Fionnar Choire, ˈfjanarxɔr, should be spelled Fionnar-choire, cold corrie, up Feshie

The Foxhunter's Path, up to Carn Ban Mor from Achlean

Gaick, ˈgaˈək, Gaig, at cleft or pass (MacBain, Watson 1926)

An Garbh-allt, nˈgarawəlt, the rough burn, SW of Monadh Mor

(The) Garbh Choire, ˈgaraxɔr, An Garbh-choire, the rough corrie, on Ben Alder

Garbh Gaick, ˈgaragaək, not on OS, but see Allt Garbh Ghaig, Garra Gaick (Roy), so Garbh-ghaig, rough Gaick, well known as a pass from Gaick to Atholl, west of the Minigaig

Geal-charn, ˈgjalxarn, white hill, carries much grass and also snow, near Ben Alder

Geal Charn, as above, near Ardverikie, others beside Beinn Sgiath, SW of A' Chailleach, E of A' Chailleach, behind Aviemore, NW of Ben Alder, at Drumochter, W of Sgoran Dubh Mor and at Dorback, should all be spelled Geal-charn, often all are called The Geal Charn locally, so from An Geal-charn, all grassy hills or with pale short heather and lichen rather than tall dark heather

Geal Charn Beag, should be Geal-charn Beag, ˈgjalxarnˈbek, little fair hill, on A' Chailleach

Glac Ghiubhsachan, glaxkˈjuˈsaxən, should be Ghiubhsachain, hollow of the little fir-wood, former croft by Feshie, below a long hollow of the same name

(The) Glas-choire, ˈglasxɔr, from An Glas-choire, the green corrie, up Glen Banchor

Glas-leathad Feshie, ˈglaʃlətˈfiʃi, Glashlet feshie (Roy), Glais-leathad Feithisidh, grey slope of Feshie or maybe stream slope of Feshie

Glas-leathad Lorgaidh, ˈglaʃlətˈlɔrəki, grey slope of Lorgaidh or stream slope of Lorgaidh

Gleann Ballach, glʌunˈbalax, glen of Ballach, Ballach meaning walled (MacBain) and this is a steep-walled glen, but note Carn Ballach to the N has gentle slopes, and even more so N of it in upper Coignafearn with Coire Ballach and Allt Ballach in peaty terrain of low gradient, which suggests that Ballach may be a collective name, not entirely local

Gleann Chomhraig, glʌunˈxɔˈrək, glen of the confluence

Gleann Einich, often mispronounced following incorrect OS name, should be Gleann Eanaich, glʌunˈɛˈnix, glen of marsh

Gleann Lochain, glʌunˈloxən, glen of lochan, below Loch Dubh in Monadh Liath

Glen Banchor, glʌunˈbjanaxar, from Gleann Beannachar or glen of horns or peaks, Irish Beannchar horns, gables, peaks (MacBain), maybe refers to horn-like bends on River Calder in the glen, Gaelic Caladar or hard water (MacBain, see Watson 1926 for other Calder cases), note Roy gives Glen Bannaker and River Bannaker within it

Glen Feshie, glʌunˈfiˈʃi, Gleann Feithisidh (MacBain), glen of bog-streams, the shortened sound ˈfiʃi also heard by me from many on Deeside as well as Speyside, but not from the best Gaelic speakers, now Anglicised, glɛnˈfɛʃe

Glen Markie, glʌunˈmarke, glen of horse-place, in south Monadh Liath

Glen Markie, as above, along upper Allt a' Mharcaidh, not on OS 1:25000

Glen Mazeran, glʌunˈmasarən, Masaran a stream-name (Watson 1926) of uncertain meaning

Glen Shirra, glʌunˈʃiˈrə, Gleann Sioro in Gaelic (MacBain), who suggested from Sir or Sior meaning long, or possible Sioradh, squinting, the nearby farm Sherramore was Siorrath Mor in Gaelic (MacBain)

Glen Tromie, glʌunˈtroˈme, in Gaelic Gleann Tromaidh (MacBain), from Trom an elder tree (Watson 1926),

Dawn sun-rays through frosty mist below Dun Da-lamh, the peak on the right, Laggan, January 1952 (AW)

named after the River Tromie, so eldery river (MacBain)

Glen Truim, glʌunˈtruim, Gleann Truim, glen of the elder tree (MacBain, Watson 1926)

Glenballoch, former house downstream from the foot of Gleann Ballach

Glenbanchor, former house E of Glenballoch and named after Glen Banchor

The Green Bothy, not on OS, green-painted corrugated-iron shooters' hut in Glen Banchor, burnt some years ago

Horseman's Corrie, not on OS, named after a former shooting tenant (Gordon 1925), note that he was Horsman, not Horseman (see notes at end of Inverness-shire section), but Burn recorded a Gaelic name, in classical Gaelic Clais Feith Inbhir Feithisidh, hollow of bog-stream of Invereshie or the mouth of bog-stream place

Inchvuilt, inʃˈvuəltʃ, Inis Mhuilt, meadow of the wether, in Glen Strathfarrar

Invereshie, from Inbhir Feithisidh or mouth of Feshie, now Anglicised, ˌɪnvɛrˈɛʃe, but to earlier Gaelic speakers was ˌinjərˈiʃi, Inner Isshie (Moll)

Invertromie, follows similar changes to above, Inner Trommy (Moll) catching the earlier pronunciation as in Invereshie

The Iosal, ˈiˈsəl, not on OS 1:25000, Iosal is low, a haugh S of confluence of Spey and Feshie

Iosel, a small holding (also on OS 6 inch) at 850063, same word as above

Kiltarlity, kɪlˈtarləte, 'in 1234 Kyltalargy, in 1289 Keltalargyn; the sound is a Pictish one – Talorgan, "fair-browed one" (MacBain), with Cill a church, up the main strath from Beauly to the SW

Kinvoonigag, not on OS 1: 25000, Kinnivonnagag (Roy), kɪnˈvunəgak, Cinn Mhunadh Ghaig (suggested by Seumas Grannd), at end of hill-range of Gaick, a former croft at 832009, disgracefully overgrown by trees planted by Forestry Commission

Knoydart, ˈnoidart, in Gaelic Cnoideart (Ainmean-Aite na h-Alba, who give a meaning as knoll fjord), Cnudeworth in 1343 suggests Knut's fjord (MacBain), in standard Norse spelling of this would be Knuds-fjorðr

The Lagan Odhar, ˌlakanˈʌur, not on OS, from An Lagan Odhar, the little dun hollow, note Allt an Lagain Odhair OS, W of Coire Bhlair

Laggan, ˈlakan, from Lagan a little hollow, was Lagan-Choinnich or St Cainneach's hollow (MacBain)

An Leitir, nˈliʃtjər, the slope, a steep hillside up Glen Banchor

An Leth-chreag or the half-rock (Mearns), not on OS 1:25000, E of Aviemore-Grantown road and S of Avinlochan beside Avie Lochan

(The) Leth-chreag, ˈljexrak, from An Leth-chreag, literally the half-rock, but often means, as here, a cliff on one side but not the other, up Eidart

Leum Uilleim, leˈmˈuˈljəm, leap of William, a peak with steep cliffs SW of Corrour Station

The Linneach Flats, not on OS, a name used by Feshie deerstalkers for flat ground by Allt Linneach, see Allt Luineag above

Loch a' Mhuillidh, ˌloxaˈvuːli, loch of the place fit for driving a mill, in Glen Strathfarrar

Loch an Eilein, ˌloxanˈeˈlən, loch of the island, often mispronounced by incomers

Loch an Sgoir, ˌloxanˈskɔˈr, loch of the peak, near Ben Alder

Loch an t-Seilich, ˌloxanˈtʃelix, loch of the willow, at Gaick

Loch Cuaich, loxˈkuˈix, loch of cup (shape)

Loch Dubh, loxˈduˈ, Loch Dou (Roy), dark loch, up Glen Banchor

Loch Ghiuthsachan, AW heard ˌloxanˈjuˈsaxən, which would be lochan of the pinewood, spelling in classic Gaelic form would be Ghiuthsachain

Loch Ghuilbinn, loxˈguləbən, Loch Golibyn (Roy), Loch Gulbin (Thomson), 'Loch Gulbin, Torgulbin etc, come from GULBAN, a beak' MacBain), and a beak of land is one meaning of Gulban (Dwelly), but the name is very similar to the Anglicised Ben Bulben (in Irish Binn Gulbain) at Sligo in western Ireland, and also to Ben Gulabin in Glen Shee, where the evidence including the same pronunciation points to its being Gulban's hill, Conall Gulban being a legendary Fingalian hero, with a cluster of Fingalian names nearby in

Glen Shee including Tobar nam Fiann, Loch an Tuirc, Carn an Tuirc, Tulach Diarmid, and Diarmid's Grave (see Watson 2013), and a cluster of names near Loch Ghuilbinn shows likewise, with Loch Ossian named after the Fingalian hero Oisin, River Ossian, Strath Ossian, Amar Srath Ossian (Amhar Strath Ossian to Thomson), Abhainn Ghuilbinn or river of Gulban, Tor a' Ghuilbinn or hill of the Gulban (giving the name to the house Torgulbin (Torgoulben to Roy, Tor gulbin to Thomson) below it), and on the S side of Torr a' Ghuilbinn is Lochan an Tuirc or loch of the boar, a hunt for a boar being again a Fingalian legend of Glen Shee, Ireland and elsewhere, note another Beinn Ghuilbin at Kinveachy N of Aviemore and, as Seumas Grannd kindly pointed out, a Torr Mhuic (hill of pigs) to the NE

Loch Imrich, lox'imərix, loch of removal or flitting, at Newtonmore

Loch Insh, lox'i:nʃ, older speakers lox'i:ʃ, with nasal sound in i, Loch Inse, loch of meadow, Diack recorded Insh parish in Gaelic as ish with nasal vowel and long i

Loch nan Cnapan, ˌloxnaˈgraˈpan, loch of the knolls, often Lochan nan Cnapan (Mearns, Gordon 1948 and in a letter to me that gave the pronunciation)

Loch Ossian, lox'ɔsiən, from Loch Oisinn, lox'ɔiʃin (U), loch of Oisin a hero of Fingalian mythology, Loch Hoishyn (Pont), Loch Hois-syn (Gordon), Loch Oyshen (Roy), a better OS Anglicisation would be Oyshin

Loch Ruthven, 'rıvən, from Gaelic Ruadhainn (Watson 1926), red place, same pronunciation for Ruthven near Tomintoul and in the Engie of lower Banffshire, but not with Ruthven at Kingussie (see below), where Gaelic persisted longer

Loch Spey, lox'spe:, loch of Spey, Loch an Spey (Thomson)

Loch Vaa, lox'va:, Loch a' Bhatha (Diack with Grant), loch of the drowning

Lochan Coire a' Choille-rais, ˌloxanˌkɔrˈxɔilˌraʃ, lochan of corrie of the wood-point, Coille-ras or wood-point lies below, and there is a wooded point projecting into Loch Laggan, the authors of the Gaelic chapter in Bearhop erroneously put the stress on rais in the name Meall Coire a' Choille-rais, not having checked local pronunciation or realised that this was a compound noun where the stress is usually on the first component, Macfarlane has Choille-ross and Cory Chailleros

(The) Lochan Gorm, ˌloxanˈgɔrəm, not on recent OS 1:25000 but was on earlier OS maps, from An Lochan Gorm, the green lochan, beside Allt a' Mharcaidh, now a swamp largely dry owing to evaporation and transpiration from tree plantations

Lochan na h-Earba, ˌloxanaˈhɛrəp, lochan of the roe deer, E of Loch Laggan

Lochan na Laire Baine, ˌloxanaˌlarˈbaˈen, lochan of the white mare, near uppermost Feshie

Lochan nam Bo, ˌloxanamˈboˈ, Lochan Druiemnabo (Thomson), lochan of the cows, Thomson version suggests Lochan Druim nam Bo, up Feshie

Lochan t-Seilich in Gleann Einich, should be Loch an t-Seilich with same pronunciation and meaning as in Loch an t-Seilich above

Luib, ˌluip, at bend, former farm on W side of big bend in river up Glen Banchor

Lundavra, ˌlunˌdaˈvra:, and Lochan Lunn Da-Bhra (OS), originally Dun-da-rath or fort of two enclosures, or Dun-da-bhra, fort of two double crests (MacBain) S of Fort William

(The) Lurg, 'lurək, from An Lurg, the path or shank, Lurg (Thomson), former croft in Glen Banchor

Lynaberack, ˌloinaˈbi:rak, Loinn nam Biorag, enclosure of the horsetails (*Equisetum* species)

Mallaig, 'maləg, Gaelic Malaig, 'malək, aig from Norse vik or inlet, but mal obscure

Mamore, ma'mo:r, from Mam Mor, big round hill (MacBain), Anglicised to Mamore as in Mamore Forest and The Mamores for the hill-range

Mealfuarvonie, mjal'fuarvone, from Meall Fuar-mhonaidh, lump-hill of cold massif or moor

Meall a' Bhuachaille, ˌmjalaˈvuaxəl, lump-hill of the herdsman

Meall a' Chrasgaidh, ˌmjalaˈxraske, lump-hill of the crossing-place, W of Glen Banchor

Meall Buidhe, mjal'bui, yellow lump-hill, W of Sgoran Dubh Mor

Meall Buidhe, mjal'bui, yellow lump-hill, between Tromie and Feshie, Meall a buighe (Thomson)

Meall Chuaich, mjal'xuəx, lump-hill of the cup-shape, rises above Loch Cuaich

Davie Duncan, Ian Crichton head stalker at Benalder Lodge and John Pottie near Culra Lodge, 28 October 2000 (AW)

Meall Dubhag, mjal'duək, lump-hill of dark place, but MacBain added evidence on Meall Dubh-agaidh apparently a correction of Meall Dubhag, and Watson (1992) followed him by writing that Meall Dubhag was
from Meall Dubh-agaidh or lump-hill of the dark cleft, but Roy mapped it as Meal Duack, so the current OS
form may be the right one

Meall Glas-choire, mjal'glasxɔr, lump-hill of green corrie, up Glen Banchor

Meall na Ceardaich, ˌmjalna'kja'rdix, lump-hill of the smithy or forge, up Glen Banchor

Meall nan Sleac, ˌmjalna'slexk, should be Meall na Sleac, lump-hill of the declivity, above a steep drop to Allt
Garbhlach

Meall Odhar Aillig, MacBain wrote that Aillig appears to have Aill a cliff as its root form, ˌmjalˌʌu'ra:lik, at
Gaick

Meall Tionail, mjal'tʃenəl, lump-hill of gathering, on upper Feshie near Carn an Fhidhleir

Meall Tionail, mjal'tʃenəl, lump-hill of gathering, S of Coire Garbhlach, but OS maps have it on a steep slope,
not a hilltop, and note that Thomson gave Meall tional Clach bhlair near Clach Bhlair about the location of
Mullach Clach a' Bhlair OS, see below

Meall Tionail, as above, lump-hill of gathering, W of Sgoran Dubh Mor

Meall Tionail Lorgaidh, ˌmjalˌtʃenəl'lɔrəki, Lorgaidh lump-hill of gathering

Meallan Dubh, ˌmjalan'du', little dark hill-lump, up Glen Banchor

Meur Aillig, mer'a:lik, finger-stream of Ailleag, see Meall Odhar Aillig, and also Eas Ailleag and Feith Ghorm
Ailleag a short distance to the E in NW Perthshire, MacBain gave Aillig at Gaick as cliff and one could
suggest rock if there is no cliff, certainly all the Ailleag or Aillig names have no cliff but some rock, though
Meur Aillig runs mostly through peaty terrain

A' Mharconaich, ə'va'rkonix, the horse-place, a hill at Drumochter

Moidart, 'moidart, probably Norse Moda-fjorðr or muddy-water inlet, Muideort (Macfarlane)

(The) Moine Mhor, mɔn'mo:r, The Moan More (Roy), so A' Mhoine Mhor, the big peat-moss

(The) Monadhliath Mountains, Englished tautology because Am Monadh Liath, ˌmˌmɔna'lia means the grey
hill-range, Monadh is 'muna in Badenoch Gaelic (Seumas Grannd), 'mona in Strathspey and Deeside Gaelic

The Moor of Feshie, mur, E of Druimanlochain, now under planted trees

Morar, 'mo:rar, was Mordhowar in early spelling so Mor-dhobhar or big water, referring to the rapid flow out
of Loch Morar into the sea (Watson 1926), Mourrour (Macfarlane)

Mullach Clach a' Bhlair, not heard locally, note Meall tional Clach bhlair (Thomson) shown nearby, Meall
Tionail being lump-hill of gathering, OS name wrongly transcribed to Mullach Chlach a' Bhlair in Bearhop,
along with an associated erroneous pronunciation of Chlach

Mullach Coire nan Dearcag, ˌmulaxˌkɔrnan'dʒɛrkak, top of corrie of the berries, a Gaick hill

Newtonmore, ˌnjutən'mo:r, Anglicised from Gaelic Baile Ur an t-Sleibhe, new town of the moor, the moor
being called An Sliabh in Gaelic (MacBain)

Onich, 'ɔ:nix, 'Offanych in 1522, is, as its older form proves, from' Omhanach, foam-frothed (MacBain),
doubtless referring to its shore

The Ord, ɔ:rd, not on OS, from An t-Ord, the round hill, a ridge between Loch Insh and River Feshie

Piccadilly, not on OS, junction of four paths at 938075 in Rothiemurchus, heard by AW back to 1946

Pitmain, pɪt'men, from Peit Mea'on or middle-town, leaving out the usual dh in Meadhon (MacBain, Watson
1926) because Gaelic speakers followed the Anglicised spelling and pronunciation in this case of a long-
established building on the main road, Peit is Pictish meaning land share or portion, but note that Nicolaisen
(1976) gave it as Pett

Pityoulish, pɪt'julɛʃ, Peit Gheollais, portion of bright station (Watson 1926), see Pitmain for Peit and Pett

Poite Coire Ardair, ˌpɔtʃˌkor'ardər, pot of Coire Ardair, a deep hollow

Port nan Dobharan, ˌpɔrʃˌtna'doran, not on OS, harbour or bay of the otters, 648889 near Arisaig, at N end of a
caravan site named Port na Doran, also ˌpɔrtˌna'doran, IM has seen otters there while he was fishing in the
bay during recent years

Port nan Luchag, ˌpɔrʃtˌnaˈluxak, pronunciation from Ewen Nicholson to IM, bay of the mice, near Arisaig

Portnalochaig, habitation named after the nearby bay Port nan Luchag near Arisaig, see above

Ralia, raˈlia, Rath Liath, grey dwelling-place (MacBain)

The Red Bothy, not on OS, a red-painted corrugated-iron shooters' hut on N side of Glen Banchor

River Calder, ˈkaldər, Water of Calder (Thomson), see under Glen Banchor

Ross's Path, not on OS but known to local people and noted by Watson (1992), along W side of Loch Einich and then up Allt Fuaran Diotach to the plateau near Carn Ban Mor

Ruigh-aiteachain, ˌruiˈɛtʃəxən, Ruighe a stretch, Aiteachain maybe from Aitneachain or juniper place (MacBain wrote that aiteachain 'may be a corruption for Ruigh Aitneachain the Stretch of the Junipers', and certainly juniper abounds there, but pronunciation like that of Etchachan names on Deeside may suggest otherwise see Watson (1904) for Feill Eiteachain in Easter Ross, and Watson & Allan (1984) for Etchachan names in Deeside), maybe Ruighe Eiteachain or cattle-run of expansive place, following Watson (1904) for Carn Eige in Ross-shire, a hut in Glen Feshie, note Thomson gives Alt Aitachan nearby, early forms of the name found by DD are Ryatichan (1773 estate records referring to a many living there, and again 1803 rental roll)

Ruigh Chreagan, ˌruiˈxrakən, shiel of the little rocky hill, should be spelled Ruighe Chreagain

Ruthven near Kingussie, ˈrʌvən, pronunciation differs from that in Loch Ruthven, see above, from Ruadhainn, red place, in Gaelic was recorded ru-ing, emphasis on ru (Diack)

Ryvoan, riˈvoˈən, Ruighe Bhothain, shiel of the bothy

Sandaig, ˈsandəg, Norse Sand-vik or sand inlet, a narrow bay and house that became well known as the abode of author Gavin Maxwell

Sgor Bhothain, skɔrˈvoˈən, peak of the bothy, at Gaick

(The) Sgor Dearg, from An Sgor Dearg, skɔrˈdʒɛrək, the red peak, at Gaick

Sgor Iutharn near Ben Alder, skɔrˈjuːarn, now commonly called The Sgor (D. Duncan), pronunciation skɔr, the OS's Sgor Iutharn probably incorrect, as in Beinn Iutharn at Glen Ey, which should be Beinn Fhiubharainn (Watson 1916, see also evidence in Wa), hill of the edge-point, which fits the shape of that hill and the one near Ben Alder, so Sgor Fhiubharainn, rocky peak of the edge-point, note that hill walkers have for many decades called it The Lancet Edge, and it is recorded as such in books by the Scottish Mountaineering Club, so it seems possible that this was partly an English translation of the correct Gaelic name

(The) Sgoran Dubh, ˌskɔranˈduˈ, so An Sgoran Dubh, the dark rocky peak, often just The Sgoran ˈskɔran

Sgorr na Diollaid, ˌskɔrnaˈdʒiˈoltʃ, peak of the saddle, a distinctive prominent little peak in mid Glen Strathfarrar

An Sguabach, nˈskuapax, the sweeping place, a hill near Kincraig

Sgurr a' Mhaim, ˌskuraˈvaim, peak of the pass, a high hill S of Glen Nevis

Sgurr Eilde Mor, ˌskurˌɛltʒəˈmoːr, big peak of hind, in the Mamore hills, Drummond (2007) stated, 'properly Sgurr na h-Eilde Mor, big peak of the hind', but gave no evidence for going against the OS form and the local pronunciation, so it is an unjustified invention, especially because place names of the form such as Sgurr Eilde Mor without a definite article are frequent across the Highlands on local lips as well as maps

Sgurr na Lapaich, ˌskurnaˈlaˈxpix, note strong local aspiration in ˈlaˈxpix, as in the same place name in Ross county, above Loch Mullardoch

The Shoonagal, Seann-choille, ʃunaˈgal, Watson & Allan (1988) gave a name ?Suidhe nan Gall, or level shelf of the lowlanders, a hollow E of Am Beanaidh and opposite Whitewell, which AW heard from Carrie Nethersole-Thompson, but since then he has heard ʃun in other Strathspey names from indigenous Gaelic speaker Donnie Smith as definitely Sean or Seann, meaning old, Seumas Grannd has informed AW that local folk knew the name as referring to the land between the rivers Luineag and Am Beanaidh opposite Whitewell, he suggests a derivation from An t-Sean-choille meaning the old wood, or possibly An Seann-ghobhal meaning the old V-shaped or forked place, so pronunciation may have been misheard by AW and perhaps should be ˈʃunagal

Sleat, slet, from Norse Sletta a plain, in Skye

(The) Slochd Beag, slɔxˈbek, from An Slochd Beag, the little gullet, a rocky channel NW of Newtonmore

(The) Slochd Beag, slɔxˈbek, Sloc Beag (Thomson), little gullet, on W side of Glen Feshie

(The) Slochd Mor, slɔxˈmoːr, Sloc more (Thomson), big gullet, on W side of Glen Feshie

An Slugan, the gullet, to incomers was The Sluggan, locally in Gaelic nˈslugan, a pass from Kincardine to Loch Morlich, also the Slugan of the Eas or gullet of the waterfall (Mearns), which would be Slugan an Easa in classical Gaelic form

Sneachdach Slinnean, snowy shoulder, W of Carn Ban in the Monadh Liath, MacBain as a native indigenous speaker of Badenoch Gaelic pointed out many instances where OS names conflicted with local usage, and corrected these, but with Sneachdach Slinnean he did not, so he had been satisfied with the OS version; nevertheless, Drummond asserted (p. 56) 'though this shoulder is "back-to-front", since the adjective should follow the noun to give slinnean sneachdach' and on p.145 ' properly Slinnean sneachdach', but Drummond's book covers all Scotland and he did not base his book on fieldwork with interviews of local indigenous informants (an impossible task by one person for all Scotland), so it was inappropriate to counter the local Badenoch work of someone of the high calibre and scholarship of MacBain who was also a native Gaelic speaker raised in Badenoch; AW in the late 1940s and 1950s heard the name from local indigenous shepherds and gamekeepers (Archie Anderson, Hamish Marshall and others) as ˈsnjexkaxˌʃlinan, in classical Gaelic form the name would be Sneachdach-slinnean, and it should be noted in counter to Drummond that many Gaelic place names have the adjective before the noun, such as Beag-ghleann and Dubh-loch and Mor-bheinn

Socach Bhran, ˌsoˈxkaxˈvraːn, snout of the Bran (Allt Bhran), the foot of a pointed broad ridge towards Allt Bhran

Spey, Anglicised from Uisge Spe, possibly water of hawthorn (Diack with Grant), note pronunciation speiˑ in northern Scots

Spiorraid an t-Seilich, ˌspiˑrətʃanˈtʃelix, spirit or ghost of the Seilich or willow, a prominent hilltop above Allt an t-Seilich up Glen Banchor

Sron Bhuirich, strɔnˈvuˑrix, hill-nose of the roaring, Stron Vurich (Roy), at Gaick

Sron Direachan, strɔnˈdjiˑrəxan, perpendicular hill-nose, has precipice on E side, up Feshie

Sron na Ban-righ, ˌstrɔnaˈbaˑnri, hill-nose of the queen (literally woman-king), up Feshie

Sron nan Laogh, ˌstrɔnanˈløˑg, hill-nose of the calves, up Gleann Lochain

Stac Mheall Chuaich, ˌstaxkˌmjalˈxuəx, pointed rock of Meall Chuaich, a crag

Steall, ʃtjʌul, a spout, often mispronounced like English word Steel, waterfall in Glen Nevis

(An) Stob Ban, n̩ˌstopˈbaːn, the white point, in Mamore, has white screes

Strath Mashie, straˈmaˑʃe, Srath Mathaisidh (MacBain), strath or valley, Mathaisidh uncertain but maybe goodness or beauty or pleasant, see MacBain, good meadow (Diack with Grant)

(The) Strone, stron, a former holding of Clan Chattan (MacBain) with farmland, a hamlet, now an upper part of Newtonmore, from An t-Sron, the hill-nose

Stronetoper, stronˈdopər, Stroinantoppar (Thomson) suggests that it was originally Sroin an Tobair, at hill-nose of the well

The Stuirteags, not on OS, ˈstjurtəks, a wet flow in the peat-mosses W of Allt Mharcaidh, where boys used to collect eggs of black-headed gulls, a species of gull that is Stuirteag in Gaelic on Speyside and Deeside

An Suidhe, nˈsui, the seat, a hill near Kincraig

The Toll, tol, a name in common use at Beauly in late 1940s, referred to a location near Beauly on the main road to Inverness, about the farm of Teawig near the junction of Struy road

Toll Creagach, tʌulˈkrakax, rocky hole, a hill in Glen Affric, has a corrie with cliffs on N side with same name, so hill named after corrie

Tolvah, tʌulˈvaˑ, Toulva (Roy), Tollbha (Thomson), Toll Bhathaidh, hole of the drowning, in Glen Feshie

Tom a' Choinich, tʌumˈxoˑinjix, OS form should be Choinnich, Tom usually a hillock but inappropriate for this high hill, but can mean any rising ground (Dwelly), a peak on N side of Glen Affric, the noun Coinneach is usually feminine, but here masculine, a feature shared with other cases nearby in Ross, as Sgurr a' Choinnich in west Monar and Sgurr Choinnich Mor above Glen Spean, here means hill of the moss

Toman nan Da Mhurach, not on OS, Toman non Du Mhurach, hilllocks of the two Murdochs (Mearns), where two held combat by bow and arrow from nearby hillocks in Gleann Einich

Tombain, land occupied by this house was Cockstreet (OS 6 inch), 'kokstrit, with a shop and several dwellings

(The) Tom Dubh, tʌum'duˑ, An Tom Dubh, the dark hillock (heathery)

Torr Garbh, tor'gara, rough hill, NW of Newtonmore

The Turn o the Feshie, not on OS, where the river turns west in the upper glen

Uath Lochan, 'uaˌloxan, dread lochan, should be spelled Uath-lochan

Uinneag Coire an Lochain, ˌuˑənjaˌkɔrn'loxən, window of corrie of the lochan, at Beinn Sgiath above Laggan

Uinneag Coire Ardair, ˌuˑənjaˌkɔr'a'rdər, window of Coire Ardair, a prominent gap in the skyline as viewed from the E

Utsi's Hut, not on OS, made by Saami native Mikel Utsi who introduced Swedish domesticated woodland reindeer to Glen More and liked to visit his hut of wood and branches, remains still visible, deep in the wood S of Loch Morlich

West Drumochter, not on OS, in Gaelic Monadh Dhruim-uachdair, hill-range of the upper-ridge (Watson 1926)

The Windy Corner (Watson 1975), not on OS, W of 930055, on track up Gleann Einich, open to south winds

Donald Milton told Davie Duncan in 2013 a rhyme about lower Feshie, as follows:-

Lagganlia for laziness
Feshieside for lies
Donn Street for poverty
and Cockstreet for pride
Dalnavert for bonnie lassies
and the Iosal for a pony ride

Hamish Marshall told me in 2011 that when Seton Gordon camped on the Cairngorms to study and photograph hill birds and plants, Mr Clark the farmer at Achlean used to climb to the camp from Achlean every 10 days with a pony, carrying food for Gordon.

Mrs Dolina Macdonald, a native Gaelic speaker raised at Kinlochewe, was wife of the deer-stalker at Glen More from 1919 till after 1947. He was paid by the Forestry Commission after the early 1920s. During 1919 till after 1947, the deer-forest covered the present FC area and the moorland and alpine land now owned by Highlands & Islands Enterprise. Dolina gave a few names:

Badaguish, bat'juˑəʃ, Bad Ghiuthais, clump of the pine

Coire na Ciste, ˌkorə'hiʃt, suggestive of Coire Chiste, corrie of chests or boxes (shape)

Coire an t-Sneachda, ˌkorə'draxt

Stalker Mr Macdonald ran a croft with arable fields enclosed by a wooden deer-fence, now the camp-site. Two horses worked the land, and Mr Macdonald grew oats and turnips to feed them, four cows and 20 sheep. In the period of food-shortage during and after the Second World War, the stock rose to 10 cows, one bull, and 120 sheep that summered on the Kincardine Hills (Donnie Smith, told to AW in 1996 Watson 1997). A seasonal under-keeper helped in the shooting season and with heather burning. Mr Cameron worked the garden at Glenmore Lodge, which is now a Youth Hostel, and he and Mrs Cameron lived in a cottage nearby. The estate paid a man to look after the woods, and he stayed at Badaguish. Mr Grant the Guislich farmer had one or two dozen sheep on Cairn Gorm in summer, and later Donnie Smith of Lurg had sheep there also, later in larger numbers. She said that sheep from Tulloch to the north of Glen More came annually in summer to the moorland parts of Glen More.

David Duncan in July 2013 sent me photocopies that he had made of hand-written papers on marches in the Glen Feshie area, from the Gordon Papers and MacKintosh Papers in the late 1700s and 1800s. These give interesting names that are not on OS maps, as well as old spellings of OS names. Because neither Mr Duncan nor AW heard local pronunciations of some of these names, the names below are spelled in the old Papers, but

AW senior high on Creag Pitridh, with Loch Laggan and Creag Meagaidh beyond, New Year 1953 (Tom Weir)

with an estimated likely form of each name in Gaelic. Also, sometimes the descriptions help identify approximate or even exact locations.

GD 44/27/25, estimated date by DD 1779-99

Aultanleime, Allt na Leuma OS, Aultanleime suggests Alltan Leime or burnie of jump

The Braes of the Glen, upper parts, mostly unwooded

Cragbheg, Creag Bheag OS

Cragnagoire, Creag na Goibhre OS

Aultfuar, Allt Fuar or cold burn, probably the burn from Loch na Bo OS

Aultearnagain, Allt Fhearnagain OS

Craglein, Creag Leathann OS

Cragghuisachain, Creag Ghiubhsachain OS

Cragmhigachie, Creag Mhigeachaidh OS

Aultmharkie, Allt a' Mharcaidh OS

Stronnabanrigh, Sron na Ban-righ OS

Lettirribhard, Leitir Ruighe Bhaird, slope of cattle-run of the enclosure, between Sron na Ban-righ and Letterrifiuntaig

Lettirrifiuntaig, Leitir Ruighe Fionntaig, slope or cattle-run of Fionntaig, note Ruigh-fionntag OS, rendered by MacBain as 'The reach of the Fair-stream', so probably the slope W of it

Craignacaillich, Creag na Caillich OS

Leadaghaill, Leathad a' Ghaille, slope of the rock, note Allt a' Ghaille OS

The Bank of the Feshie, just meant as in English

Ault badantorcain, Allt Bad an Torcain, burn of clump of the little pig, on W side of lower Feshie, probably at Stronetoper

Toulbha, Tollvah OS

Coirrebhlair, Coire Bhlair OS

Lagganobhir, note Allt an Lagain Odhair OS, so An Lagan Odhar the grey little hollow at c880915

Clachblair, Clach Bhlair

Corresullagach, Coire Suileagach, corrie full of eyes or springs (see MacBain for another one north of Drumgask), note that the author wrote of two Corresullagachs, there are two shallow corries with a number of springs, one at 885933 and a larger corrie at 897933, maybe they were Coire Suileagach Beag and Coire Suileagach Mor

Tombuie na hamoire, Tom Buidhe a' Chadha Moire, yellow hillock of the big pass, 891945 at OS 953 m point, close to the big steep pass and descent to Coire Garbhlach

Tombuie Luinaig, Tom Buidhe Luineig, yellow hillock of Luineag, maybe 910950 at OS point 937 m, this also likely because Thomson showed a Tombuich there on SW side of Allt Sgairnich OS

The foord of Luinaig, the Foord of Luineag, Scots Foord is Ford, maybe the ford at 914953 on way to Allt Luineag OS

Caochan ban na Liachry, Caochan Ban an Liath-choire, white burn of the grey corrie, 935973, it follows that the earlier name for Horsman's Corrie was An Liath-choire ot the grey corrie, and that Ronald Burn's Clais Feith Inbhir Feithisidh in alphabetical list under Horseman's Corrie above may have referred to the lower hollow, and Horseman's Corrie and An Liath-choire to the whole corrie

Feanacraoibh Caorin, Feith na Craoibh Chaoruinn OS

Snaim a Naultainchraggich, Snaim an Alltain Chreagaich, knot or bind or fetter of the rocky burnie, note Alltan Creagach OS runs into Bhran and Tromie, has many rocks on the nearby hillsides in its upper section, would have been An t-Alltan Creagach, and Snaim was a point on the march with Bhran, so on the flat col at c827866 near OS point 766 m

GD 176, Box 40, MacKintosh of MacKintosh Papers, 1875

The papers refer to the Right Honorable Edward Horsman M.P. and to Mr Horsman, so the name Horseman's Corrie on Braeriach (Gordon 1925) should be Horsman's Corrie

Invermarkie, not on OS but obviously land at foot of Allt a' Mharcaidh around Blackmill and Lagganlia, was a separate estate that later became part of Invereshie, see MacBain

Eilean Vean 'is good and superior as a grazing if it were protected from floods', in Kingussie parish, Eilean an island or riverside meadow, maybe Mheadhoin of the middle

Eilean Dubh is shingle, marked on OS 6-inch to mile maps, just upstream from present Kincraig Bridge, was in Alvie parish

GD 44 27 15, 1769

Inishreoch, Inshriach OS

Baddenach, Badenoch OS

GD 176, Box 50, 1854

Achloamchoit, marginal notes added by a different hand

Achleumchoit, Achadh Leim Choit, field of jump of boats or huts

Achleam in notes added by a different hand, Auchleum OS, Achadh Leim, field of jump

Achlean, marginal notes added by a different hand, Auchlean OS

Alt Cist Maret, Allt Ciste Mearaid not on OS, burn of Margaret's hollow, 886971

Ciste Maret, Ciste Mhearad OS which should be Ciste Mearaid

The Furan, Am Fuaran, the spring, not on OS, at top of Allt Ciste Mearaid

Thomson's map gave names in Glen Feshie and nearby, not on OS maps or heard by me.

Achnahoid, former farm SE of Stranlia and on E side of Feshie

Alt Chiola, Allt a' Caoileig OS is ungrammatical, if Caoileig accepted it should be Chaoileig

Balnrioch, a farm NE of Milton, Baile an Fhraoich, stead of the heather

Birchwood, a building E of 870889, on W side of burn at foot of birch wood

Blarduith, Blar Dubh or dark moor, W of lower Allt a' Mharcaidh

Bray cory cregach, 878837, from Braigh Coire Creagach, upland of rocky corrie

Corry Attachan, c858931, Coire Aiteachain, above Ruigh-aiteachain, corrie of Aiteachain, for meaning see Ruigh-aiteachain

Cruitbeg for Croftbeag OS, a farm N of Feshieside and S of Kepoch, Cruit Beag, little croft

Cuachana Satuy for Allt Leac an Taobhain OS

Cuachan clash tamff for Allt Clais Damh OS, from Caochan a hidden burn

Cualnaneach, flattish area near the top of Allt Sgairnich, Cul nan Each, back-place of the horses

Cual nan Scor, high area NW of Sgor Gaoith and E of Meall Tional, Cul nan Sgoir, back of the Sgor with Sgor referring to Sgor Gaoith

Fendaich, same as Fionntag Burn OS

Ilrick, hill slope N of Creag Bheag, from Eileirig a deer-trap

Inver Endiart, but Thomson spread the name across the foot of both Allt Eindart OS and River Eidart OS and used the same spelling Endiart for both streams

Kepoch, a farm N of Feshieside and near Spey, Ceapach or stump-place

Knockanbuidh, Knockinbui (Roy), from Cnocan Buidhe, yellow little hill, former farm opposite Corarnstilbeg and slightly further S

Lup Vorar, a building probably a shiel at c882860 on S bank of Feshie, from Lub Mhoraire, bend of the laird or lord

Maitin, 834945, hill NW of Carnachuin, Meadan a meadow

Snowy Tom a' Choinich left and Toll Creagach from above Loch Beinn a' Mheadhoin in Glen Affric with Beinn a' Mheadhoin far left and Old Caledonian pinewood on its lower slopes and on an island that had been formerly a promontory before a dam for a hydro-electric scheme raised the level of the loch, from a helicopter, November 1988 (AW)

Maul Clash Tamff, 831m top, 832849, from Meall Clais Damh, lump-hill of hollow of deer

Maul cory na Keistachan, 837m top at 864832, from Meall Coire nan Cisteachan, lump-hill of corrie of the hollows

Muineadh Miarnach for the hill on N side of uppermost Feshie opposite Allt Clais Damh, Muineadh a fair representation of the Badenoch pronunciation of Monadh, which is like Munadh in Badenoch, so in classical Gaelic form Monadh Mairrneach, Mar-men's hill

Pry Clash Tamff, steep slope, 840846, from Braigh Clais Damh or upland of hollow of deer, note that Scrope named Mal Corriechragach which was probably the round 845m hilltop at 872830, from Meall Coire Creagaich

Rea Birack not marked as a building, to E of Rea Leame and about half way to Allt Eindart, Rea Birack from Ruighe Bioraig, shiel of horsetail (plant)

Rea Leame marked as a shiel W of the foot of Allt na Leuma OS, note OS has Ruigh nan Leum (jumps plural) E of the burn-foot and yet Allt na Leuma (jump singular) for the burn, Thomson version suggests Ruighe Leim or shiel of jump

Stranlia, former farm SE of Creag na Sroine, on W side of Feshie, Srathan Liath, grey little riverside flat

Taluin Cragach, on N side of Allt Creagach, maybe Talamh Uaine Allt Chreagaich, green land of Allt Creagach

Tombeulan Fliumhaur, 2nd and 3rd letters in Fliumhaur not very distinct, 953 m top E of Coire Garbhlach, Tom a hillock, Beulan a little mouth or opening, rest uncertain

Trie ma bow cloich, a small rise on county boundary and N of main path to Geldie, Tri nam Bogha-cloiche or trio of the stone-bows

Thomson gave, Carna bhan for Carn Ban Beag, Corra Gormadh for Coire Gorm a' Chrom-alltain, and Monadh Ruaidh for the high ground around Sgor Gaoith

He showed a building, presumably a former farm, Alt mharcaidh, uphill and S of the main big bend of Allt a' Mharcaidh

Towards Tromie he gave

Bad a Ducha, OS Bad an Dubh-chadha or clump of the dark path or pass

Cailleach Feith mhoir, OS Cailleach na Feithe Moire seems fussy compared with Thomson version, which suggests Cailleach Feith Mhor or old woman of Feith Mhor or big-bog-stream

Ducharridh which is An Dubharach OS

Knockchoilloch, farm N of Lower Mains at Drumguish, from Cnoc Choilich, round hill of the cock

Laggan leath a farm E of Tromie Bridge, Lagan Liath on OS, grey little hollow

Lupanriach, Luibean Ruadh on OS

Lubin not on OS, former farm at 793965, Luban, little bend

Meall an ducha, OS Meall an Dubh-chadha or lump-hill of the dark path or pass

Rith Bhaidmhor, OS Ruigh a' Bhaid Mhoir

An Tonach More, Aonach Mor OS, so An t-Aonach Mor, the big hill or moor

Torbreck a farm, Torr Breac OS or speckled hill, tɔr'breaxk

Thomson is a particularly rich source of names of shiels on the mid and upper Dulnain, not covered in this chapter.

Roy gave Stronavoity marked as a shiel below and just W of the main turn of River Feshie, Sron a' Bhoitidh, hill-nose of the calling to pigs, note that MacBain gave this name Sron a' Bhoitidh and its location and meaning

Richard Perry gave names from near Drumguish, heard from Gaelic speakers, but his spelling was inconsistent. If AW heard a name in the 1940s or 1950s, the pronunciation is given below

Cladhan a deep hollow, lay in birchwoods N of the pinewoods at Drumguish

Lower Drumguish and Upper Drumguish separate farms

For Drumguish he gave Druim-a-Ghuibhais, OS has Druim a' Ghiubhais or ridge of the pinewood, ˌdruimˈjuˑiʃ

Balguish was Baileguish OS, and he gave Dell of Balguish or Dail Bailaghuibhais, Dail a haugh, last word should be spelled Baile a' Ghiubhais or stead of the pinewood, ˌbalˈjuˑiʃ

Glait-a-Ghuibhas obviously was Glac a' Ghiubhais or hollow of the pinewood

Gnaicanmair or bed of the dam was doubtless Glac an Amair or hollow of the channel

Toran Buidhe the yellow hillocks, should be Torran Buidhe

Blar-a-Mhinistir or the minister's moss, Blar a' Mhinisteir OS

Fluich-adagan the wet stooks of rushes, should be spelled Fluich-adagan

Blar nan Saighead the moss of the arrows, Blar na Saighde OS

Perry named three former farms at Cnoc-a-Chanaich the hill of cotton grass, should be Cnoc a' Chanaich or round hill of the cotton grass, a second was at

Tor Dhu the black hillock, Tor Dubh OS, ndɔˈrˈdu, from An Torr Dubh, the black hill, and a third at Cnoc-a-Chenn the head of the hillock, maybe Cnoc-cheann or round hill-head

Another farm noted as on green land was Tom-fad the long hillock, Tamfad (Thomson) at 825964, ndʌumˈfat, from An Tom Fada, the long hillock, shown on Perry's map as Tom Fad

AW did not hear the OS name Cadha na Coin Duibh above the crags of Coire Garbhlach, supposedly path of the black dog, but spelling ungrammatical, must be Cadha a' Choin Duibh, path of the black dog

Argyll

Achnacon, ˌaxnaˈgon, Auchnacoan (Thomson), Achadh nan Con, field of the dogs

Aoineadh Beag, ˌøːinagˈbek, g throaty, little precipice, at Loch Aline, pairs with nearby

Aoineadh Mor, ˌøːinagˈmoˑr, g throaty, big precipice, at Loch Aline, a district with quite a number of names starting Aoineadh, all steep rocky slopes rising from the sea

(The) Aonach Dubh, from An t-Aonach Dubh, ndˌøːnaxˈdu, the black hill, ø as in Danish, Norwegian, or French oeu or German ö

(The) Aonach Eagach, from An t-Aonach Eagach, ndˌøːnaxˈekax, the notched hill

Ardnamurchan, ˌardnaˈmurəxan, perhaps Ard nam Murchon (Watson 1926), heights or capes of the sea-hounds or otters

Ardtornish, ardˈtorniʃ, Ard is Gaelic point, the rest Norse from Thori's cape (Watson 2002), so Thori-nes, Point is tautological Englishing

(The) Baile Mor, mˌbaləˈmoːr, Am Baile Mor, the big town, the village on Iona

The Bah Lochs (Scrope, Whitehead), part Englished name, obviously from Ba Lochs, by deerstalkers for a chain of lochs at the start of Rannoch Moor towards the main road

Ballachulish, ˌbalaˈxøːliʃ, Baile a' Chaolais (Ballachulish ferrymen in 1947, and Dwelly), stead of the ferry

Barrguillean, barˈguələn, Barrgillan (Thomson), maybe from Barr nan Cuilinn, hilltop of the hollies

Beinn a' Bheithir, biňˈveˑhər, Bin vehir (Pont), hill of the bear or wild beast or thunderbolt, at Ballachulish

Beinn an Lochain, ˌbiňanˈloxən, hill of the lochan, N of Torloisk on Mull

(The) Beinn Bhuidhe, biňˈvui, from A' Bheinn Bhuidhe, the yellow hill, from its grassy colour, N of Torloisk on Mull

Beinn Dubhchraig, biňˈduːxrek, emphasis on Dubh is so strong that the g in the last syllable is barely or not sounded, ˈduːxre, Beinn Dubh-chreag, hill of black crag, near Tyndrum

(The) Beinn Ghlas, biňˈglas, from A' Bheinn Ghlas, the green hill, E of Oban

Ben Cruachan should be Cruachan-beann (Dwelly, Gordon 1934, Ballachulish ferrymen, MacCalum Cameron to me), ˈkruaxanˌbjʌun, haunch of peaks (Watson 1934), but this would be Cruachan Bheann, so maybe a compound noun as haunch-peaks, often just Cruachan locally (Dwelly), Dwelly gives Cruachan as a conical hill

Bidean nam Bian should be Bidean nam Beann, pinnacle of the hills (Watson 1926, Ronald Burn notes,

Watson 1934, Ballachulish ferrymen in 1947, MacCalum Cameron to me), nam Bian means of the hides ˌbidʒanaˈbjʌun, but Pont in his 1500s maps gave it as Pittindeaun, Poddindeaun, and Boddindeaun (Drummond), and Drummond rightly suggested from this that it was originally Bod an Deamhain or penis of the demon, the same as the original Gaelic name for the Englished misleading euphemistic version The Devil's Point in the Cairngorms, note that there is a third Bod an Deamhain at Glen Canness in Caenlochan Glen at the top of Glen Isla (Watson 2013)

Black Corries OS, Blackcorries (McConnochie) The Black Corries are a translated name of two corries and also a deer forest called Blackcorries (McConnochie), the corries are along the N side of A' Chruach and the OS form is translated with a Scots/English plural from Coire Dubh Mor and Coire Dubh Beag, both OS names, note Corrie du mor and Corrie du beag (Thomson)

(The) Black Mount, from Am Monadh Dubh (Watson 1926), ˌmonaˈduˑ, the dark hill-range

(The) Cam Ghleann, ˈkaːmglʌun, from An Cam-ghleann, the crooked glen

Carn Mor, karnˈmoːr, big hill, or maybe refers to the cairn of archaeological significance on the top, N of Torloisk

A' Chruach, əˈxruax, the rounded hill standing alone, a long high hill W of Loch Laidon, Pont wrote of 'the great hill Crowach Luydon' between Loch Ba and Loch Luydon (Laidon OS), and also of Monie na Crowach, i.e. Monadh na Cruaiche or hill-range of the rounded hill standing apart, Crowach Luydon (Gordon), Cruach Loyden (Roy), Stack Hill (Stobie) Englishing from one meaning of Cruach which is a stack

(The) Clach Leathad, ˈklaxleət, compound noun, so An Clach-leathad, the stone-slope, authors of the Gaelic chapter in Bearhop erroneously put the stress on Leathad and give a false associated translation as stone of the slope, a warning of place-name study without checking local pronunciations, a hill in Black Mount

Coire an Easain, ˌkɔrənˈjɛsən, corrie of the little waterfall, on Meall a' Bhuiridh

Coire Pollach, ˌkɔrəˈpulax, corrie of pool place, holds the ski tows on Meall a' Bhuiridh, Ronald Burn had the corrie on Meall a' Bhuiridh as Coire na Cubhaig or corrie of the cuckoo, but did not state which corrie he meant

Coireach a' Ba, ˌkɔrəxˈbaː, literally corrie of cow, the OS a' Ba being incorrect and ungrammatical, but Coireach was used in a collective sense for a large corrie that included other small ones, as in Coireach Bhuth in Deeside (Watson & Allan 1984), which in local Gaelic was corrach voo, corrach gives a collective sense (Diack), and included several corries between Carn an Tuirc, Cairn of Claise and Sron na Gaoithe as well as towards the Cairnwell (Watson & Allan), in the case of Coireach a' Ba, it is a 'super-corrie' or collective corrie that includes at least two others named on the OS map, Coire an Dhomhnaill and Glas Choire, and stretches E for a few miles, Coryba (Pont), the name Ba appears in the River Ba which drains the super-corrie, in Ba Cottage along the Wade road to the north, in Ba Bridge where the Wade road crosses the river, in Loch Ba, a large loch below the main road, and in the Ba Lochs, a part Englished name for the lochs on either side of the main road, so it seems as if Ba is more than just cow, but refers partly to an area and is used for a few names, such as the name Ballach in the Monadh Liath and the name Ailleag which appears in several place names in Atholl, north-west Perthshire

Coireach Ba Forest (McConnochie, Whitehead), Corrichibah (Scrope), the former name of the deer forest now known as the Black Mount Forest, it held Coireach a' Ba and a much larger area including the Ba Lochs, the second i in Corrichibah may well have been a svarabhakti extra vowel to ease pronunciation, as common in Gaelic, such as in Gorm, gɔrəm

Creag Dhubh, kregˈguˑ, black rocky hill, below Meall a' Bhuiridh

(An) Cruachan Odhar, nˌkruaxanˈʌuər, from An Cruachan Odhar, the dun conical hill, N of Torloisk on Mull

Deadh Choimhead, ˌdjeˈxoˈit, good watching, a hill that is a good viewpoint SE of Oban

Dervaig, ˈdjɛrvək, from Norse Djurvik or deer inlet, a village on Mull at the head of an inlet

Eas Criche, ɛsˈkrixə, cascade of boundary, a torrent in a rocky gorge near Kilbride

Eilean Balnagowan, ˌelənˌbalnaˈgʌuən, ylen Balenagaun (Pont), Balnagowan I. (Thomson), Eilean Baile nan Gobhainn, island of stead of the smiths, or Gamhainn of the stirks, I did not ask local folk which was meant, an island in Loch Linnhe

Fishnish Point, ˈfɪʃnəʃ, Norse Fisknes or fish cape, point is tautological Englishing

Garbh Bheinn, from Garbh-bheinn, ˈgarəviň, rough hill

Glen Coe, glʌunˈkoˈən, Glen Koen (Pont), from Gleann Comhann, Comhann obscure (see Watson 1926)

Kilninian, kɪlˈnɪnjən, in Gaelic Cill Naoinein (Watson 1926), St Ninian a frequent church name

Loch Aline, loxˈaˈlən, in Gaelic Loch Alainn, lovely loch (Watson 1926)

Loch an Easain, ˌloxənˈjesən, loch of the little waterfall, in Coire Loch an Easain

Loch Sunart, loxˈsunərt, Sunart from Norse Sveinn fjord (MacBain), in Norse spelling Sveinn-fjorðr

Meall a' Bhuiridh, ˌmjalaˈvuːri, hill of the roaring

Mishnish, ˈmɪʃnəʃ, from Norse, nish from Nes a cape, Mish maybe from Missa or loss, a near-peninsula and parish W of Tobermory

Quinish Point, ˈkwɪnəʃ, from Norse kvi a fold or pen and nes a cape, Point is tautological Englishing, a cape on N coast of Mull near Dervaig

Ross of Mull, rɔsˈmulax, in Gaelic An Ros Muileach (Watson 1926), the Mull promontory

Stob a' Ghlas Choire, ˌstupaˈglaʃxɔrə, point of the grey-green corrie, high hill NW of Meall a' Bhuiridh, with Glas Choire below it into Cam Ghleann, leads to NE to Sron na Creise (The Craish in Scrope), in classic Gaelic form would be spelled Stob a' Ghlais-choire

Stob Coir' an Albannaich, ˌstupˌkɔranˈalapanix, peak of corrie of the Scotsman, authors in Bearhop give an erroneous pronunciation with the e in Coire sounded as well as the a in an, but the OS form should have warned them that the two vowels run together in such cases, and checking the local pronunciation would have shown them this, a hill S of Black Mount

Stob Coire Sgreamhach, ˌstupˌkɔrəˈskrevax, point of abhorrent corrie, the authors of the Gaelic chapter in Bearhop were incorrect in stating that this name is 'properly Stob a' Choire Sgreamhaich' and giving a pronunciation that fitted their invention, in this and many other cases such as Stob Coire Sgreamhach where there is no definite article, they erroneously state that OS names are properly or more properly X or Y, with an invented definite article added and an associated invented pronunciation, despite this form without a definite article being common in place names both published and unpublished, a peak S of Glen Coe

Stob Ghabhar, stupˈgʌuər, point of goats, a high peak S of Black Mount

Torloisk, tɔrˈloisk, from Torr Loisgte, burnt hill, on Mull, small settlement

Treshnish, ˈtreʃnəʃ, Trese-ne (Blaeu), nish from Norse nes a cape, as in Fishnish, rest obscure, maybe Norse traustr which is firm

White Corries, a name coined by developers of a downhill ski area on Meall a' Bhuiridh, called more commonly by later developers the Glencoe Ski Centre, although not in Glen Coe, and recently by current developers Glencoe Mountain, after CairnGorm Mountain

North-west Perth

Airgiod Bheinn, ˈarəkətvin, silver hill, Arragetvean (Thomson), Argiodvane (Scrope), should be spelled Airgiod-bheinn, at Beinn a' Ghlo

(The) Alder Burn, ˈaldərˈbʌrn, was Auld Auler (Thomson), so Allt Allair, burn of Alder or rocky place, see Ben Alder in Inverness-shire list above

Allt a' Chaorainn, altˈxuˈrn, Auld Churn (Thomson), burn of the rowan, up Tarf

Allt a' Ghlas Choire, altˈglasˌxore, Auld Glasschorry (Thomson) suggests that the name may have been Allt Glas-choire, OS spelling if accepted should be Allt a' Ghlas-choire to follow classical Gaelic form, burn of the green corrie, S of An Sgarsoch

Allt Bhuideanach, altˈvuːənjax, burn of the yellow place, on Bhuidheanach hills see below

Allt Craoinidh, altˈkrone, Allt a burn, rest uncertain, runs into Tilt

Allt Cro-chloiche, altˈkroˌxloix, burn of stone-cot, at Rannoch

Allt Diridh, altˈdʒiri, straight or perpendicular burn, drains Gleann Diridh W of Glen Tilt

Allt Eigheach, altˈeˈjax, Alt Eijach (Macfarlane), Avon Eyach (Blaeu), so Abhainn Eigheach, noisy river, Eyach (Moll), noisy or shouting burn, but nearby Coire Eigheach (see below) drained by the burn and Loch

Jim Hunter on ferry to Iona, Ross of Mull beyond, August 1984 (AW)

Eigheach into which the burn runs suggest a collective use of Eigheach as in Ailleag names in Perth and Inverness and Ballach in Inverness

Allt Feith Lair, ˌaltˌfəˈlaːr, burn of bog of mare, at Fealar Lodge

Ardlarach, ardˈlarax, Arlarich (Gordon map), Ard Laraich, height of site or habitation, a farm at Loch Rannoch

Auchtarsin, axˈtarsən, from Achadh Tarsuinn, cross or athwart field, a set of former farms at Dunalastair

Aulich, ˈaːlix, sometimes now ˈʌulɪx following OS spelling, Avalick (Gordon map), Avalich (Moll), in Gaelic Abhlaich, the root is Abh a stream or river (Watson 1926), so stream-place, and the farm is at a stream running into Loch Rannoch, the OS spelling with Au is misleading as often with their spellings of Auch when local pronunciation is Ach

Bac na Creige, ˌbaxknaˈkrek, bank of the rocky hill

(The) Bachd Ban, baxkˈbaːn, Am Bac Ban, the white (i.e. grassy) bank

Ballintuim, ˌbalənˈduəm, Baile an Tuim, stead of the hillock, at Dunalastair

Barracks (Whitehead), short for Barracks Deer-forest, named after former military redcoat barracks at W end of Loch Rannoch, which are now Rannoch Barracks OS

Beinn a' Chait, binˈxatʃ, Ben chatt (Stobie), hill of the cat, probably wildcat meant, N of Glen Tilt

Beinn a' Chuallaich, ˌbinˈxualəx, Bin Chouldach (Blaeu), Binchouldach (Moll), Benchualach (Thomson), hill of the herding, above Dunalastair

Beinn a' Ghlo, ˌbineˈgloˑ, to those with local Gaelic was ˌbiňəˈgloˑ, with ň like that in piň'on pine, hill of the veil or hood

Beinn Bhoidheach, binˈvoˑiax, beautiful hill, at Rannoch

Approaching the village on Iona, with monastery building on right, August 1984 (AW)

Beinn Bhreac, binˈvrexk, speckled hill, up Tarff, Ben Vreachk (Roy), Benebreck (Thomson) and Ben y Breck (Knox) retain a sign of the Gaelic pronunciation which was close to biň' or even biŋ as in Braemar Gaelic, in this name and the other Beinn names in this Perth list

Beinn Dearg, binˈdʒɛrək, red hill, above Glen Bruar

Beinn Mhaol, binˈvul, Ben Voule (Thomson), hill of the bald top, S of Beinn a' Ghlo

Beinn Mheadhonach, binˈveˈnax, Ben venoch (Stobie), middle hill, between Gleann Mhairc and Gleann Diridh

Beinn Mholach, binˈvoˈlax, rough hill, above Loch Rannoch

Beinn Pharlagain, binˈfarlagən, hill of?, no meaning heard, Farlough in Ireland was from For-loch, outlying or exposed loch (Joyce), so maybe Beinn Far-lagain, hill of outlying or exposed hollow, Ben Farligan (Roy)

Beinn Vuirich, binˈvu:rix, from Beinn Bhuirich, hill of the roaring, W of Gleann Fearnach

A' Bhuideanach, ˈvu:ənjax, the yellow place, Vuinnach (Scrope), a hill E of Drumochter Pass

A' Bhuidheanach Bheag, ˌvu:ənjaxˈvek, the little yellow place, a hill near A' Bhuidheanach

(The) Blath Bhalg, ˈblaˈvalag, Am Blath-bhalg, the warm bag, bag here being the hill's shape

Braigh Coire Chruinn-bhalgain, ˌbraiˌkorˈxruinˌvaləgən, upland of corrie of round little bag (shape) to follow the OS spelling, but quite likely a variant plural Chruinn-bhalgan, or round bags, perhaps referring to hillocks in the corrie

Bruach nan Iomairean, ˌbruaxnanˈimaran, brae of the ridges, NW of Dalnapsidal

Bunrannoch House, bunˈranəx, Bun Raineich, bottom of Rannoch, near Kinloch Rannoch

An Caisteal, nˈgaʃtəl, not on OS 1:25000, the castle, Top of Carrie Chastail or The Castle Hill (Scrope), a prominent rocky top on Beinn a' Ghlo when seen from Glen Tilt, above Coire a' Chaisteil

Cama Choire, ˈkamaxor, crooked corrie, at Gaick

Camasericht, ˌkamasˈɛrəxt, Camas Eireachd, bay of Ericht, where River Ericht from Loch Ericht enters Loch Rannoch, also a farm, but the current Camusericht Farm is well to the W, Camiserich-beg and Camiserich-more (Stobie), also Camiserich beg and Camiserich more (Thomson) were farms beside the current Camusericht Lodge, the former above the road, the latter below it, hence Camas Eireachd Beag and Mor

Caochan Dubh Mor, ˌkuxanˌduˈmoˑr, big dark hidden burn, runs out of Loch Tilt

Carn a' Bhutha, karnˈvuˑa, hill of the anthill shape (Watson 1975), the very summit having a tiny peak, a hill above Fealar Lodge

Carn a' Chlamain should be Carn a' Chlamhain, ˌkarnˈxlaˈvən, hill of the buzzard

Carn an Righ, karnənˈriˑ, Cairn rie (Thomson), usually stated as hill of the king, but maybe the less fanciful Carn nan Ruighe or hill of the shiels, would fit the shiels below it

Carn Dearg, karnˈdʒɛrək, Carn Dearg (Thomson), red hill, at Rannoch

Carn nan Gobhar, ˌkarnaˈgʌuər, hill of the goats, highest hill in Beinn a' Ghlo range

Carn Torcaidh, karnˈdorke, Ben Turkie (Stobie), Benturkie (Thomson), Cairn Torkie (Scrope), hill of boar place, on Beinn a' Ghlo, the early forms Ben Turkie suggest Beinn Tuircidh a genitive Tuirc

An Cearcall, nˈkjerkal, Bin Kerkil (Moll), Kerkle (Stobie, Thomson), Carkel (Scrope), the circle, a steep slope above Loch Garry, Moll and Stobie and Thomson put it as hill behind

Cnapan Loch Tilt, ˌkrapanˌloxˈtëlt, little hill of Loch Tilt

Coire a' Chaisteil, ˌkorˈxaʃtəl, Carrie Chastail (Scrope), corrie of the castle, which is a rocky top above the corrie, see An Caisteal, a corrie on Beinn a' Ghlo

Coire an Loch, kornˈlox, corrie of the loch, above Loch Tilt

Coire Bhachdaidh, korˈvaˈxke, maybe corrie of the obstruction, but Bhacaidh is an old locative of Bhacach (see Watson 1904, p.90), and is pronounced the same as Bhachdaidh, so could be Coire Bhacaidh or corrie at the bent place, the deer-forest here is sometimes Anglicised to Corrievarkie (Whitehouse)

Coire Bhuirich, korˈvu:rix, corrie of the roaring, above Loch Ericht

Coire Cas-eagallach, korˈkaseklax, frighteningly steep corrie, on Beinn a' Ghlo

Coire Creagach, korˈkrakax, rocky corrie, SE of Loch Ossian

Coire Earra Dheargan, ˌkorˌerˈjɛrəgan, corrie of red clothes, an old resident told Davie Duncan in the 1970s that a clan fight occurred there between the Robertsons with Donnachadh Reamhar (fat Duncan) and the Domhnullachs or MacDonalds

Coire Eigheach, kor'ejax, see Allt Eigheach, Kory-eiiach or 'Showting corie' and Kori-eiyach (Pont)

Coire na Cloiche, ˌkorna'kloix, corrie of the stone, Coire na cloiche (Thomson), near Alder Burn

Coire na Conlaich, ˌkorna'konələx, corrie of the fodder, W of Glen Tilt

Comyns' Road, see Rathad nan Cuimeineach

Conlach Bheag, ˌkonələx'vek, little Conlach or fodder (place), hill W of Tilt

Conlach Mhor, ˌkonələx'voˑr, big Conlach or fodder (place), Cairn liannaconalich (Stobie and Knox), Cairnliannaconalich (Thomson) obviously Carn Liath na Conlach or grey hill of the fodder (place), Conaloch (Scrope), hill W of Tilt

Creag an Loch, not on OS, ˌkrakən'lox, Craig Loch Tilt (Roy), Crag-an-loch (Stobie), Craiganloch (Thomson), rocky hill of the loch, W of Loch Tilt

Creag na h-Iolair, ˌkrakna'hilər, Craig na heilar (Thomson), rock of the eagle, in Gleann Bruar, OS has two Creag na h-Iolair Mhor (big) and nearby the smaller rock of Creag na h-Iolair Bheag (small)

Creagan Odhar, ˌkrakan'ʌuər, dun rocks or dun little rocky hill, Craiganour Lodge and Craiganour deer-forest named after it, first meaning may fit, from the long lines of rocks on this hill N of Loch Rannoch

Croftnacoille, ˌkroftna'kɛil, Croit na Coille, croft of the wood

(The) Crom Allt, 'kroməlt, Auld Crumald (Knox) but this was a tautology with Allt (Auld, ald) twice, An Crom-allt, the curved burn, SE of Fealar Lodge

(The) Cruaidh Alltan, 'kruiˌaltan, from An Cruaidh-alltan, the hard little burn, Auld Crualdan (Thomson), far up Tarf

Dalnacardoch Lodge, ˌdalna'kjardəx, Dail na Ceardaich, haugh of the smithy

Dalnamein Lodge, ˌdalna'miˑn, Dail na Mine, haugh of the meal

Dalnaspidal, ˌdalna'spitəl, Dail na Spitil, haugh of the hospice, Dalnaspeedal (Roy) fits Gaelic pronunciation better than the usual current pronunciation like Spittal

Dirnanean, ˌdɪrnan'jen, Doire nan Eun, copse of the birds

(The) Dubh Alltan, n'duəltən, from An Dubh-alltan, the black little burn, also The March Burn as tape-recorded by IM in the 1990s, near the march between Tilt and Dee

An Dun, ndun, the heap or fort-like hill, south of Gaick

Dunan, 'dunan, Dunnan (Thomson), little hill, a farm W of Loch Rannoch

Dun Beag, dun'bek, Dun-beg (Stobie), little fort-like hill, above Tilt

Dun Mor, dun'moˑr, Dun-more (Stobie), big fort-like hill, above Tilt

Dunalastair, dʌn'alastər, Dun Alasdair, fort of Alasdair, at Rannoch

Dunie, 'duni, Dunaidh, little hill or fort

Eas Ailleag, ɛs'a:lək, waterfall of Ailleag or possibly rock, see Meall Odhar Aillig nearby in Inverness-shire list, spelling should probably be Eas Aillig, a section of fast stream in a narrow steep rocky glen, with a waterfall, in NW corner of Atholl

Enochdhu, ˌenax'du, in Gaelic An t-Aonach Dubh (Watson 1926), the dark moor

Fealar Lodge, fə'la:r, Fealair Lodge (Thomson), from Feith Laire, bog of mare

Feith Ghorm Ailleag, ˌfeˌgɔrəm'a:lək, green bog-stream of Ailleag, see Eas Ailleag, same stream as at Eas Ailleag but further up, in NW corner of Atholl

Feith Seasgachain, fe'ʃeskəxən, bog-stream of barren or reedy place, or of farrow cattle, runs into Tarf, see Drimliafeaheaskichan in notes on Scrope below

(The) Feith Uaine Bheag, ˌfeˌhuan'vek, originally would have been An Fheith Uaine Bheag, the little green bog-stream, green referring to the grassy ground by the burn, runs into Tarf Water

(The) Feith Uaine Mhor, ˌfeˌhuan'voːr, originally as above would have been An Fheith Uaine Mhor, the big green bog-stream, pairs with the above burn, note Thomson and Knox gave Auld Fevuany, which may suggest Allt Feith Mhonaidh, burn of bog-stream of the hill

The Garra Buidhe, not on OS, ˌgaraˈbui, the burn running into Glen Tilt from near Loch Tilt is Allt Garbh Buidhe or rough yellow burn, but the old stalkers on Mar and Fealar often spoke of "gaan ower (going over) the Garbh Buidhe" to mean the low pass west of Meall a' Chrombaig to Fealar Lodge, a handy short-cut to Fealar from Allt Garbh Buidhe below Loch Tilt, and also on good going with mainly grassy terrain, D suggested from Gearradh Buidhe or yellow cut, so this would be from An Gearradh Buidhe

Gaur, ˈgʌuər, the River Gaur flows into Loch Rannoch below Bridge of Gaur, in Gaelic was Gamhar (Watson 1926), Avon Gaur (Blaeu) so Abhainn Gamhar, river of Gaur, Gamhar a wintry stream or winter stream (Watson 1926), alluding to its flooding, Gawyr syd (i.e. Gaurside) in Pont

An Glas Choire, ˈglasˌxor, the green corrie, should be An Glas-choire, S of An Sgarsoch

Glas Choire Lodge, ˈglasˌxor, from An Glas-choire, the green corrie

Glas Feith Beag, ˈglaʃeˈbek, Glashy beg (Thomson), should be Glais-fheith Bheag, little green bog-stream, up Tarf

Glas Feith Mhor, ˈglaʃeˈvoːr, Glashy more (Thomson), should be Glais-fheith Mhor, big green bog-stream, up Tarf

Glas Tulaichean, glasˈtulxan (one old resident), commonly glasˈtʌlxan, Glashtulchan Hill (Stobie, Thomson), Glasstulchin (Brown), Glash Tulchan (Knox), OS form suggests green hillocks or little hillocks, not fitting such a big wide-spreading hill, so maybe Glas-thulchann, Tulchann a gable or backside or stern, with Glas green (Watson 2013), pronunciation has changed to have stress on second syllable and not on the first as expected from Gaelic speakers, but AW did not hear any stressing the first

Gleann Beag, glauŋˈbek, little glen, pairs with Gleann Mor below Fealar

Gleann Craoinidh, glauŋˈkrone, Glen Crony (Stobie, Thomson, Knox), Gleann a glen, rest uncertain, a small glen N of Glen Tilt

Gleann Diridh, glauŋˈdʒiːri, Glen Deery (Stobie), straight or perpendicular glen, a steep-walled glen at Atholl

Ben Cruachan from Barguillean near Taynuilt, Argyll, April 1998 (AW)

Sandy Walker, Peter Weir and Stuart Rae on Meall a' Bhuiridh view Buachaille Etive Mor (Buachaille Eite Mor, great herdsman of Etive), June 1991 (AW)

Gleann Fearnach, glen'fernət, see Glenfernate Lodge (OS) at glen foot, Gleann Fearnaid, glen of alder-water (Watson 1926), note Glen Fernacht (Blaeu, Moll), in local Gaelic was pronounced glen farnatsh, faurnatsh (Diack),

Gleann Mhairc, glauŋ'mark, glen of the horse, at Atholl

Gleann Mor, glauŋ'mo:r , big glen, pairs with Gleann Beag below Fealar

Glen Banvie, glen'banvi, Gleann Banbhaidh, glen of pig-stream (Watson 1926), near Blair Castle

Glen Brerachan, glen'breraxan, Gleann Briathrachan, glen of little talkative one, referring to the stream (Watson 1926)

Glen Bruar, glen'bruar, glen of Bruar Water, Bruar probably represents an early Celtic word meaning bridge-stream (Watson 1926)

Glen Derby, glen'derbi, in Gaelic was Gleann Geunaid, glen of (probably) goose-stream (Watson 1926), so a strange Anglicisation to Glen Derby

Glen Errochty, glen'erəxte, Gleann Eireachdaidh, glen of assembly (Watson 1926)

Glen Garry, glen'gare, was Gleann Garadh in Gaelic, and thought to be from Garadh a den or copse, and in Perthshire Gaelic dialect the adh of Garadh was not sounded (Watson 1926)

Glen Loch, glen'lox, dark glen, E of Beinn a' Ghlo, holds Loch Loch

Kenaclacher, ˌkena'klaxər, Kinachlachar (Gordon), Kenachlacher (Stobie), Ceann a' Chlachair, end-land of the stonemason, habitation at W end of Loch Rannoch

Killichonan, ˌkɪle'honan, Killyhounan (Thomson), Cill Chonain (Watson 1926), church of Saint Chonan, a settlement on N side of Loch Rannoch

(The) Killichonan Burn, Scottishing from Auld Killyhounan (Thomson) from Allt Cille Chonain, runs into Loch Rannoch at Killichonan

Kinloch Rannoch, ˌkɪnlox'ranəx, Ceann Loch Raineich, end of Loch Rannoch, but earlier was just Keanloch (Blaeu, Moll), Kenloch (Roy), but by time of Stobie's map Kinloch Rannoch

Leacann an Sgailein, ˌljexkanan'skalən, hillside of the shade, N-facing above Loch Ericht

Leathad an Taobhain, ˌleətan'duvən, slope of the rafter, but Roy's Leitten na Tooven suggests Leathadan nan Taobhan or slopes of the rafters, Liateranduva (Thomson) suggests Leitir or hillside, a hill bordering upper Tromie, Lekke-nyn-Tewnan (Macfarlane) suggests Leac nan Taobhan or slope of the rafters, and note Leac an Taobhain OS is marked on E side of the hilltop, as a slope leading into upper Feshie

Loch Eigheach, lox'ejax, see Allt Eigheach for more detail, given as Loch Eyracht (Pont)

Loch Ericht, lox'erəxt, Loch Eireachd, loch of assembly (Watson 1926), Loch Eyracht (Pont), Loch Eyrachty (Roy)

Loch Errochty, see Glen Errochty, from Loch Eireachdaidh, loch of assembly (Watson 1926), Errochty pronounced as in Glen Errochty, note that the current River Ericht flowing out of Loch Ericht was Avon Eyrachty (Pont) from Abhainn Eireachdaidh, Abhainn a river, so the aidh seems a mere suffix, River Eyrachty (Roy)

Loch Loch, lox'lox, dark loch, E of Beinn a' Ghlo

Lochan a' Chlaidheimh, ˌloxana'xlae, lochan of the sword (story noted by Grimble), Loch Achlay (Roy), Loch-anachly (Stobie), Lochan Chlaimh (Thomson), note how mh at end of Chlaidheimh is not sounded in Perthshire Gaelic, as in Strathspey, near Rannoch Station

Lochan Sron Smeur, ˌloxanˌstroin'sme:r, following the OS spelling, Lochan Sron Smeur, lochan at hill-nose of fruit resembling a blackberry, see Sron Smeur for detail, and note that it is Loch Stronier (Roy), Loch-an-Stron-muin (Stobie), Lochan Stronmuin (Thomson), see Sron Smeur for explanation, W of foot of Loch Ericht, an interesting name of a tiny lochan E of Lochan Sron Smeur is Lochan Ruighe na Doire Macmhadagain (OS), a name that is not on earlier maps such as Thomson's and that I did not hear from local people, but a straight translation is lochan of cattle-run or shiel of the copse of son of a small wolf

(The) Lochan Uaine, ˌloxan'uan, from An Lochan Uaine, the green lochan, E of Fealar Lodge

(The) Mam Ban, mam'ba:n, Mam ban (Thomson), from Am Mam Ban, the fair or white pass, W of Loch Ericht

Mam Ban, mam'baːn, Mam-bane (Stobie, Thomson), fair or white pass or hill, W of Dalnaspidal

The March Burn, see Dubh Alltan

Am Meadar, 'metar, the milk-pail, refers to hill's shape, Meeter (Stobie), Medher (Scrope)

Meall a' Chrombaig, mjal'xrombi, Meal chrombeg (Thomson), Crom is curve, and the rest may be a mere suffix, but uncertain, note that Water of Crombie at Glen Livet in local Gaelic speech was uisg chromi (Diack), hence chromaidh meaning curved one (Watson 2013), so Meall a' Chrombaig may be Meall a' Chromaidh, especially as a map at Blair Castle by Stobie in 1780 had it as Benecrombie with no g (see Watson & Allan 1984), and as Camas in Anglicised or Scotticised form is often Cambus with a redundant unsounded b in local dialect but a sounded b among outsiders, a hill near Fealar, has a marked curved shape

Meall a' Mhuirich, mjal'vuːrəx, Malvourich (Scrope), I got no meaning, literally the OS form means hill of the leper but Dwelly gives Muireach as an obsolete form, one wonders whether Meall a' Bhuirich or hill of the roaring, as in Beinn Vuirich, is better for this hill which is part of the Beinn a' Ghlo deer forest

Meall Gorm, mjal'gorəm, green hill-lump, N of Loch Rannoch

Meall na Mucarach, ˌmjalna'muxkarax, Meall na Mucaireachd, lump-hill of the swine-herding, at Rannoch

Meall nan Eun, ˌmjalnan'jeːn, Meall nanean (Thomson), lump-hill of the birds, NW of Beinn a' Chuallaich

Meall na Spionaig, ˌmjalna'spiːnək, Meal na spinaig (Thomson), Meal na Spinaig (Knox), OS form means literally poorly nourished hill, but maybe from Spion or torn out, as with the Spion Rocks in Glen Avon, and Meall na Spionaig has many protruding rocks on its E shoulder, SW of Fealar Lodge

(The) Miadan Mor, ˌmiadan'moːr, Am Miadan Mor, the big meadow, S of Fealar Lodge, Miadan in Deeside and east Perthshire as against a dialect form Meadan in Strathspey Gaelic

Minigaig, given by Roy as Minigag, Anglicised from Monadh Mion-ghaig, ˌmona'minəˌga'ək, hill-range of smooth Gaick (see MacBain), locally Monadh Ghaig (Diack with Grant) presumably on Speyside, where Grant was raised, but AW recorded Perthshire pronunciation as in first line above

Pitcarmick, pɪt'karmək, Pit is from Pictish Peit a share of land, in this case Cormac's share (Watson 1926), so Peit Cormaic, now a house, estate and moor in Strath Ardle, see Pitmain in Inverness list for spelling Peit or Pett

Poll Tarf, not on OS which has Falls of Tarf, pol'tarf, Pol Tarff (Roy), pool of Tarff

Rannoch, 'ranəx, from Raithneach or bracken (Watson 1926), a district name as well as in place names such as Loch Rannoch, Rennoch (Macfarlane)

Rathad nan Cuimeineach, ˌraətna'gumənax, road of the Comyns or Cummings, according to AW's Perthshire informants on Atholl in the late 1960s, this path runs north over Sron a' Chleirich and Bac na Creige to Gaick, also known to them more commonly as Comyns' Road or Cummings' Road, see Watson (1992), path rendered by OS on Inverness side as Rathad nan Caoirneach is erroneous

River Tilt, tëlt, in Gaelic (Watson 1926) was Abhainn Teilt, Abhainn a river, Teilt uncertain

Schichallion, ʃi'haljən, Suy Challen (Pont), Sidh Chailleann (Watson 1926), fairy hill of Caledonians

Sgairneach Mhor, ˌskarnjax'voːr, big stony place, a hill at south Drumochter

Sgor Choinnich, skor'xuːnjix, peak of the moss, at Rannoch

Sgor Gaibhre, Sgur Gaoibhre (Thomson), skor'gaiər, rocky peak of goat, W of foot of Loch Ericht

An Sgulan, n'skulan, the basket, a hill above Loch Ericht

An Sligearnach, n'ʃligərnax, the shell-place, shelled snails abound there, up Tarff

An Sligearnach, ðr'ʃligərnax, the shell-place, up from Dalnamein Lodge

An Sligearnach, ðr'ʃligərnax, in local Gaelic was pronounced sliogarnach (Diack), the shell-place, above Glen Tilt

(The) Sow of Atholl or Meall an Dobharchain, I heard only the English name, the Gaelic one means lump-hill of the otter, should be Meall an Dobharchoin (literally water-dog)

Sron a' Chleirich, ˌstrona'xliːrix, Stronachlirach (Stobie), Stron Achlirach (Knox), hill-nose of the cleric

Sron Gharbh, stron'gara, following OS spelling, but Thomson had Meal garrow na glashy, obviously from Meall Garbh na Glais-fheith, however there may well have been two names, and the OS location on a flat

In the warmth of a temperature inversion at sunset on 6 January 1973, Adam Christopher Watson looks at a Perthshire panorama from Glas Maol, with Beinn a' Ghlo in the distance rising out of frost fog and Glas Tulaichean to its right (AW)

hill-top does not fit a hill-nose, so Sron Gharbh may have been the obvious hill-nose with many boulders, facing S towards Tarf and about a km S of the hilltop, and Meall etc for the hilltop

Sron Smeur, ˌstroinˈsmeːr, following the OS spelling, from Sron Smeur, hill-nose of fruit that is a bramble or resembles a blackberry, and in this situation it is too acidic and wet for bramble, so the cloudberry is a likely possibility for it thrives on thick peat, however, Stobie has Stron-muine and Thomson has Stronmuin, so Sron Moine or hill-nose of peat-moss, which seems more likely than Smeur, and note muine and muin resemble the pronunciation of Moine in the Gaelic dialect of Badenoch nearby, W of foot of Loch Ericht

Sronphadruig Lodge, stronˈfatrək, Sron Phadruig, hill-nose of Patrick

Talla Bheith, ˌtalaˈveː, from Tall a' Bheithe, crag of the birchwood (Watson 1926), a deer-forest at Loch Rannoch and a settlement by the loch

Tarf Water, tarf, from Tarbh a bull

An Torc or Boar of Badenoch, ndɔrk, the boar, Tork, or The Duke of Atholl's boar (Scrope), a hill near Dalnaspidal

Uchd a' Chlarsair, ˌuxkaˈxlarsər, Ochnichlarser (Roy), hill-brow of the harper

Uchd na h-Analach, ˌuxknaˈhanalax, Oucht nahannaloch (Thomson), Ought na Hannaloch (Knox), hill-brow of the breath (i.e. steep ascent), on the Minigaig track

Vinegar Hill, should be A' Mhin-choiseachd, əˈvinˌxoʃaxk (see Scrope 1894, MacBain 1922, also Alick Sutherland to me), means the easy walking (MacBain), absurd OS Anglicisation

Below are a few interesting names not heard by AW, not on OS 1:25000 maps, but published by Scrope in his book Scrope's lists of Gaelic names include many others that are not on OS 1:25000 maps and appear to be unpublished. His book would repay detailed study along with searching of old estate plans and other estate documents.

North side of Tarf

Corrie Stock Guise, from Coire Stoc Giuthas, corrie of pine-stump with Giuthas in an adjectival sense to judge from Scrope's spelling, obviously the corrie drained by Allt Coire an Stuic Ghiuthais OS

Drimliafeaheaskichan, from Druim Liath Feith Sheasgachan, ˌdruimˌliaˌfeˈheskixan, ridge of bog-stream of barren or reedy places, 911808, note Leachdann Feith Seasgachain OS marked at hilltop to N, a ridge on N side of Tarf

Druim Minagag, from Druim Mion-ghaig, see Minigaig, ridge of Minigaig, 818822, runs S into Atholl

Glengarry Forest (now Dalnacardoch Forest and Dalnamein Forest)

Mal cham corrie, from Meall Cham-choire, obviously a round hill beside Cama Choire OS, maybe the one E of A' Bhuidheanach Mor

Sroin Craig an Loch, from Sron Creag an Loch, nose of Creag an Loch, the only hill-nose is to the SE, N of An Sligearnach

Sroin Glasechorrie, from Sron Glas-choire, nose of green corrie, ridge E of Glas Choire OS

After reading Watson (2013), Dr Iain Smart sent AW a letter about names in Glen Shee. He wrote that 'the presence of Persey Kirk and Manse is not noted in the book. We lived in the Manse for fifty years! The Kirk in 1961 when we arrived was unused but in working order with pews and pulpit and even a gallery in good wood. Then one day we found the woodwork had gone. Next, a door was knocked in the side and it was used as a barn for storing hay. Then it was bought and a conversion started for a dwelling house. They ran out of money and it is now deteriorating again.'

'There is a big pool on the Ericht half a mile south of the Manse known as Poldronach. Two interesting stories about that: Fergusson of Shieldrum, the farm high on the opposite side of the river, used to say, "if I can hear the Poldronach singing I know there will be rain." i.e. when there is a strong wind from the SW. Lady

Ashmore wrote a poem about it, saying Fingal's golden goblet fell in and can still be seen glinting on sunny days. I have never seen it myself".

'Drumore, I was told, was originally Druim odhar and not Drum mor, and was so pronounced by the older people' (AW also heard Druim Odhar, as noted in Watson 2013).

'There used to be a house in Glen Beg about the level of Iron Bridge that was entered on old maps as Cronachri. Geordie Livingstone, a glen native, knew of it and pronounced it Cro na Chri. It is barely traceable now but once was considered a desirable holding. possible because of the grassy corrie to the east below Creag Leacach.' AW reminded Iain of Cro na h-Airighe OS, but it lies further down Gleann Beag. Iain is aware that he might have mistaken it with Cronachri, but is fairly sure that he heard it pronounced as Cronachri, stress on chri.

Iain thought that Poldronach would be Poll Dronnach, white backed or white rumped pool, which would fit, because he wrote that a short white waterfall tumbles into it.

Cro is a cot, as in Cro na h-Airighe further down Gleann Beag. The meaning of na Chri is uncertain, might be Cro na Chridhe or cot of the heart or centre, as suggested by Iain, but Cridhe is usually a masculine noun.

Moray

Anagach, usually now pronounced 'anagax, following OS spelling, but Pont gave it as Anacach, and Roy likewise, and Roy in addition a nearby Loch Anacach, Diack recorded it in local Gaelic speech as ankach, anakach and angach with emphasis on an, and Hamish Marshall told me that old folk called it 'aŋgax, it is by Spey, so first part maybe Ath or ford

Auchnahannet, ˌaxnaˈhanət, Achadh na h-Annaide (Watson 1926), field of the ancient church, a farm NE of Grantown

(The) Beachan Wood, 'beˈaxan, Am Beitheachan, the little birch place

Ben Aigan, binˈeˈgən, Beinn Eiginn, hill of difficulty (Watson 1926), in local Gaelic pronounced bing aikin, ping ekin (Diack 1944), has a steep face on one side

Beum a' Chlaidheimh, ˌbemaˈxlaˈe, gash of the sword, Thomson gave it as Scournan Chlai, so Sgoran a' Chlaidheimh or rocky points of the sword, a rocky gap N of Duthil

Cawdor, 'kaˈdər, a regional name, now in Nairnshire but formerly included part of Inverness-shire and Moray, also name of an Earldom, and a Thanedom in King Macbeth's time, was Caladair in Gaelic (MacBain), meaning hard water, pronounced in local Gaelic caladir, chalter (Diack), the OS past habit of altering an a sound into au or aw in numerous place names has resulted in the official formal pronunciation of Caw being as in English cawing of rooks

(The) Craggan, from An Creagan, n'grekan, the little rocky place, crofts Upper and Lower Craggan named after the general area

Craigellachie, kreg'elaxe, Creag Ealachaidh, cliff of stony or rocky place, note the cliff by River Spey below the village

Dallas, 'dalas, Dail a haugh, Fas a level stance or station and in combination Dallais (Watson 1926), in local Gaelic speech dallash (Diack)

Darnaway, in Gaelic tarranich, tarnich (Diack), Taranaich (Watson 1926) and he gave 1300s forms as Ternway and Terneway, and quoted Lachlan Shaw as writing that it was probably from taran or tarnach, thunder, thunder in Gaelic is torunn and in Cornish taran, and Watson concluded that Taranaich represented an early British Taranu-magos or thunder-plain

Dava, 'daˈva, in local Gaelic speech was n dava (Diack), from An Damh-ath, the ox-ford

Divie, 'duvi, usually now 'dɪvi following misleading OS spelling, in Gaelic Dubhaidh or Duibhidh maybe for dubh-dhea or black goddess , and sometimes was Dubhag or little black one (Watson 1926), duibhidh or little black burn (Diack 1944)

Duffus, 'dʌfəs, from Dubhais (Watson 1926) or black stance, in local Gaelic speech du-ash with long u (Diack), see Dallas

Dulsie, was 'dulasi to oldest speakers, now usually 'dʌlsi, in Gaelic was Dulasaidh for Dulfhasaidh, and Dulsie Bridge was Drochaid Dhulfhasaidh, Dul a meadow and Fasadh a stance, so meadow-stance (Watson 1926), Diack recorded it in Gaelic speech as tullasi, and the bridge as droichet ullasi

Elchies, 'elaxe, in local Gaelic ellachie (Diack 1944), Ealachaidh, at stony or rocky place, as in Craigellachie, with s an Anglicised plural

Elgin, 'elgən, in Gaelic Eilginn (MacBain, Watson 1926, Diack), recorded in Gaelic speech as elikin with palatal n (Diack), derivation uncertain, see discussion on it in Watson (1926)

Feakirk, fe'kёrk, from Feith Circe, bog-stream of hen, Circe often refers to grouse or greyhen, former farm up Divie, near the Falls of Feakirk

Findhorn, in Gaelic was Eire, in local speech er (Diack), from Fionn-eire or white water where Fionn was added later to identical original names as with Dubh-eire or black water in Deveron (Nicolaisen 1976), and the rivers Earn as well as Ahr and other rivers on the west European continent (Nicolaisen 1976), the river in Gaelic local speech was 'uisg eir rather than abhainn eir' (Diack)

(The) Gaich, 'gøəx, An Gaothach, the windy place, an exposed farm on a long wide flat

Inverallan, ˌɪnjər'alan to oldest Gaelic speakers, usually now ˌɪnvər'alan, an old parish name and a house Inverallan which stands near the mouth of a stream, in Gaelic was Inbhir Ailein (Watson 1926), Allan a common stream name in Scotland, suggested by Watson (1926) as from Old Irish ail a rock, can also mean stone, the burn at Inverallan has long been known as the Glenbeg Burn (OS), but Diack wrote that older folk knew it as Allan

Kylintra, ˌkɛilən'traˑ, Coille an t-Srath, wood of the valley, at Grantown

Carn an Righ from Glas Tulaichean during a ski-mountaineering tour, 5 April 1980 (AW)

Loch na Bo, ˌloxnaˈboˑ, from Loch nam Bo, loch of the cows

(The) Moidach More, ˌmɔˈindjaxˈmoˑr, Am Mointeach Mor, the big peat-moss, at Dunphail

The Mossie, ˈmɔse, not on OS 1:25000, Scots little moss, a bog at Grantown

Muckrach, from Mucrach, ˈmuxkrax, pig-place

Relugas, rəˈluˑgəs, in Gaelic was ri-llugash with long i and u, raoi-lukash with long u, perhaps Ruighe Luig-fhais, shiel or cattle-run at hollow stance, like Dunlugas on Deveron with Dun a hill (Watson 2013)

Rothes, ˈroθəs, from Rathais (Watson 1926) or fortunate stance, ra-ash (Diack)

(The) Shennach, ˈʃɛnax, Diack recorded it in Gaelic speech as n dshennach, An Sean-achadh, the old field, two farms Wester and Easter in north Cromdale

Spynie, ˈspini, Gaelic Spiathanaigh at little hawthorn place, Spey in Gaelic was Abhainn or Uisge Spe, where Spey or 'Speith is genitive of a noun, Spiath, whose diminutive is Spiathain' (Watson 1926) as in river Spean, Spey being 'hawthorn stream', and a 'broch near Lentran, Inverness, is called Caisteal Spiathanaigh, Castle Spynie'

The Streens, striˈnz, in Gaelic was Na Srianaibh meaning at the bridles (Watson 1926), na strianu (Diack), a long gorge on Findhorn

Toperfettle, ˌtopərˈfetəl, Tobar Feudail, maybe well of cattle or booty, farm near Grantown

Upper Banff

In this section, the term 'early maps' refers to unpublished estate plans, the original copies of which are held at Register House in Edinburgh. AW inspected them while preparing his book on place names published in 2013. Other early maps available online from the National Library of Scotland are referred to by the map-maker's name, such as Pont, Gordon, Roy, Thomson etc.

The Ailnack Gorge, not on OS, see Water of Ailnack for pronunciation and meaning of Ailnack, a long gorge that runs for miles

Alltachbeg, ˌaltaxˈbeg, a house near Tomintoul, beside a burn Alltach Beag

(The) Alltach Beag, ˌaltaxˈbek, from An t-Alltach Beag, Allt a burn, and the suffix ach may be emphasis such as the burn-place, a long burn running straight downhill

Alltach Mor, ˌaltaxˈmoˑr, big burn-place, a burn further E and also running straight downhill

Allt an t-Seallaidh, ˌaltənˈdʒɔl, burn of the view, below Beinn Mheadoin

Allt Coire Ruairidh, ˌaltkoˈruːari, burn of Rory's corrie, drains N into River Avon

Allt Cumh na Coinnich, see Cumh na Coinnich for pronunciation, plus alt in front, a burn draining from Cumh na Coinnich into Glen Avon

(The) Allt Dearg, altˈdʒerək, from An t-Allt Dearg, the red burn, on A' Choinneach

Allt na Ha, ˌaltnaˈhaˑ, Allt na h-Atha, burn of the kiln, in Strath Avon

Alltnaha, as above, a farm at foot of Allt na Ha

Allt Nathrach, ˌaltanˈarax, Altenarrow, Altan Arach, Aultan Arrach, Shealings of Aultan Arach on old maps suggest that the name is Alltan Aireich, burnie of grazier or possible Alltan Nathrach of serpent (Watson 2013), note also the Pass of Alltanarrach in Glen Avon and Coire Nathrach at the head of the burn could be Coire an Aireich or Coire Nathrach

Allt nan Stacan Dubha, ˌaltnaˌstaxkanˈduˑ, burn of the black cliffs, runs down to Loch Avon

Allt Ruigh Mhath, altˌraˈvaˑ, should be Allt Ruighe Mhath, burn of good cattle-run, S of Delnabo

Altrava, pronounced as above, a house beside above burn

Auchnarrow, axˈnara, Auchenarraw (Roy), Achadh an Arbha, field of the corn, crofts and settlement at Glen Livet

Avonside, aˈnˈseid, not on OS but in Peck who also gave A'anside, a name for anywhere beside the River Avon

The Back Dykes, not on current OS but noted by Gaffney (1976) and Peck, on either side of the main road through Tomintoul is a parallel narrow road, and this name refers to the stone dykes that formed the back of the row of tenants' houses and accompanying land on the inner side of each of the two roads

Badivochel, ˌbadiˈvoxəl, Bad a' Bhuachaille, clump of the herdsman, crofts, there were two former farms Badowachall more and beg (Pont), so Bad a' Bhuachaille Mor (big Badowachall), and Bad a' Bhuachaille Beag (little Badowachall) below the Bochel

Ballindalloch, common pronunciation has long followed the OS spelling, but in Gaelic sounded bal n dalach, bal na dalach (Diack), Balnadalach (Pont), from Baile na Dailich, farmstead of the haugh place

(The) Barns Corrie, on E side of Beinn Mheadhoin below the tors or barns

(The) Barns of Bynack, ˈbarnzaˈbaenək, tors on Bynack More, in Gaelic were Sabhalan Mora Beidhneig or big barns of Bynack (Watson 2013)

(The) Big Brae, a flat-topped shoulder of Ben Avon with a steep brae to the S, was The Bruach More on an old map, so A' Bhruthach Mhor, the big bank or brae (Watson 2013)

Big Garvoun, ˈgarawon, following OS spelling, but on old maps Garrowhome more, so Garbh-thom Mor or big rough knoll (Watson 2013), in upper Glen Avon

The Bishop's Well, waˈl in local Scots, not on OS, 246195, a few metres downstream from the Scalan in Glen Livet, visited by IM in September 2013

(The) Black Water, ˈblakˈwatər, in Gaelic the sound was tushk du (Diack), hence An t-Uisge Dubh, the black water, runs into Deveron, also (The) Blackwater Forest (deer forest) and Blackwater Lodge named after it

Blairnamarrow, ˌblarnaˈmara, Blar nam Marbh, field of the dead, former farm, now house, first one towards Tomintoul from the Lecht

The Bochel, ˈboˈxəl, Bochill (Roy), in upper Banffshire Gaelic was buachil (Diack), from Am Buachaille, the herdsman, prominent hill below the Braes of Glen Livet

Bothan Dubh, ˌbohanˈduˈ, black bothy, Shealings of the Boandu on an old map show the location as 974951 (Watson 2013), SW of Faindouran Lodge

Bothan Robaidh, ˌbohanˈrobi, bothy of Robbie, in upper Glen Avon

The Braes of Avon, not on current OS but in Gaffney (1976), ˈbrezaˈaˈn, hills around lower Glen Avon

(The) Bridge of Brown, (The) Burn of Brown, and Glen Brown, locally The Brig o Broon, ˈbrɪˈgaˈbrun, also The Burn o Broon, and Glen Brown locally Glen Broon, now pronounced brun, originally bruin, as noted correctly by Queen Victoria, Brown is absurd Englishing from Gaelic Allt Bruthainn, burn of sultry heat (Watson 1926), Nicolaisen (1976) gave Bruthainn as raging

The Bruach, ˈbruax, A' Bhruathach, the bank, a steep hill facing down Glen Avon

Bruach Mholach, ˌbruaxˈvoˈlax, rough bank, in Glen Avon

The Buck, locally The Buck o the Cabrach ðrˈbʌkəðrˈkabrəx, in Gaelic was pronounced bochk na cabrich (Diack), Gaelic Boc and English Buck mean a buck such as roebuck, a prominent hill overlooking the Cabrach upper basin

(The) Burn of Loin, loin, Watson (2013) indicated that Loin must be a stream-name like the River Loyne in Inverness-shire, and not the genitive case of Lon a marsh, for there are also Glen Loin, Drum Loin from Druim Loin or ridge of Loin, a freely drained ridge with no marsh, Little Drum Loin which should be Druim Loin or ridge of Loin, Allt Loin Bheag or little Loin burn, which on an old map was Burn of Little Loin (Watson 2013) to the W, Allt Loin Bheag signifying that Loin was feminine, Cnap Loin Bheag, Coire Loin Bheag, and to clinch it Inverloin, as heard by AW ˌɪnvɛrˈloin, from Inbhir Loin or mouth of Loin at the mouth of the burn, all these names heard by AW, Loyne is given in Gaelic as Leana by Dwelly, but MacBain and Watson (1926, 2002) apparently did not investigate the names Loyne or Loin

(The) Burn of Lochy. ˈloxe, locally The Burn o Lochy, in Gaelic Lochaidh a stream-name, dark one (Watson 1926), runs down Glen Lochy to Inverlochy (see Inverlochy below), and then into River Avon

The Cabrach, ˈkaˈbrəx, in Gaelic was a' chabrich (Diack), so from A' Chabraich, the place for growing cabers or tree poles, a basin on upper Deveron

(The) Ca-du Ford, from An Cadha Dubh, kaˈdu, the black pass, a ford on upper Ailnack

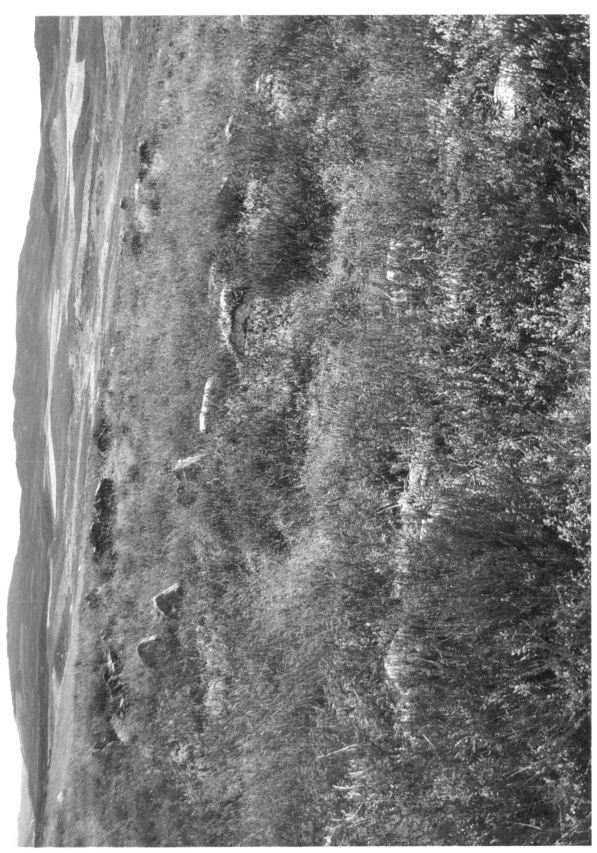

Foundation of a rectangular prehistoric house on an exposed stretch of Pitcarmick Moor far above today's upper fields, soil pits dug by Sandy Walker revealed a cultivated soil that has remained rich for thousands of years, and now contributes to the lush growth of moorland vegetation (Ian Shepherd)

(The) Caiplich, ˈkaˈplix, An Caiplich, the horse-place

Cairnacay, kjarnˈmakae, in Gaelic sounded carn mach ky "Mackay's cairn" (Diack), so Carn MacAoidh, hill or cairn of Mackay, a hill above lower Glen Livet

Campdalmore, ˌkamdalˈmoːr, Camedull (Pont), Camdelmore (Roy, Robertson) for there were two farms, Mor and Beag or big and little, Cam-dail Mor, big crooked haugh, a farm down Strath Avon from Tomintoul, current OS maps

(The) Campdalemore Wood, Campdalemore pronounced as in the name above, with no p sounded, current OS maps increase the Englishing by adding e after dal, as if it were dale, local Scots usage for Wood is Wuid, pronounced as wɪd

(The) Caol Ghleann, ˈkulglən, An Caol-ghleann, the narrow glen, N of Ben Avon

Carn Dearg, karnˈdʒɛrək, red hill, a small hill with reddish gravel above Ailnack

Carn Dubh, karnˈduˑ, black hill, a peaty hill above upper Ailnack

(The) Carn Fiaclach, karnˈfiaxklax, An Carn Fiaclach, the toothed hill, a ridge NE of Ben Avon with a jagged skyline because of rocks

Carn Ruabraich, from Carn Ruadh-bhruthach or hill of red brae, named from a slope of reddish gravel below the hill, a slope which was shown to IM and AW by Donnie Smith, who called it the Ruadh-bruthach (not on OS but in Watson 2013) and gave its meaning, classical Gaelic form would have An Ruadh-bhruthach, the hill Carn na Ruabraich to the S on an old map was Cairn-a-huracher (which Watson (2013) decided was from Carn a' Chorcuir or hill of the white lichen on stones), named after reddish gravel scree below it towards Ailnack, and the hill Carn Ruadh-bhreac W of Ailnack should also be Carn Ruadh-bhruthach and again named after reddish gravel scree towards Ailnack

Carn Ulie, karnˈuli, Carn Ulaidh hill of treasure (Alexander), above Loch Builg

Carnagaval ford (Gaffney 1976), ˌkarnaˈgavəl, Carn a' Ghabhail, cairn of the fork, was across River Avon below Fordmouth

Casfuar, kasˈfuar, cold foot or leg, a former farm above upper Conglass

The Castle, from An Caisteal, ˈkastjal, AW also heard ˈgastjal with k after n becoming a g sound, meaning the Castle, a prominent rock on upper Ailnack gorge

Cathar na Feithe Buidhe, ˌkaharnaˌfeˈbui, boggy ground of the yellow bog-stream, above Ailnack

A' Choinneach, ðrˈkuːnjax, A' Choinneach has now become Anglicised to The Coinneach, both meaning the moss

Ciste Mhearad of Cairn Gorm, should be Ciste Mearaid, Margaret's hollow, kiʃtˈmerət

Clach Bhan, klaxˈvaːn, stone of women, tors on Ben Avon, where women seeking a baby used to bathe in the water held in the pot holes of the granite (Gordon 1925)

Clach Fiaraidh, klaxˈfiare, leaning stone, a tor on Ben Avon

Clach Bun Rudhtair, ˌklaxˌpunˈrutər, Dwelly shows no word Rudhtair, early maps showed Clachpune-ruter, Clach Pune Rutter, and Clach-pune Rutter, so Watson (2013) suggested maybe Clach Buinne Rodeir (should have been Rodair) or stone of statue of wayfarer, Clach Bun Rodair also possible as stone of foot of wayfarer, a group of big tors on Ben Avon

Clashnoir, klaʃˈnoːr, Clais an Fheoir, hollow of the grass, a farm in Glen Livet

Cnapan a' Mheirlich, ˌkrapanˈvjaˈrləx, little knoll of the thief, note that here and in the nearby Lagan a' Mheirlich, as well as more generally in Strathspey, Upper Deeside and upper Banffshire, the OS maps all have the form Meirlich for a thief, whereas it should be the local dialect form Mearlach, pronounced quite differently, on old maps was Cneap Lagganvearlich and Knap Lackanvarlich (Watson 2013)

Cnap Leum an Easaich, Cnap is pronounced krap, meaning a knoll, for pronunciation and meaning of rest see Coire Leum an Easaich, should be Cnap Leum an Easain

Cnap na Cul-ath, ˌkrapnaˈkuˈla, knoll of the Cul-ath, for latter see Glasath Beinn a' Chaorainn, on an old map was Chula beg, which Watson (2013) decided was from A' Chulath Bheag or the little back-place

Cnoc Lochy, kroxkˈloxe, Cnoc Lochaidh, hill of Lochy referring to the stream Lochy (Gaelic Lochaidh meaning dark one), a hill N of Tomintoul, looks down to Inverlochy

Coire an Luichan Shalaich, OS form incomprehensible, ˌkorˌloxanaˈʃarax. should be Coire Lochan nan Searrach, corrie of lochan of the foals (Watson 2013)

(An) Coire Buidhe, nˌkorˈbui, the yellow corrie, named after its extensive grass which is yellow outside the summer, on Beinn Mheadhoin

(An) Coire Buidhe, as above, on upper Ailnack

Coire Domhain, often mispronounced, from An Coire Domhain, nˌkorˈdo:ən, the d at tips of one's teeth and hence almost a t sound, the deep corrie

Coire Leum an Easaich, ˌkorˌlemanˈjesən, should be Coire Leum an Easain, corrie of leap of the little waterfall (see Watson 2013), on N side of Beinn a' Bhuird

Coire Lochan nan Gabhar, not on OS, ˌkorˌloxananˈgʌur, corrie of lochan of the goats, N of Ben Avon

Coire na Coinnich, ˌkornaˈku:njəx, corrie of the moss, S of A' Choinneach

Coire na Coise, ˌkornaˈkoʃ, corrie of the foot, a corrie at foot of a slope in upper Glen Avon

Coire nan Clach, ˌkornaˈglax, corrie of the stones, on N side of Beinn a' Chaorainn

Coire Odhar, korˈʌur, dun corrie, N of Ben Avon

Coire Raibeirt, often mispronounced following OS spelling as Corrie Raybert, should be Coire Robaidh, Robbie's corrie, korˈope, note another Coire Robaidh, this time OS, in upper Glen Avon above Faindouran Lodge

Coire Ruairidh, koˈru:ari, corrie of Rory or Roderick, on N side of Beinn a' Bhuird, near another of the same name on the Dee side of the hill

Conglass Water, ˈkoːnglas, in local Gaelic was uisg conlass, usig chonghlas (Diack), recorded on early maps as Avon Konlash (Pont), Water of Connalash (Gordon), Uisge is water in a stream, Avon from Abhainn a river, the other forms indicate Uisge Chon-ghlais, water of dog-stream, where in Gaelic the Chon would have carried the main stress, with the gh in ghlais almost unsounded

Corryhabbie Hill, korˈhabi, earlier known as Hill of Corchabbie to indigenous residents of Glen Livet as told to AW in the 1940s, on old maps was Hill of Corchabbie and Summit of the Great Hill of Corhabie (Watson 2013), Coryhabbie H. (Thomson), Corryhabbie from Coire Chabaigh or corrie of the little gap (see Watson 2013)

(The) Corrie of the Barns, downhill from Barns of Bynack and Little Barns of Bynack, OS 1:25000 has it in wrong place in the bottom of the glen

(The) Craggan, ˈkragan, in Gaelic was pronounced n grekan (Diack), An Creagan, the little rocky hill, a farm in Strathavon, named after an outcrop of bedrock to the S that projects into the foot of the strath, resulting in a blind summit for the public road

Creag Chailceach, krakˈhalki, not on current OS but on first OS 6-inch map, in Gaelic was pronounced crek halki (Diack), on an early map was Craig Chalky (Watson 2013), Craighalkie from Creag Chailcaidh or limestone rock (Gaffney 1976), Craig Halkie (Peck), was originally an abrupt cliff above the main road, later quarried back as a limestone quarry that is now disused SE of Bridge of Avon at Kylnadrochit, pronunciation would fit Creag Chailcidh or crag of the chalk (Watson 2013)

Creag Dhubh, krakˈduˑ, black crag, above Loch Avon

(The) Creag Mhor, from A' Chreag Mhor, əˌxrakˈvoːr, the big rocky hill, a hill with tors in Glen Avon

Creag na Feithe Buidhe, ˈkraknafeˈbui, (Watson 1975), rock of the yellow bog-stream, above Loch Avon, often now called the Feith Buidhe Slabs

Creagan a' Chaise, ˌkrakanˈhaʃ, I did not hear a meaning in English from an indigenous Gaelic speaker, OS form literally means little rocky hill of the cheese, and the nearby burn Allt a' Chaise, altˈhaʃ, that runs steeply into Glen Lochy is literally burn of the cheese, but these seem unlikely derivations, maybe little rocky hill of the steep place and burn of the steep place, these would fit, for the burn runs straight down a fairly steep hillside and the hilltop is a conical summit, obvious in the view from Grantown on Spey, rising fairly steeply from a plateau, with the rocks on the S and E sides forming a small broken crag

Croughly, 'kruxle, r sounded nasal, on the basis of old forms such as Cruichly recorded in Watson (2013), he suggested Cnuiclidh, at place of hills, Cnuic being the plural of Cnoc, a farm on a slope near Tomintoul

Cul-ath, 'ku:la, back-place, see Glasath Beinn a' Chaorainn for explanation, a burn running into Ailnack

Cul-ath Croise, ˌku:la'kroʃ, following OS spelling, back-place of crossing, but on an old map was Ault na Chula, which Watson (2013) inferred was from Alltan a' Chulath or burnie of the back-place, and certainly it seems more fitting that a burn should be Allt or Alltan rather than Cul, a burn running into Cul-ath (OS), but the old map was not very precise and so may have intended Ault na Chula as covering Cul-ath as well as Cul-ath Croise, and note that two old maps gave The Chulath for the wide corrie E of Cnap na Cul-ath, inferred by Watson (2013) as A' Chulath or the back-place, interesting that although Cul is a masculine noun, Culath was feminine in the cases above Ailnack and on Deeside with The Coolah and Ruighe na Culath (Watson & Allan 1984)

Cul-ath Dubh, ˌku:la'du·, black back-place, a burn running into Cul-ath

Cul na Bruaich, ˌkulna'bruəx, back of the bank, a burn running into Avon, but on an old map was Ault Chulae-na-Bruich, from Allt Chulath na Bruthaich (Watson 2013), more fitting that a burn is Allt rather than Cul

Cumh na Coinnich, ˌkuvna'ku:njəx, OS Cumh does not fit, Cumhang na Coinnich, defile of the moss, E of Beinn a' Chaorainn, with the last syllable ang of Cumhang not sounded as was usual with the last syllable of many nouns in Braemar Gaelic

Da Dhruim Lom, 'da·gruim'lom, following OS spelling, two bare ridges, but on old map was clearly Dagrum Loin and similar with Loin on two other maps (Watson 2013), so Da-dhruim Loin, two ridges of Loin, opposite Glen Loin and Inverloin in Glen Avon

Dagrum, 'da:gruim, Dagriem (Roy), Da-dhruim, two ridges, a hill in Glen Avon

Dail Neilead, dal'neləd, old maps had Dellenislet and Dellen Ilet, so Watson (2013) inferred maybe Dail an Ailleid, haugh of the rugged bank, below The Neilead OS a rough steep slope above the haugh, maybe from An Ailleid the rugged bank (Watson 2013)

Dalestie, dal'ɛste, following OS spelling, but Delesley and Dilleysley on old maps indicate Dail Sleibhe or haugh of moor (Watson 2013), a former farm in lower Glen Avon

Delachule, ˌdela'hul, from Dallachoil, Dellachoil and Dellachcoul on old maps, Watson (2013) inferred Dail Choille, haugh of woods, in Gaelic speech was tallachul (Diack) and Diack wrote of it as Dailchaoile, which might suggest Dail a' Chaoile or haugh of the narrow place, a farm on upper Conglass

Delnabo, ˌdalna'bo·, pronunciation by a Strathspey Gaelic speaker, but commonly now follows the OS spelling which is Scotticised from Dal to Del, as in Aberdeen pronounced Aiberdeen and a glass pronounced a gless,. Dalnabo (Pont), Dalnamboe (Roy), Dail nam Bo, haugh of the cows

Down to Coire Bhachdaidh Lodge and across Loch Ericht to Beinn Bheoil and the snow patches of Ben Alder, July 1974 (David Duncan)

Delnalyne, ˌdalnaˈlɛin, note on pronunciation of Delnabo also applies to Delnalyne via Scotticisation of Dal to Del, Dalnaloin (Roy), from Dail na Loinne, haugh of the enclosure

Drumin, drʌmˈën, in Gaelic sounded drum-yaun, drim-yann, some think it means "kid" (Diack), so Druim Mheann, ridge of kids

(The) Dubh Lochan, ˈduˈloxan, Na Dubh Lochain, the black lochans, below Beinn Mheadhoin

Faindouran Lodge, fenˈdʌurən, Feith an Dobhrain or bog-stream of the otter, lodge named after a nearby burn of that name, in Gaelic sounded fe-an-dobharan (Diack)

Feith an Dobhrain Moss, Gaelic part is pronounced as in name above, on an old map was Faindowran Moss (Watson 2013), which is a good representation of the pronunciation, a small stream and peat-moss at the N end of Tomintoul, Moss is pronounced mos locally

(The) Feith Buidhe, feˈbui, with a few indigenous speakers the b, voiced at their lips, sounded as a p, Feith is usually feminine and so the original would have been An Fheith Bhuidhe, the yellow bog-stream, named after the great expanse of mat grass which is pale yellow except in high summer, rises on Ben Macdui plateau and runs into Loch Avon

(The) Feith Buidhe, as above, a small boggy stream S of Cairn Gorm

(The) Feith Buidhe, as above, a boggy stream draining peaty ground into Ailnack

The Feith Buidhe Slabs, see Creag na Feithe Buidhe

Feith Ghiubhasachain, feˈjuːsaxən, bogs-stream of the little pine wood, runs off N side of Beinn a' Bhuird, on old maps was Ault Faeguisachan and similar on two other maps (Watson 2013), so All Feith Ghiubhsachan, burn of bog-stream of the little pine wood

Feith Laoigh, feˈlui, bog-stream of calf, runs off E side of Ben Avon

(The) Feith Musach, feˈmusax, dirty bog, a flat peat-bog NE of Tomintoul, used for peat production

Fetterletter, ˌfɛtərˈletər, Fotherletter (Roy), in local Gaelic was fo-lehtir with long e (Diack), Fothair Leitir. slope of hillside

Findron, ˈfinrən, Finderin (Roy), Finoron (Thomson), and on two old maps was Findron (Watson 2013) who suggested Fionn-dronn or white ridge, but in view of pronunciation likely Fionn-roinn or white land-portion, a farm near Tomintoul

(The) Folds of Corhabbie, falz, Scots Faulds (outer lands dunged by cattle) here is Anglicised to Folds erroneously but OS spelling of Corhabbie is more accurate than for Corryhabbie Hill, pronounced Falz in local Scots, see Corryhabbie for the rest

Fordmouth, furdˈmuˈ, Scots foord is ford and moo is mouth, on an old map of 1771 was Foordmouth (Watson 2013), which shows the indigenous Scots pronunciation, in local Gaelic bel-ai with long a (Diack), so Beul Atha, mouth of ford, farm near Tomintoul

The Fords of Avon, on old map was Ain na Feann (Watson 2013), Ath nam Fiann, ford of the Fingalians (Gordon 1925), ˌaˈnaˈviˈan with last n almost like ng in English or Scots

Gaffney's Cairn, not on OS but in Peck, a cairn commemorating local historian Victor Gaffney on the site of one of his favourite views, a short distance up the road to Campdalmore farm NW of Tomintoul

The Gallowhill Road, not on current OS but in Peck, public road past Gallowhill Cottage in lower Glen Livet

Garbh Uisge Beag, ˈgaruʃkˈbek, little rough water, on Ben Macdui, drains into Garbh Uisge Mor

Garbh Uisge Mor, ˈgaruʃkˈmoːr, big rough water, was sometimes earlier called An Geur-uisge the vehement water, on old maps Burn of Gaeruisk and Burn of Geruishk (see Watson 2013)

The Garlet, ˈgarlət, An Garbh-leathad, the rough hillside, a rocky slope down from the Lecht

The Garlet, not on OS modern 1:25000 maps, as above, a ruined house below the above slope, also was known as Topliss's Hoose (not on OS), after criminal Mr Topliss on the run took refuge there and shot at an approaching policeman, was later apprehended elsewhere, a former farm

Gaulrig, ˈgʌulrəg, in Gaelic speech was noted as gyaullak,.giaullak, kaulik, kyaulak, and West Gaulrig was gyaulak suas (Diack), the last meaning upper or west Gaulrig, so the original Gaelic would have been Geallaig as in the hill near Crathie, which means white one (Watson & Allan 1984)

Gearr a' Bhogha, ˈgaravoˑ, should be Garbh-bhogha or rough bow, see evidence from old maps in Watson 2013, Gearr as a noun is incomprehensible, a rough low shoulder of Glen Builg

Glasath, ˮglaʃa, so Glaiseath, old maps show Burn of Glasha Bynack, Ault Clasha, Ault Glasha, Burn of Glasha-bynack, so Watson (2013) decided that the original was Allt Glaiseath Beidhneig, which would have distinguished it from Glasath Beinn a' Chaorainn

Glasath Beinn a' Chaorainn, ˌglaʃaˌbinˮxuˑrən, so Glaiseath Beinn a' Chaorainn, stream-place of hill of the rowan, a set of burns, but note Glasath in previous name, Cul-ath Croise and Cul-ath Dubh running into Cul-ath and it in turn are burns that run into Ailnack, Cul being back, and there are no fords, so it seems that ath may be a suffix meaning place, as also in Deeside with names such as The Coolah and Ruighe na Cula (Watson & Allan 1984), see Glasath in above name

Glen Livet, from Gaelic Gleann Liomhaid, glen of shining or flooding one (Nicolaisen, Diack with Grant), glʌunˈliːvətʃ, in Scots Glen Leevit, ˈliˑvət

Glenconglass, for pronunciation see Conglass, Glen pronounced as in Scots, now a farm above lower Conglass Water, but early maps also gave the name for the glen extending from upper Conglass Water to lower

Glenmulliach, a name invented about 1990s by owner of a former cafe and then put on Forestry Commission signs, tourist leaflets and OS maps, was Glen Mullie (OS before the 1990s) ˈmuli, Glen Mule (Roy), Glenmullie on an old map of 1775 (Gaffney 1976), Glenmullie (Thomson), Gleann Muillidh, glen fit for driving a mill, Glenmullie (OS) also a former farm, modern OS maps now extend the error by inventing the name Allt Mulliach, for the burn draining the glen

(The) Hill of Three Stones, locally The Hill o Three Stanes, the Scots word Stanes means English Stones and in upper Banffshire is pronounced stinz like Steens, a hill above upper Cabrach

Inchnacape, ˌinʃnaˈkep, in local Gaelic was pronounced innis-na-ca-ap, innish-na ga-ip, and meant stocks (Diack), Inis nan Ceap, meadow of the tree stocks, a farm near Tomintoul

Inchrory, inʃˈruːari, Innis Ruairidh, meadow of Rory

Inverlochy, ˌinverˈloxe, mouth of Lochy, Inner Lochay (Pont), Innerlochy (Gordon), and Inner lochie (Moll) all kept the Scotticisation Inner, from the Gaelic Inbhir which was pronounced ˈinjər in the Gaelic of Deeside and Strathspey, and as was kept with Innerleithen S of Edinburgh, but Roy gave Inverlochie, and Thomson also continued the Anglicised Inver as did the OS later, note that Diack recorded it in local Gaelic as inner-lochi, a farm at the mouth of the stream

Jock's Hill, ˈdʒoksˈhël, Englished from probable Carn an t-Seabhaig, hill of the hawk, in lower Glen Rinnes

The Kirk o the Craggan, not on current OS but in Peck, a church built on S side of the blind summit of the road above the Craggan, now ruinous

The Kirkie, not on current OS but in Peck, Scots Kirkie is little kirk, on first OS 6-inch map was marked as Church, Chapel of Ease, by Culraggie Bridge below the Bochel in upper Glen Livet

(The) Ladder Hills, Englished from Monadh an Araidh (Watson 1926), hill range of the ladder, on Robert Gordon's surveys Monagan Arie or the Mountains of the Ledder, Araidh and Fharaidh pronounced the same, both mean ladder, Scots laider or ledder is a ladder

Lagan a' Mheirlich, ˌlakanˈvjaˑrləx, little hollow of the thief, see Cnapan a' Mheirlich for explanation of local spelling of Mearlach a thief, and local pronunciation

Lagganauld, ˌlakanˈaˑl, early map shows Laggan Ail, so Lagan Aoil, little hollow of the lime (Watson 2013), which abounds there, a former farm above Inchrory

Lagganvoulin, ˌlakanˈvuˑlən, Lagan Mhuilinn, little hollow of the mill, ruined house SE of Tomintoul

Leacann nan Aighean, ˌljexkananˈaeˑən, hillside of the deer, up Glen Avon

Leachd a' Bhainne, declivity of the milk, or Sleac a' Bhainne, Sleac is a Badenoch and Deeside alternative to Leachd, of same meaning, for pronunciations and other details see Watson (2013)

The Lecht, lext, from An Leachd, the declivity

(The) Liater, ˈliˑxtjər, An Leitir, the slope, steep hillside above Ailnack

Liath Bheinn, 'li·avən, now usually 'liabən or 'liapən, Liath-bheinn or grey hill, prominent from Tomintoul up the E side of Glen Avon

(The) Little Barns of Bynack, 'barnza'baenək, tors on Bynack More, in Gaelic were Sabhalan Beaga Beidhneig or little barns of Bynack (Watson 2013)

Little Garvoun, Garvoun pronounced as in Big Garvoun, but spellings in early maps show Garrowhome beck and Garrowhome peck, so Garbh-thom Beag or little rough knoll, see Watson (2013), a lower hill near Big Garvoun in upper Glen Avon,

(The) Loch Brae, 'lox'bre·, Scots name for a slope W of Loch Builg

Loch Builg, lox'bulək, loch of bag (shape)

Loch Dagrum, ˌloxan‖da:gruim, AW heard it as Lochan, a small loch beside Dagrum

Lochan a' Bhainne, ˌloxan'va·n, following OS spelling, lochan of the milk, but on old map was Lochandu Dagrum, Lochan Dubh Da-dhruim (Watson 2013), below the hill Dagrum

Lochan Beinn a' Chaorainn, ˌloxanˌbin'xu·rən, lochan of hill of the rowan

Lochan Buidhe, ˌloxan'bui, yellow lochan, often was Lochan Feith Buidhe to natives, or lochan of yellow bog-stream, source of the main Feith Buidhe on Ben Macdui plateau

Lochan gun Doimhne, ˌloxanˌkun'do·n, lochan without depth (i.e. shallow), pool on Banff side of the Lecht

Lochan nan Gabhar, ˌloxana'gʌur, lochan of the goats, a lochan below cliffs N of Ben Avon

Lynachork, lɪn'hork, Loinn a' Choirce, enclosure of the oats, former farm W of Tomintoul

Lynavoir, ˌlɪna'vjo:r, in Gaelic was loinn vyor, vyor being grass (Diack), so Loinn Feoir, enclosure of grass, with F becoming a v sound after nn in Loinn, former farm on upper Conglass

Maggieknockater, ˌmagi'nokatər, Magh an Fhucadair, field of the fuller, a settlement

Meall Gaineimh, məl'ga:ne, lump-hill of sand, a sandy shoulder of Ben Avon

Meall Tional, məl'tʃenəl, should be Meall Tionail, lump-hill of gathering, Watson (2013) on old maps noted Maul Tiennal Feagusachan and others similar, so would have been Meall Tionail Feith Giubhasachan, above the burn Feith Giubhasachan

Meur Gorm, mer'gorəm, green finger-stream, after its grassy banks, runs off N side of Ben Avon

Meur Gorm Craig, mer'gorəm'krag, a part Gaelic-part Scottish construction, Craig a rock, there is a West Meur Gorm Craig and an East one

Meur na Banaraich, ˌmerna'ba:narix, finger-stream of the milkmaid, at top of Loch Avon

The Mointeach Dhu, ˌmointjəx'du, not on current OS but in Peck, and in Gaffney (1976) was Moiteach Dhu, on two early maps was Motachow Hill, so A' Mhointeach Dhubh or the black peat-bog (Watson 2013), Carn Meadhonach OS

Monadh nan Eun, ˌmunən'je·n, early maps show Mune as does the pronunciation, so Watson (2013) decided it was Moine nan Eun, peat-moss of the birds, N of upper Glen Avon

Mulben, məl'ben, often mispronounced by radio announcers with stress on mul, in Gaelic was muln pan or white mill (Diack), so Muileann Ban

Mullach Lochan nan Gabhar, ˌmulaxˌloxana'gʌur, summit of lochan of the goats

The Old Packhorse Bridge, not on current OS but in Peck with a drawing, locally in Scots The Aal Packhorse Brig, crosses Livet at Bridgend of Livet

The Pass of Alltanarrach, not on OS, see Gaffney (1960) and name heard from others by AW, see Allt Nathrach for meaning, a pass that went uphill by this burn

Rhynamarst, ˌrəna'marst, Rinnamart (Roy), rui-na-marst "cow" (Diack), so Ruighe nam Mart, cattle-run of the cows, former farm down from the Lecht

The Saddle, pronounced as in English, in Gaelic was An Diollaid, 'dialtʃ, same meaning, on Cairn Gorm

St Bridget (Chapel, Site of), pronounced now as in English, an interesting ancient name after a female Saint Brigid, see Watson (1926) for full account, including his citing of an old record of 'Cromdale Bhrid' which Watson corrected as Camdale and not Cromdale, St Bride's Camdale near Ruthven, Tomintoul, but Watson was incorrect in inferring that it must be the Camdale near Ruthven, well down Strath Avon, for St Bridget was close to Tomintoul village on the site shown on OS maps, Roy marked buildings on the OS site, as Camdelvride, hence Cam-dail Bhride or crooked haugh of Bride or Brigid, Gaffney (1976) gave Wester Camdel (Wester here meaning further upstream, as is common in Gaelic and Scots in Badenoch, Strathspey, Deeside, and upper Banffshire) or Camdell Beag (i.e. Cam-dail Beag or little crooked haugh), also known as Brigid's Camdell or St Bridget's

(The) Scalan, 'ska:lan, in local Gaelic was pronounced skalan with a long a, and meant shelter (Diack), in Gaelic was Sgalan or shelter (see Diack on whether there might have been a definite article in Gaelic), a remote former Roman Catholic college far up Glen Livet

Sgor Riabhach, skor'ri·ax, two early maps show Scorran, so should be Sgoran Riabhach (Watson 2013), brindled rocky points, small cliffs on E side of Ben Avon

The Sgriodan, 'skri·tən, not on OS, An Sgriodan, the stony ravine, a steep scree slope at 133127 above Ailnack

(The) Shelter Stone, locally Stone is Steen in Scots of Dee, Don and Avon, in Gaelic Clach Dhion, klax'yi·n, or stone of the shelter, the coat of arms of the Cairngorm Club is named after Clach Dhion but erroneously is Clac-dian, Clac not being a stone and dian meaning vehement (Watson 1975), a large stone at Loch Avon

(The) Shelter Stone Crag, in Gaelic An Sticil, n'stjixkəl, the rafter, Donnie Smith did not know this name but spoke of The Sticean of Loch Avon, 'stjixkən, Na Sticean, which means the kiln-rafters, referred to precipices jutting out towards Loch Avon (Watson 2013) and hence the Shelter Stone Crag and the cliff of Carn Etchachan

The Silver Bridge, not on current OS but in Peck, in local Scots is Brig, 'sëlvər'brıg, 155265, bridge over River Avon

(The) Slios Min, ʃli·s'mi·n, An Slios Min, the smooth side, on Bynack More

The Snowy Corrie, not on OS, but in Watson (1975, 2013), NE of the summit of Ben Macdui, this is the snowiest corrie in the UK during early and mid summer

The Soldier Stone, not on current OS but in Peck, in local Scots The Sodger's Stane, stane pronounced steen, among birches on W side of main road opposite Cnocfergan Quarry in Strathavon, where a soldier died in 1690, the stone carries the inscription 1690, more details in Peck

(The) Spion Rocks, 'spiən, pluck up or tear, in upper Glen Avon

Sron Ghorm, stron'gorəm, blue hill-nose, on Beinn Mheadhoin

Sron na Bruaich, 'strona'bruəx, hill-nose of the Bruach or bank, in Glen Avon

Stac an Fharaidh, staxka'na·re, cliff of the ladder, above Loch Avon

(The) Stacan Dubha, ˌstaxkən'du·, Na Stacan Dubha, the black cliffs, on Beinn Mheadhoin

Stob an t-Sluichd, ˌstupən'tluixk, point of the Slochd or pit, in Glen Avon

Stob Bac an Fhurain, ˌstupˌbaxkan'u·arən, should be Stob Bac an Fhuarain, point of bank of the spring, on Ben Avon

(The) Suie, 'sui, in Gaelic sounded n sui (Diack), An Suidhe, the level place or seat, a former farm high on thr Braes of Glenlivet, other OS names nearby (The) Suidhe Burn, (The) Tor of Suie which is a protruding low hilltop in Glen Suie, Glen Suie, Suidhe Beag or little Suie, which is a hillside, and Carn an t-Suidhe or hill of the Suie, which is a high hill to the N of Suidhe Beag, all of which AW heard, Carn an t-Suidhe on an old map was The great Hill called the Sowie (Watson 2013), the Suie was Suiarthour in 1638, so Suidhe Artair, Arthur's seat (Watson 1926)

Tom na Bat, ˌtamna'bat, Tom nam Bad, hillock of the clumps, above Tomintoul

Tomintoul, ˌtamən'tʌul, Tom an t-Sabhail, hillock of the barn, now the name of a village

Tomnavoulin, ˌtamna'vu·lən, Toman a' Mhuilinn, little hillock of the mill, a settlement at Glen Livet

Topliss's Hoose, see The Garlet

(The) Torrans, 'toranz, Torran a little hillock, because there were two former farms, Upper and Nether, as shown on an old map (Watson 2013), the collective name is now the Torrans with s a Scottish or English plural

Uisge Dubh Poll a' Choin, ˌuʃk'duˌpol'xo·n, black water of pool of the dog, a burn N of upper Glen Avon

Schichallion framed by a silver birch on the shore of Loch Rannoch, July 1983 (David Duncan)

Water of Ailnack, 'a·lnak, from Ailneag or little stony one (Watson 1926) or more appropriately little rocky one, referring to the stream, which runs down a gorge with cliffs

Water of Caiplich, uʃk'ka·plix, stream of horse place

Native Strathspey Gaelic speaker and farmer Donnie Smith gave many more names than in the above list, as well as pronunciations from Glen Avon, Caiplich and Glen Brown including some that were then unpublished, now published in Watson (2013)

A few Englished names in the Glen More area

The Angel's Peak (OS), from Sgor an Lochain Uaine (OS)

Chalamain Gap (OS), Eag Coir' a' Chomlaich (OS 1902), Eag Coire na Comhdalach or Eag Coire a' Choinneachaidh both meaning gap of corrie of the meeting (Grannd 1999), also Eag Saobhaidhe (Mg), The Chalamain Gap named after the hill Creag a' Chalamain to the north-west, means rocky hill of the dove, and it seems possible that there might have been stock doves in the crags at The Chalamain Gap in former decades (Watson 2013)

CairnGorm and CairnGorm Mountain, the hill Cairn Gorm (OS) was often Anglicised to Cairngorm, and in the mid 1990s the former Cairngorm Chairlift Company changed to CairnGorm Mountain Ltd, an absurd Englishing and tautology because Carn and its Anglicised Cairn means hill or mountain, the description accompanying the web-camera at Loch Morlich mentions the Northern Corries of CairnGorm Mountain, another absurdity

The next few, widely used by climbers and skiers on Cairn Gorm, are not on OS maps.

The Coronation Wall, 004043, steep slope W of Cairn Gorm summit

The Goat Track, E of 990030, steep path in Coire an t-Sneachda, made by red deer, not goats

The Gunbarrel, 996051, straight gully of Allt a' Choire Chais above foot of Coire Cas Tow

The Headwall of Coire Cas, steep top of the corrie, holds a snow-wreath A' Chuithe Chrom or the curved wreath

The 105, on a track E of 000045

The Ptarmigan Bowl, 007048, wide basin at top of Allt na Ciste E of Ptarmigan Restaurant

The Saddle (OS), An Diollaid, the saddle

The Sugar Bowl, 986072, sheltered bowl often holding soft snow in winter

The Traverse, 001047, vehicle track that often has a ski-run

The West Wall, 003061, steep slope in mid Coire na Ciste on W side of Allt na Ciste

The White Lady, 000050, large snow wreath that fancifully resembles a lady with skirt

The Windy Col, E of 999038, slope S of cairn at Fiacaill a' Choire Chais towards the col at Coire an t-Sneachda, an off-piste skiers' name

The Windy Ridge is at An t-Aonach (OS) which means the hill and was known to Gaelic speakers as The Aonach, note The Windy Ridge also covers Sron an Aonaich (OS), nose of the Aonach or hill

The Windy Ridge Path, up the Windy Ridge

The following careless English incorrect translations appear on maps of Glenmore Forest Park by the Forestry Commission and on FC signs, The Green Loch from An Lochan Uaine (OS) which means the green lochan, Serpent's Loch from Lochan nan Nathrach or lochan of the serpents (plural), and Shepherd's Hill, Meall a' Bhuachaille (OS) or hill of the herdsman.

Chapter 9. Misleading OS spellings of Anglicised names in Upper Deeside and other parts of north-east Scotland

The first name in each pair is from current OS maps, followed by an Anglicised spelling nearer to the indigenous pronunciation

Upper Deeside

Auchallater, Achallater, all Auch names are Ach throughout Aberdeenshire

Auchelie, Acheerie

Auchendryne, Achendryne

Auchnerran, Achnerran

Aucholzie, Achylee

Auchtavan, Achtavyann

Aultdourie, Altdowrie, all Ault or Aulton names are Alt or Altan throughout Aberdeenshire

Aultonrea, Altanree

Balhalloch, Balhylach

Ballaterach, Ballaitrach, stress on lait

Balnaut probably printer's error, Balnalt

Baltndory probably printer's error, Balindory

Ben Avon, Ben Aan

Birkhall, Birkha (i.e. Birk Haugh)

Braeriach, Bry Reeach

Brown Cow Hill, The Broon Coo

Burn of Mohamed, The Burn o Mahomet from MacThomaid

Bush, The Buss, also Bush Crathie and Bush Lawsie often printed as if two places, but The Bush is one place, Lawsie another and now changed to Knock Gallery

Cac Carn Beag, Mor, Ca Carn Beag, Mor

Cairn Bannoch, Cairn Byannoch

Cairn of Claise, Cairn na Glasha

Cairn of Gowal, The Cairn o the Gowal

Cairn Toul, Carn Towl

Cairnwell, The Cairnwall

Cambus o' May, Camas a Mei

Carn Aosda, Carn Osh from Aoise

Claybokie, Clabokie

Cnapan Nathraichean, Cnapan Errachar from Cnapan Fhearchair

Coilacriech, Kylachreech

Conachcraig, Conna Chraig stress on Conn

Corbyhall, Corbyha (i.e. Corby Haugh)

Corrienearn, Cornairn

Corrie of Corn Arn, The Corrie o Cornairn

Corrour. Corrower

Coyles, Kyles

Craig Coilich, Craig Kylich

Creag Ghiubhais, The Creag Ewes from Creag-ghiubhas

Creag Moseen, Creag na Sheen

Croft (Muick), The Craft
Daldownie, Daldoonie
Dalmochie, Dalmuchie
Drummargettie, Drum Argity
Ey in Glen Ey and Inverey, Ei
Feardar, Fyarder
Felagie, Filaigie, stress on laig
Glen Fenzie, Glen Fingie
Invercauld, Invercal
Inverchandlick, Inverchanlick
Inverenzie, Inveringie
Khantore, Kintore
Lair of Aldararie, The Lair o Allt Darrarie
Lary, Lairy
Lawsie, Laazie
Lebhall, The Laivel
Loch Kander, Loch Kyander
Loch Ullachie, Loch Yoolachee
Knockie Branar, Knockie Brander
Mealldarroch Cottage, Mildorrach Cottage from A' Mhile Dorcha
Meikle Kinord, Muckle Kinner, all Meikle names are Muckle
Meikle Pap, The Muckle Pap
Micras, The Meecras
Milton of Brackley, Milton of Braichlie
Mount in Mount Battock and Mount Keen, Mun
Muir (Inverey), The Meer
Muir of Dinnet, The Meer o Dinnet
Poolagach Burn, The Poolach Burn
Quartz Cliff, The Slate Quarry (OS 1860s has Slatequarry)
Raebush, Ribuss
Rinasluick, Rinaslake
The Stulan, The Styoolan
Tom Glady Wood, Tam Glaidy Wid
Tornauran, Tornooaran
Turnerhall, Turnerha (i.e. Turner Haugh)
White Mounth, The White Munth

Other parts of north-east Scotland
Aberdeen, in dialect Aiberdeen
Aberlour, Aberlowr
Aboyne, Abyne
Alford, Aford, long a, often mispronounced with short a
Alvah, Aava
Altens, often mispronounced as if Aultens
Alves, Aaviss
Alyth, Ailyth
Ardo, Ardi, in dialect Airdi, second i as in hit

Auch at start of names, Ach
Auchnarrow, Achnarra
Auldearn, Aldairn
Avoch, Ach
Badaguish, Bad Yewish, from Bad a' Ghiuthais
Banchory, Bangchree
Bellabeg, Baillabeg, long e
Benaquhallie, Benachylie, long e in Ben
Birselawsie, Birselaazie
Blackchambers, Blekchammers
Blackhall, Blackhaa
Boltingststone, Bowtensteen
Boyndie, Beenie
Boyndlie, Beinlie, ei as in height
Boynds, Beens
Brimmond Hill, Brimmon without the 'hill'
Brindy, the Breenie
Bucksburn, in rural dialect Boxburn
Bunzeach, the Boonyach
Burnhervie, Burnervie
Cairnacay, Cairn Mackay
Campdalmore, Camdalmore
Careston, Cariston, stress on Car
Catterline, Cetterlin
Causewayend, Cassie Ein
Causey Mounth, The Cassie Munth
Clashnoir, Clashnore
Clatt, Clett
Corsemail, the Corsemal, stress on mal
Cove Bay, the Cove
Covesea, Cowsea, stress on Cow
Coylumbridge, Coylyumbridge
Craibstone, Craibston
Craiglich, Craiglik, stress on lik
Crimond, Creemon
Crimondmogate, Creemonmogit, stress on mog
Crovie, Crivie
Culsalmond, Culsamon, stress on sa
Dalmunzie, Dalmungie
Dalrulzion, Dalrullion
Daugh, Dach, long a
Daviot, Davit, long a
Davoch, Dach, long a
Deskford, Deskert
Downies, Doonies
Drumlithie, Drumleethie
Duncanstone, Duncanston

Dunsinane, Dun Sinnan
Durris, Doars
Edzell, Aigal
Faindouran Lodge, Faindowran Lodge
Findochty, Finechty
Findon, Finnan, i sounded as in e in her
Findrack, Finrack, i sounded as in e in her
Finella, Finlay
Fingray, stress on Fin, i sounded as in e in her
Fintry, also Fintray, Fintree, stress on Fint
Finzean, Fingin
Fisherford, Fisherfyoord
Floors, Fleers
Forbes, Forbiss, castle, parish
Fortrose, stress on fort
Forfar, Farfar
Foudland, Fowdlan
Fourman Hill, The Foreman
Forglen, Foreglin
Fowlsheugh, Fools Heugh
Frendraught, Frendrit, stress on Fren
Friockheim, Freekam
Garioch, The Geerie
Garmond, The Garmon
Garmouth, Germich
Gight, Gicht, i sounded as e in her
Glen Dye, The Glen o Dye
Gourdon, Gurdon
Grandhome, Grannam
Haddo, Haddi, i as in hit
Hazlehead, Hessilheed
Hopeman, Howdman
Inglismaldie, Ingilzmaddie, oldest folk Ingilzmaldie
Johnshaven, Johnshiven
Kerloch, stress on loch
King Edward, Kinedder
Kingussie, Kin Yoosie, from Cinn a' Ghiuthsaich
Kirriemuir, Kirriemair
Knock Hill, The Knock, both k sounded
Knockando, Knock Ando, stress on An
Knockespock, stress on es and each k sounded
Laigh of Moray, The Laich of Moray
Lessendrum, stress on drum
The Ley, Leys, pronounced like ei in height
Lindertis, stress on dert
Lintrathen, Lintraithen
Loch of Strathbeg, Loch of Strabeg (as in Stracathro)

Logie Coldstone, Logie Coalstin
Longmanhill, Langmanhill
Lonmay, Lonmei, ei as in height, stress on mei
Maud, Mad with long a
Mearns, Mairns
Meikle at start of names, always Muckle
Meikle Loch, The Muckle Loch o Slains
Memus, stress on mem
Menmuir, The Maimer, stress on maim
Methlick, e as ai in hair
Mintlaw, Mintla
Montcoffer, Muncoffer
Montgarrie, Mungeerie
Montreathmont, Muntrimmon
Mountblairy, Munblairy
Moray, Murra
Mormond hill, The Moremon
Mosstodloch, stress on tod
Mounthooly, Munheely
Mugiemoss, Muggiemoss
Muir of Fowlis, Meer a Fools
Muirden, Meerden, stress on den
Muirskie, Mairskee
Netherley stress on ley and pronounced lei with ei as in height
Newburgh, The Neebro
Newe, The Nyow
Oldmeldrum, Al Meldrum
Oldwhat, Alfat
Pole of Itlaw, The Pole o Itla, stress on it
Prosen, Prossin with long o, often mispronounced Prozen following OS spelling
Rannagulzan, Rannagullion
Rosehearty, Risartie, stress on ar
Rothiemay, Rothiemei, ei as in height
Ruthven near Rothiemay, Rivvin
St Cyrus, Sin Ceeris, Ceer as in French Cyr
Sandend, San Ein
Strachan, Straan
Strathbogie, Strabogie
Strathfinella, Stra Finlay
Tarland, Tarlan
Tillynaught, Tillynacht, i sounded as in e in her
Tillypronie, Tillapronie, i sounded as in e in her
Tilt, i sounded as in e in her
(The) Toll of Birness, long o in Toll, stress on Bir, i sounded as in e in her
Torry, Tory, long o
Turriff, Turra
Wardhouse, Waardiss

Whinnyfold, Funnyfaal
Whitehills, Fitehills
Whiterashes, Fiterashes
Wogle, The Waggle
Womblehill, Wummelhill
Wrae, Vrae

The Cromdale Hills rise beyond the colourful autumn woods and a clover field at Inverallan near Grantown, November 1953, (AW)

Bibliography

Alexander, W.B. (1952).The place-names of Aberdeenshire. Third Spalding Club, Aberdeen.

Allan, E. (1995), Burn on the hill. Bidean Books, Beauly.

Bearhop, D.A. (Ed). (1997). Munro's Tables. Scottish Mountaineering Club District Guide, published Scottish Mountaineering Trust.

Bennet, D. (Ed). (1999). The Munros. Scottish Mountaineering Club Hillwalkers' Guide, published Scottish Mountaineering Trust.

Blaeu, J. (1654). Atlas novus. Scotiae et Hiberniae pars quinta. Amsterdam. National Library of Scotland.

Broadhead, D., Keith, A. & Maden, T. (2004). North-west Highlands. Scottish Mountaineering Club Hillwalkers' Guide, published Scottish Mountaineering Trust.

Brown, G. (1808). Plans of the estate of Invercauld in Perth-shire. Register House, Edinburgh.

Burn, R. (1910s & 1920s). Notes on place names from his diaries, originally sent to AW by a London bookseller, deposited by AW at Special Collections in library of University of Aberdeen, notes abstracted and typed by Elizabeth Allan, copied to AW, original typing now at School of Scottish Studies, Edinburgh, copied there by Jake King in 2012.

Burn, R. (1925). Finishing the three thousanders in the Cairngorms. Cairngorm Club Journal 11, 147–153.

Cleasby, R. (author) & Vigfusson, G. (contributor) (1874, republished 2011 by V.L. Agnarsson (compiler). The Cleasby-Vigfusson Old Norse to English dictionary. Create Space Independent Publishing Platform.

Diack, A.M.G. with Grant, J.H. (2006). Place-names of the Cairngorms National Park. Cairngorms National Park Authority, Grantown-on-Spey.

Diack, F.C. (1944). Inscriptions of Pictland. Spalding Club, Aberdeen.

Dorward, J. (2012). Lowdown on the upland of Mar. Disintermediation, Bracknell, and Kindle edition (2011), also website joedorward.squarespace.com.

Drummond, P. (1991). Scottish hill and mountain names. Scottish Mountaineering Trust.

Drummond, P. (2007). Scottish hill names. Scottish Mountaineering Trust.

Dwelly, E. (1901–11). The illustrated Gaelic-English dictionary. Reprinted 1971 by Gairm Publications, Glasgow.

Gaffney, V. (1960). The Lordship of Strathavon. Third Spalding Club, Aberdeen.

Gaffney, V. (1976). Tomintoul, its glens and its people. 2nd edition. Sutherland Press, Golspie.

Gordon, R. (1636–52). Maps at National Library of Scotland.

Gordon, S. (1925). The Cairngorm hills of Scotland. Cassell, London.

Gordon, S. (1934). Highways and byways in the west Highlands. Macmillan, London.

Gordon, S. (1948). Highways and byways in the Central Highlands. Macmillan, London.

Grannd, S. (1999). Donnchadh Grannd. In the shadow of Cairngorm (Ed by J.K. Campbell), Appendix IX, 373–374.

Grannd, S. (2013). Gaidhlig Duthaich Mhic Aoidh. The Gaelic of the Mackay Country, dialect and vocabulary. Taigh na Gaidhlig Mhealanais.

Grant, W. & Murison, D.D. (1929–76). The Scottish National Dictionary. SND Association, Edinburgh.

International Phonetic Association (1963). The principles of the International Phonetic Association. University College, London.

Joyce, P.W. (1869, 1871). Irish names of places. Vols 1 and 2, and (1913) Vol 3, all Dublin. Reprinted 1976, E.P. Publishing, Wakefield.

Knox, J. (1850). Map of the basin of the Tay including the greater part of Perth Shire, Strathmore and the Braes of Angus or Forfar. In National Library of Scotland.

Loader, C.M. (1952). Cairngorm adventure. William Brown, Edinburgh.

MacBain, A. (1922). Place names Highlands and Islands of Scotland. Eneas Mackay, Stirling.

McConnochie, A.I. (1923). The deer and deer forests of Scotland: historical; descriptive; sporting. H.F. & G. Witherby, London.

Macfarlane, W. (c1725). Geographical collections relating to Scotland made by Walter Macfarlane. Ed. by A. Mitchell for the Scottish History Society, published 1906–08. Some collections are based on much earlier notes by Pont and Gordon.

Mearns, S.N. (late 1940s). Around Strathspey. Mearns Publications, 7 Union Row, Aberdeen.

Milne, R. & Brown, H. (2002). The Corbetts and other Scottish hills. Scottish Mountaineering Club Hillwalkers' Guide, published Scottish Mountaineering Trust.

Moll, H. (1745). A set of thirty-six new and correct maps of Scotland divided into shires. National Library of Scotland.

Murray, I. (1998). A tribute to an aald Deeside residenter. Leopard Magazine No 235, 18–20.

Murray, I. (1999). The Dee from the far Cairngorms. Lochnagar Publishing, Alt na Craig, Ballater.

Murray, I. (2010). The Cairngorms and their folk. Lochnagar Publications, Alt na Craig, Braemar Road, Ballater.

Murray, J. (2014). Reading the Gaelic landscape. Whittles Publishing, Caithness.

Nicolaisen, W.F.H. (1976). Scottish place-names. Batsford, London.

Nicolaisen, W.F.H. (1979). Field-collecting in onomastics. Names 27, 162–178.

Ordnance Survey (1973). Place names on maps of Scotland and Wales. OS, Southampton.

Peck, E.H. (1983). Avonside explored. Published Edward H. Peck, Tomintoul.

Perry, R. (1948). In the high Grampians. Lindsay Drummond, London.

Pont, T. (1583–1601). Maps of Scotland. National Library of Scotland.

Robertson, J. (1822). Topographical and military map of the counties of Aberdeen, Banff and Kincardine. National Library of Scotland.

Roy, W. (1747–55). The military survey of Scotland. National Library of Scotland.

Scrope, W. (1894). Days of deer-stalking in the Scottish Highlands. Hamilton Adam, London.

Stobie, J. (1783). The counties of Perth and Clackmannnan. Map in National Library of Scotland.

Thomson, J. (1823–30). Maps of Scottish counties. National Library of Scotland.

Watson, A. (1975). The Cairngorms. SMC District Guide.

Watson, A. (1992). Book review of Drummond (1991). Scottish Mountaineering Club Journal 35, 169–170.

Watson, A. (1997). Human-induced changes in numbers of red deer in the Cairn Gorm area. Deer 10, 278–281.

Watson, A. (2013). Place names in much of north-east Scotland. Paragon Publishing, Rothersthorpe, Northampton.

Watson, W. J. (1904). Place-names of Ross and Cromarty. Northern Counties Publishing, Inverness.

Watson, W. J. (1904–05). The study of Highland place-names. Celtic Review 1, 22–31.

Watson, W.J. (1916). Some place-names in the Cairngorm region. Cairngorm Club Journal 8, 133–136.

Watson, W. J. (1926). The history of the Celtic place-names of Scotland. Blackwood, Edinburgh.

Watson, W. J. (1934). Glossary of place-name elements, both Norse and Gaelic. In Gordon (1934), pp. 409–414.

Watson, W. J. (2002). Scottish place-name papers (republished from W. J. Watson's collected published works). Steve Savage, London & Edinburgh.

Weir, T. (1948). Highland days. Cassell, London.

Whitehead, G.K. (1960). The deerstalking grounds of Great Britain and Ireland. Hollis & Carter, London.

Zoega, G.T. (2013). A concise dictionary of Old Icelandic. Dover Language Guides.

Acknowledgements

We are grateful to Mrs Lydia Thomson, then Editor of CCJ, for welcoming our plans to republish, and thank Joe Dorward for sending some information (see also Dorward 2012).
Above all we thank our many informants for their patience, interest, generosity and hospitality, and we have named them individually in several chapters. This book would not have been possible without their help. They are a tribute to the value of local identity and its continuance into the future.

The Ailnack Gorge near Tomintoul, Banffshire, October 1979 (AW)

Tom Weir, Stuart Rae and IM at Loch Builg in Banffshire, with Carn Ulie rising to Meikle Geal Charn beyond, June 2000 (AW)

Other books by the authors

Adam Watson

1963. Mountain hares. Sunday Times Publications, London (by AW & R. Hewson)

1970. Animal populations in relation to their food resources (Editor). Blackwell Scientific Publications, Oxford and Edinburgh

1974. The Cairngorms, their natural history and scenery. Collins, London, and 1981 Melven Press, Perth (by D. Nethersole-Thompson & AW)

1975. The Cairngorms. Scottish Mountaineering Club District Guide, published by Scottish Mountaineering Trust. Second edition published 1992

1976. Grouse management. The Game Conservancy, Fordingbridge, and the Institute of Terrestrial Ecology, Huntingdon (by AW & G.R. Miller)

1982. Animal population dynamics. Chapman and Hall, London and New York (by R. Moss, AW & J. Ollason)

1982. The future of the Cairngorms. The North East Mountain Trust, Aberdeen (by K. Curry-Lindahl, AW & D. Watson)

1984. The place names of upper Deeside. Aberdeen University Press (by AW & E. Allan)

1998. The Cairngorms of Scotland. Eagle Crag, Aberdeen (by S. Rae & AW)

2008. Grouse: the grouse species of Britain and Ireland. Collins, London, New Naturalist Library No 107 (by AW & R. Moss)

Ruin of Wester Scalan, Glen Livet. 29 September 2013 (IM)

2010. Cool Britannia: snowier times in 1580–1930 than since. Paragon Publishing, Rothersthorpe (by AW & I. Cameron)

2011. It's a fine day for the hill. Paragon Publishing, Rothersthorpe

2011. A zoologist on Baffin Island, 1953. Paragon Publishing, Rothersthorpe

2011. Vehicle hill tracks in northern Scotland. The North East Mountain Trust, Aberdeen, published imprint Paragon Publishing, Rothersthorpe

2011. A snow book, northern Scotland: based on the author's field observations in 1938–2011. Paragon Publishing, Rothersthorpe

2012. Some days from a hill diary: Scotland, Iceland, Norway, 1943–50. Paragon Publishing, Rothersthorpe

2012. Human impacts on the northern Cairngorms: A. Watson's scientific evidence for the 1981 Lurcher's Gully Public Inquiry into proposed Cairn Gorm ski developments, and associated papers on people and wildlife. Paragon Publishing, Rothersthorpe

2012. Birds in north-east Scotland then and now: field observations mainly in the 1940s and comparison with recent records. Paragon Publishing, Rothersthorpe (by AW & Ian Francis)

2013. Place names in much of north-east Scotland. Hill, glen, lowland, coast, sea, folk. Paragon Publishing, Rothersthorpe

2013. Points, sets and man. Pointers and setters, stars of research on grouse, ptarmigan and other game. Paragon Publishing, Rothersthorpe

2013. Hill birds in north-east Highlands. Field observations over decades – ptarmigan, red grouse, golden plover, dotterel, bird counts. Paragon Publishing, Rothersthorpe

2013. Mammals in north-east Highlands – red deer, mountain hares, others. Paragon Publishing, Rothersthorpe

2014. More days from a hill diary: Scotland, Norway, Newfoundland, 1951–80. Paragon Publishing, Rothersthorpe

2014. Plants in north-east Highlands - timing of blaeberry growth, tree regeneration, land use, plant orientation. Paragon Publishing, Rothersthorpe

2014. The place names of Upper Deeside. Facsimile reprint of the 1984 book of the same title. Paragon Publishing, Rothersthorpe

Ian Murray

1992. In the shadow of Lochnagar. Lochnagar Publications & Marketing, Alt na Craig, Braemar Road, Ballater

1999. The Dee from the far Cairngorms. Lochnagar Publications & Marketing, Alt na Craig, Braemar Road, Ballater

2010. The Cairngorms and their folk. Lochnagar Publications, Alt na Craig, Braemar Road, Ballater

Authors

Adam Watson

Born in 1930 at Turriff on Deveronside, he graduated BSc in Pure Science with First Class Honours in zoology at the University of Aberdeen. A native speaker of the north Aberdeenshire variant of the Scots language, he took to English as his main subject at Turriff Secondary School. In the mid 1970s, after attending evening classes for three years, he passed the Gaelic O Grade examination of the Scottish Education Department. A lowlander, he became a mountaineer and ski-mountaineer from boyhood. In 1939 he developed a deep interest in the Cairngorms and their place names when reading a book by Seton Gordon. As a biologist studying animal populations, he was promoted to Senior Principal Scientific Officer with Special Merit in Research. Author of many books and hundreds of scientific papers, he is a Fellow of the Arctic Institute of North America, Centre for Ecology and Hydrology, Royal Meteorological Society, Royal Society of Edinburgh, and Society of Biology, an Emeritus Member of the Ecological Society of America, Honorary Life Member of the Cairngorm Club, and since 1954 a member of the Scottish Mountaineering Club. He was author in 1984 of *The place names of Upper Deeside*, and later combined with Ian Murray interviewing local residents in preparation for the present new book.

Ian Murray

His work background is in engineering, leaving school in Deeside to join Otis Elevators in 1980, where he became a lift engineer, moving from apprentice to senior management during his time with three companies. He has always enjoyed exploring, walking and skiing o the hills and glens of Scotland and fishing the rivers and lochs.

He now works with people from many countries as a fishing and wilderness guide, and travels to the West of Scotland to fish from his creel boat. A qualified Winter Mountain Leader, he still works as a lift consultant at times, and has had a near 20 year association as a volunteer with Braemar Mountain Rescue Team. He has been collecting information on folklore and exploring the hills, glens and former habitations of his home area centred on Ballater from an early age. Author of three books on the folklore, history and place names of Upper Deeside and the Cairngorms, he is passionate about recording and preserving these important aspects of local identity and culture.

Lightning Source UK Ltd.
Milton Keynes UK
UKOW06n1206270115

245210UK00005B/56/P